The Triumph of Provocation

The Triumph of Provocation

Józef Mackiewicz
Translation by Jerzy Hauptmann,
S. D. Lukac, and Martin Dewhirst
Foreword by Jeremy Black

Yale University Press
New Haven & London

Published with assistance from the foundation established in memory of
Henry Weldon Barnes of the Class of 1882, Yale College.

Copyright © 2009 by Nina Karsov. All rights reserved. This book may not be reproduced, in whole or in part, including illustrations, in any form (beyond that copying permitted by Sections 107 and 108 of the U.S. Copyright Law and except by reviewers for the public press), without written permission from the publishers.

First published as *Zwycięstwo prowokacji,* copyright © 1962 by Józef Mackiewicz.
Set in Garamond and Stone Sans types by The Composing Room of Michigan, Inc.
Printed in the United States of America.

Library of Congress Cataloging-in-Publication Data
Mackiewicz, Józef.
   [Zwycięstwo prowokacji. English]
   The triumph of provocation / Józef Mackiewicz ; translation by Jerzy Hauptmann, S.D. Lukac, and Martin Dewhirst ; foreword by Jeremy Black.
     p. cm.
   First published in Polish in 1962 under title Zwycięstwo prowokacji.
   Includes bibliographical references.
   ISBN 978-0-300-14569-4 (cloth : alk. paper)   1. Poland—Relations—Soviet Union. 2. Soviet Union—Relations—Poland. 3. Communism—Poland. 4. Poland—Politics and government—1945–1980. 5. Mackiewicz, Józef. I. Title.
   DK4185.S65M313 2009
   327.438047—dc22

                                                                                                  2008051565

A catalogue record for this book is available from the British Library.

This paper meets the requirements of ANSI/NISO Z39.48-1992 (Permanence of Paper).

10 9 8 7 6 5 4 3 2 1

Extracts from Norman Davies, *God's Playground: A History of Poland,* vol. 2 (Oxford: Clarendon Press, 1981) are reprinted by permission of Oxford University Press and Columbia University Press. The extract from Kyril FitzLyon and Tatiana Browning, *Before the Revolution. A View of Russia Under the Last Tsar* (London: Allen Lane, 1977) is reprinted by permission of Kyril FitzLyon. Extracts from Jan T. Gross, *Revolution from Abroad: The Soviet Conquest of Poland's Western Ukraine and Western Belorussia* (Princeton: Princeton University Press, 1988) are reprinted by permission of the publisher. Extracts from "To the New Moon" by Salvatore Quasimodo are taken from *Complete Poems,* trans. Jack Bevan (London: Anvil Press Poetry, 1983) and are reprinted by permission of the publisher. Extracts from Alfred Erich Senn, *The Great Powers, Lithuania and the Vilna Question 1920–1928* (Leiden: E. J. Brill, 1966) are reprinted by permission of Alfred E. Senn.

Contents

Foreword by Jeremy Black, vii

Part One The Downward Slope, 1

   1 "Censored," 3

Part Two Poland No Longer Between Germany and Russia, 27

   2 Does Russia Still Exist?, 29

   3 Between Bolshevism and Nationalism, 48

   4 Mikaszewicze, 60

   5 "Gomułkaism" (National Communism) of the Twenties, 73

   6 The First Great Provocation About the Alleged "Evolution of Communism," 82

Part Three Between the Quality of Life and the Boredom of Communism, 89

  7 The Second Phase of National Communism, 91

  8 Alliance or Collaboration with the Soviet Invader?, 97

  9 The Origins of "PAX," 114

 10 Pharisaism Versus Subversion, 123

 11 The Second Great Provocation, 133

 12 Along the Road of Classic "Poputnichestvo" [Fellow-Traveling], 144

 13 The German Complex, 156

 14 Culture in the Stranglehold of Compulsory Infantilism, 168

 15 The Real German Threat, 180

 16 "Realisms" Versus Reality, 185

 17 Pathos Versus Pestilence, 191

Part Four Let Us Hope . . . [1982], 197

Józef Mackiewicz: His Life, Work, and Views (A Chronology) by Nina Karsov, 213

Notes, 239

Foreword

This salutary book is a reminder of the terrible damage wrought by Communism and of the need, amid the War on Terror, not to lose sight of other ideological challenges to Western values. As the chronology at the end of the book makes clear, Józef Mackiewicz (1902–85) in his life and views bore testimony to the extraordinary changes in Europe over the twentieth century. Growing up in Vilnius, now the capital of the independent state of Lithuania, he experienced the shattering shifts of control and ideology that were particularly acute in 1915–21 and 1939–45. In his novels and journalistic and historical writings, Mackiewicz sought to make sense of his times and to explain and encourage. His was an account of the recent past designed to shape the response to the present and thus the future. Mackiewicz's targets were many, understandably so if one's perspective was that from Vilnius, a city that is very much one of contested memories, to use the expression of Timothy Snyder in *The Reconstruction of Nations: Poland, Ukraine, Lithuania, Belarus, 1569–1999* (Yale University Press, 2003). The evil that was Nazism comes in for appropriate vilification in his writing, and Mackiewicz does not pull his punches:

Hitler's terror . . . Hitler's mad policy. He also underlines the harsher treatment meted out to Jews than to other Poles, a point that was deliberately neglected by the government during the Communist years.

It is Communism, however, that was Mackiewicz's prime target, Communism and the willingness of non-Communists to propitiate it and to seek coexistence. His work published in this book is at once an attempt to recover a history totally misrepresented by Communist propaganda and to warn about Communism. Indeed, one of the criticisms made of the German occupation is that it made the way easier for Communism. The latter is presented as a totalizing experience, with the Communist government set on absolute control and unwilling, because of its ideology and teleology, to accept any limits. These themes are central to Mackiewicz's account of recent Lithuanian and Polish history and give it a powerful character. Indeed, those interested in the history of the period will find his perspective instructive.

So what, you might say. Is not Communism one with Shelley's Ozymandias, "that colossal wreck, boundless and bare"? This is certainly the case as far as the particular iteration of totalitarianism that Mackiewicz challenges, but the importance of this work in part rests on the degree to which the autocracy, and indeed the accommodation of the autocracy, that he depicts are not restricted to the case of Communism. As Mackiewicz points out, the problem is posed more generally by illiberal ideologies and governments: "democracy is not freedom. Democracy is only equality, while freedom results only from liberalism. The combination of equality and freedom constitutes the ideal we would all like to achieve." Moreover, as he repeatedly drives home, it is necessary to look at what governments did, as well as what they claimed to do. This is even more the case today, when all regimes, whatever their character, proclaim a support for human rights for all. Thus, although an Islamic dictatorship, the Sudanese government issued a new constitution in 1999 that promised freedom of religion, expression, and association. The Green Book that contained the thoughts of Colonel Qaddafi, ruler of Libya from 1969, declared that "Wealth, weapons and power lie with the people," but there was neither democracy nor free debate in the country. Hafez Assad, leader of Syria from 1970 (officially President from 1971) until his death in 2000, gained power as a result of a coup and relied heavily on the secret police but claimed to rule in accordance with the constitution and preserved a parliament. The governing Baath party in Syria was socialist and republican, but the reality of power was a dictatorship, and Assad was succeeded by his son. The same situation was true of post-Soviet Uzbekistan under Islam Karimov and of post-Soviet Belarus under Alexander Lukashenka.

Mackiewicz also attacks those who, through self-interest and folly, aided Communism, by active support or by an accommodation that undermined opposition. Thus, he is very critical of Piłsudski for undermining the Whites in 1919–20, of those, notably in the Church and among intellectuals, who were willing to support Gomułka, and, more generally, of the idea of *détente*. In a postscript of 1981, Mackiewicz complained that "dissidents" and "evolution" were permitted but not "(counter-)Revolution." This is particularly instructive because the end of the Cold War lent a somewhat benign air to those who pushed for coexistence. As Communist rule collapsed, they could be made to seem prescient. Mackiewicz died too soon to see the return of freedom to Eastern Europe, but it is worth considering whether his depiction of Communist distortion and tyranny and his call for vigilance would not, instead, have seemed prescient if this unexpected collapse had not occurred. This point extends to a critique of those willing to hobnob or cooperate with recent and current dictators. One can debate the merits of Realpolitik in such cases as Richard Nixon's exploitation of the Sino-Soviet split, but in many cases there appears to have been an unacceptable tolerance of tyranny on the left that is, correctly, not offered to dictators on the right. One thinks of Neil Kinnock's visit to Fidel Castro. Mackiewicz will have none of the idea that dictatorial systems are inherent to particular countries or cultures, for example Russia. He is particularly critical of the propiation of Communist tyranny by intellectuals, notably the International PEN Club, and of the perversion of language such that "those who revolt are called 'reactionaries' and those who bend their necks under the yoke of Communist tyranny call themselves 'progressive'."

There is room to debate Mackiewicz's arguments and conclusions, but to ignore him is to slight a powerful voice that recovers a set of beliefs too often neglected. His writings remind us of the range of views that should be borne in mind when considering the political thought of the past century, and, not least, of the potency of an anti-Communist voice that is still all too valid today.

Jeremy Black

Part One **The Downward Slope**

Chapter 1 "Censored"

In the famous trial of the seventy-nine nihilists (all of them followers of Nechaev and used by Dostoevsky as models for his *Devils*) conducted in 1871 in St. Petersburg, one of the most distinguished Russian lawyers of the nineteenth century, a Pole named Włodzimierz Spasowicz, stated in his defense plea: "A Pole . . . may look back at many past events which will quicken his pulse. When he re-creates the grandeur of this past, all in gold and purple, he takes refuge in the arms of history so that his dreams of democracy are wreathed in the national romanticism. The Russian . . . past is very poor indeed, and the present is as dry, pitiful, and naked as the rolling steppe, where you can all too easily go the whole hog, but it's almost impossible to stop halfway! . . . The radicalism of the Russian character . . . stems from the lack of a past, from the lack of culture, from the fact that there is nothing solid which would give support."[1]

It would be difficult in a few words to give a more precise idea of the typical Pole than the above, an idea that has been sanctioned over the generations and largely adopted by the literature and philosophy of history of Poland. All the insurrections and revolutions prior to World

War One are seen in accordance with this view; even all the ideas of the Polish national romanticism after the partitions in the eighteenth century (including the well-known saying of Piłsudski that he "boarded the Red tram in order to leave it at the stop called Poland") are tinged with it. This national characteristic can also explain the scornful reaction of members of the Polish Underground when, in Warsaw in early 1944, I tried to spell out to them the dangers of a Soviet occupation. They replied: "If we were able to engage in successful resistance despite massive terror, if we were able to shoot somebody like Kutschera in broad daylight! . . . if we were able to kill leaders of the Gestapo and the SS, are you suggesting that we won't be able to take care of a Wasilewska, or a Putrament, or an Osóbka and other Soviet agents?! This will simply be child's play for people like us." These were the voices of ordinary Poles educated in the popular tradition.

How, then, did the present situation come about?

Several years before World War Two, the Prime Minister of Poland, Sławoj-Składkowski, ostentatiously offered his resignation to the President of the Republic as a protest against the decision of the archbishop of Cracow [Kraków], taken on the latter's own initiative, to move the body of Marshal Piłsudski to the vault of the Silver Bells in Wawel Castle, which he interpreted as a case of lèse-majesté. A terrible rumpus erupted all over Poland, and the number of the archbishop's enemies increased substantially. However, had somebody said at that time: "The Metropolitan Archbishop Cardinal, Prince Sapieha, is a man capable of recognizing an NKVD [Narodnyi Komissariat Vnutrennikh Del, or the People's Commissariat for Internal Affairs] agent as *President of the Republic* and of calling the Bolshevik occupation the *liberation of Poland*," one would have to agree that even the greatest enemies of the archbishop would have called such a calumny a tasteless exaggeration. Had one predicted not only that this would happen in the not-too-distant future but that, in addition, after Sapieha's death, many of the most patriotic Poles would call him "The Steadfast Prince," everyone would have taken this as a nihilistic joke, a libel, or a sign of downright insanity.

Yet, this unuttered prediction came true. *Tygodnik Powszechny* [Everyone's Weekly], published since 1945 and (at first) the official organ of the Metropolitan Curia of Cracow, called the entry of Bolshevik troops the "liberation of Poland"; the former NKVD agent Bolesław Bierut assumed the title of "President of Poland" in 1947 and was recognized as such by the Polish Episcopate; Cardinal Sapieha died in 1951, and the Polish émigré press dubbed him "The

Steadfast Prince," since he had resisted the transformation of the Church into a tool of atheistic Bolshevism.

In comparison with the present, however, those times seem very far away.

In the years 1945–47, the majority of Polish émigrés regarded the former prime minister Stanisław Mikołajczyk as a "traitor," since he had agreed to collaborate with the Communists in a coalition government. At that time of general indignation and despair, after the Western powers had ceased to recognize the legal Polish government, nobody would have believed that soon the entire Polish community in exile would not only favor the establishment of diplomatic relations with the Communist government in Warsaw but even try to obtain foreign loans for this government and that, furthermore, it would regard as "traitors" those Poles who wanted to oppose these efforts. Similarly, at that time nobody would have believed that, in 1957, the Primate of Poland would support an election based entirely on a single Communist list of candidates or that the Catholic group represented by *Tygodnik Powszechny* would cooperate with the Communists more actively than PAX had done in its early years but would still be accepted as a group of patriots. In brief, nobody would have believed in the possibility of these or other examples of present-day reality. I chose the above examples not in order to criticize anyone personally. On the contrary, it is my intention to avoid as much as possible the emotional ad hominem aspects that, unfortunately, are so popular in Polish political writings and to present as detached an assessment of reality as possible. The brilliant essayist Wacław Zbyszewski correctly reminded us Poles that we make too many moral assessments and too few factual ones.

By profession I am a biologist. One of my professors, the late zoologist Konstanty Janicki, used to say that only a comparative science is an exact science; only by comparisons can objective knowledge be attained. All my life, I have tried to use this maxim as a guide, since it seems to me to be the only correct method in the assessment of all the truth that is accessible to man.

The events in Poland after 1945 obviously cannot be treated without reference to the reaction against the preceding German occupation. The phrase quoted above about the "liberation of Poland" by the Red Army, for instance, can be used only in reference to the liberation from the Nazi occupation. Only the Communists and their supporters extend it to include the liberation from a capitalist government. This, however, is merely an illustration, a commentary on these events. It emphasizes the psychological shift that has occurred and that has all the characteristics of the so-called downward slope. What has happened in Poland is a change from fundamental rejection of the Bolshevik system to mere opposition to the Bolshevik system. The term "Bolshevik," which is irritating to all conformists, is used here quite deliberately. It is a very precise term, even more so than in the past. Some correctly point out that there has been of late a return to so-called pure Leninism. With a small amendment, however: namely that Leninism did not exist in practice during Lenin's lifetime and that the very term originated after his death. During his lifetime, only Bolshevism existed, and this, with its numerous tactical manifestations, including the Bolshevik NEP [New Economic Policy], was Lenin's own creation in its classic form. This Bolshevism, which, at one time, was unacceptable to all Poles with the exception of a small group of Communists, has now become accepted de facto. At the same time there appeared a kind of concurrence between the "Polish road to Socialism" in Poland and the road to surrender outside the country, among the émigrés.

It is obvious that we do not live in a vacuum but are affected by the general processes of change taking place in the world, as will be discussed below. One should not, however, as is frequently done, blame the world around us, the Western powers (and the policies of the United States in particular), for all that has happened. The failure, the "blindness," and the "stupidity" of the Western powers are a favorite subject of Polish émigré journalism. It is easy to forget that these countries, with their "short-sighted" policies toward the Soviet Union, of which we have always been critical, do not operate in a vacuum, either, and that they frequently base their policies on premises discerned in the attitude of Poland and other nations conquered by the Soviets. In the meantime, any criticism of our own attitudes toward the Soviets and toward Communism is most unpopular, avoided and even forbidden in Polish émigré journalism. There is a special taboo on any suggestion that the political attitudes of certain Polish circles contribute considerably to a false assessment of the real dangers inherent in international Communism and that these circles are in part responsible for the disinformation that prevails today in Western public opinion. If a discussion of this theme does happen to emerge in the émigré press, it follows the conventional, prearranged formula; it is limited to ambiguities and restricted by the censorship imposed by "national desiderata." Similarly, there is a predetermined control over any criticism of our national characteristics should it exceed the boundaries established in the plea of Spasowicz quoted above.

Contemplating the train of events that brought about the current situation in Poland and in exile, I have tried several times to break through these barriers that inhibit Polish journalism, generally without success. In this book, the reader will find many things that could not be printed elsewhere because of the censorship of the Polish émigré press.

FOR THE SOVEREIGNTY OF THOUGHT

It is not my intention to impose my views upon anyone. I take it for granted that these might be contravened by some other undoubtedly serious ones. I am, however, deeply convinced that Polish émigré circles—like any other group in exile from Communist rule—have one great mission to fulfil and, indeed, have the chance to fulfil it. Namely, having lost their national sovereignty, they can at least protect the sovereignty of thought.

The sovereignty of thought will not be saved by solemn resolutions, assertions, and patriotic demands, and it will be helped even less by slogans and taboos.

No one in this world knows the whole truth. What we human beings call "truth" is merely the search for it. This, however, is possible only when there is a conflict of ideas, and such conflict is possible only where there is free discussion. The Communist system, which prohibits any conflict of ideas, is bound therefore to be one great falsehood. We who live in countries that recognize the freedom of the individual and the freedom of thought should do all we can to expand the horizons of thought and not to limit them, not to limit the discussion but to extend it. Should my book contribute in the smallest measure to such an extension, I will be happy that I have achieved my purpose.

One has to admit that the conditions of the middle of the twentieth century are not favorable to such a goal, even in the part of the world free from Communism. Since 1914, this world has effected substantial changes and has achieved a great deal: it has removed most kings, emperors, and tsars and enthroned the principle of total Democracy. Whether it is because this new "sovereign" is so total or because it caters to the mass of people, it has nevertheless facilitated the emergence of a by-product: a collective way of thinking. The old, exuberant individualism is out of fashion. Like any old-fashioned object, it has been thoroughly reshaped, on occasion perhaps too radically. Unfortunately, this has been happening in an era when world Communism, which is both total and totalitarian, has elevated collectivized human thought to the rank of a symbol. There is much evidence that after World War Two, the Western democracies have been inclined less to fight Communism than to compete with it. Out of this, a tendency toward uniformity and one-sidedness, toward an almost undeniable conformity, has come into play.

Pope Leo XIII, speaking to the German Chancellor von Bülow years ago, expressed his conviction that Socialism and democracy were the greatest of evils. These, of course, were times we may rightly call reactionary. However, some comparisons spring to mind. After all, it was often easier to be a revolutionary in those days of emperors and kings than to be a counterrevolutionary today, to be a Socialist then than to be an anti-Socialist out of conviction today. The creator of the greatest form of slavery in human history and the greatest enemy of the old world, Lenin, when deported to Siberia under the tsars, lived in conditions that, when compared to present-day Siberia, have been jokingly described as a "Cherry Orchard."

When we look at other human liberties, the comparison does not always favor those established by the democracies of today. Let us take, for instance, the attitude toward war. All wars, not only today but always, have been regarded as a misfortune. The desirability of peace was discussed in times past, as well as today. Conferences were organized and the best means to maintain peace discussed. The first Peace Conference at the Hague, convened in 1899 by Emperor Nicholas II to discuss the reduction of armaments, had twenty-six countries participating; the second conference, in 1907, had as many as forty-four and drew up a number of Conventions for the maintenance of peace. The word "peace" was on everybody's lips, but it was also possible to talk and write about, even to glorify, wars of liberation. If we cast a glance over the cities of Europe, we will find in them many monuments to people who in their time initiated wars of liberation. In Italy, the tourist will find in nearly every town a statue of Garibaldi with saber in hand or holding a flag, calling people to war. Some of these statues are of quite recent origin. When, however, we compare the tyranny of old Austria, against which Garibaldi called people to arms, with the tyranny of today's Soviet Union, against which nobody is allowed to call people to arms, any thinking person will find himself in a quandary. The question is bound to arise: how did it happen that today, despite the existence of the greatest tyranny in history, which has subjugated hundreds of millions of people, the word "war" is virtually prohibited by democratic public opinion in an almost policeman-like fashion? Anyone who dares to utter the word is called a criminal or insane. In this case, the opinions of the Vatican and of the atheists are in absolute agreement.

In reality, this is even more one-sided than it may appear, because not every "war of liberation" is condemned today, only wars that aim to liberate people from Soviet rule. Not every revolution is condemned; sometimes the opposite happens—since the word "revolution," under American influence, has assumed positive connotations, revolutions against colonial powers, for instance, have even met with considerable sympathy. Only (counter-)revolution against Communism is condemned. All this is happening at a time when this same Communism, increasing its dominions, can openly and in the sight of all glorify its conquests as "revolutions" and "wars of liberation." It is true that many people resent this, but nobody calls the Soviet Union "insane"!

This brings us to another phenomenon of our times: to the attitudes of so-called intellectual circles all over the world, of artistic and literary groupings, of students, and so on. In the past, these circles produced the greatest percentage of "lunatics" whose revolutionary ideas shocked the solid citizens who supported the status quo. Suddenly these zealots have disappeared. Where are those individualists of bygone days, those unkempt idealists calling for unrealizable goals? It is true that on the boulevards of big cities we can find similarly unkempt people, the existentialists, but they are no longer individuals but members of a fashionable collective. They are not so much people in favor of the abolition of tyranny as proponents of peaceful coexistence with the major tyranny of our time. We are dealing here with an unusual paradox.

Physical violence and mass murder are not qualities that are peculiar to the Communist system. Nazism, in many instances, was able to outdo it in terms of these ordinary crimes. The most characteristic feature of the Communist system is the total enslavement of the human spirit, the subjugation of human thought and of the human intellect. It would appear, therefore, that the greatest enemies of this system should be found not among the workers, peasants, craftsmen, bourgeoisie, and "ordinary" men and women in the street but in the so-called progressive circles that have traditionally proclaimed to the masses the ideal of free thought and that have regarded matters of the spirit as more important than daily bread. Logically, one would have expected that these intellectual circles in all countries would become the avant-garde of the battle against Communism. Nothing of this sort has happened. What has happened was the opposite of the logical prediction: those who revolt are called "reactionaries," and those who bend their necks under the yoke of Communist tyranny call themselves "progressive."

The best example of this paradox can be seen in the stance of those literary circles throughout the world that are organized as the International PEN Club.

It is well known that the Soviet régime has transformed Russian literature, once a great literature, into worthless kitsch. In all other countries, the advent of Communism has brought about the undermining or, indeed, the destruction of free literature. Yet, the PEN Club, which, in accordance with the fine words of its Charter, is meant to foster freedom of spirit, thought, and creativity, instead of fighting for these great ideals, behaves in a completely contrary manner and collaborates with those who trample on these ideals. It invites Communists to become members and elects as chairmen writers with soft attitudes toward Communism who periodically visit Moscow; recently it elected as vice-chairman a representative of a Communist state, the Polish writer Jan Parandowski, who may not himself be a Communist but who most certainly will vote with the Communists on all important matters.

This stance, found among the most eminent representatives of world literature, is, however, not an isolated example. Rather, it reflects a widespread attitude within the intellectual world, and the literary world in particular. This is true not only in Western Europe but also in America. The area over which these attitudes have spread is very large, indeed.

In 1955, the Nobel Prize for literature was awarded to the Icelandic Communist H. Laxness, hardly a writer of world stature. The same year, an Italian poet, Salvatore Quasimodo, published in *L'Unità,* a newspaper of the Communist Party of Italy, a poem that includes the following lines:

> In the beginning God created the heaven
> and the earth, and in due time
> set moon and stars in the heavens
> . . . .
> After a thousand ages, man,
> . . . .
> one October night, without fear,
> set in the tranquil heavens
> other bodies like those
> that had been spinning
> since the creation of the world. Amen.[2]

This refers to the Bolshevik October Revolution. Four years later, in 1959, Quasimodo received the Nobel Prize for literature. The writer Jarosław Iwaszkiewicz, an agent in literary matters of the Communist government in Warsaw, wrote about Quasimodo's prize: "A friend of our culture . . . a friend of our nation! He attended the congress of intellectuals in Wrocław in 1948; the Peace Congress in 1950; the Mickiewicz celebrations in 1955."[3]

One hardly has to add that all the events listed were organized by Communists. Soviet writers also sent a telegram to Italy: "You are the first Western poet who wrote a poem about our Sputnik!"

A correspondent of *Figaro Littéraire* asked Quasimodo whether it was true that he had refused to sign the protest against the jailing of Hungarian writers. "Yes," said the Nobel Prize winner, "since I did not know the circumstances in Budapest." Asked about the literary life of Moscow, which he frequently visits, he answered: "The literary life of Moscow is developing normally, without any pressure from outside ... obviously there are some limitations characteristic of every political society. It was the same in the Greece of Pericles."

If we are looking for classic examples of hypocrisy, it is certain that this kind of answer should be counted among them. Clearly, nobody in the West would assert that Quasimodo and other writers and artists like him receive prizes or make careers because they are Communists or pro-Communists. Such a claim would normally be scornfully rejected with a shrug of the shoulders. As far as their views are concerned, they are referred to as people who are in favor of "peace." Thus, the "peace" slogan is elevated above all other absolute values such as truth, freedom of thought, freedom of movement, the welfare of the individual, and so on. Everything is less important than relative "peace": it is obvious that, in fact, an absolute peace is not what is meant, but only peace with the Communist world.

One can understand that, once such a position is taken by leading intellectual representatives of the "Weltgeist," there is no point in wringing one's hands over the conformism of the hoi polloi or of contemporary mass culture.

It was in December 1958, while I was still a member of the International PEN Club (which I left during the Congress in Frankfurt when the Hungarian Communists were admitted as members), that I delivered a speech at the convention of the "PEN in Exile" in Munich. Excerpts from this speech are quoted below.

> I read Boris Pasternak's *Doctor Zhivago,* and I have to admit that I was enchanted. I should like, however, to express my opinion that as a work of literature it does not reach the same level of talent as that of Bunin, for example. As far as a philosophical analysis of the course of the revolution is concerned, the memoirs of Professor Fedor Stepun, for instance, are more interesting. I say "for instance," since among Russian writers in exile there are many first-rate talents which remain unknown. One must, therefore, doubt whether *Doctor Zhivago* would have received the same renown had the author been living in exile. This doubt is further strengthened by what happened

with Ehrenburg's *The Thaw* and Dudintsev's *Not by Bread Alone*. *The Thaw* is a book without any literary value, and Dudintsev's work is definitely kitsch, but why are they published in every language, and why do people run to bookshops to spend good money on bad books? Because they fit contemporary political views. Whatever one says about Djilas's *The New Class,* one thing is certain: during the last forty years that Bolshevism has been in control in the East, dozens of authors have defined the nature of Communism better and more accurately than Djilas. Why is it that those books have been forgotten and that Djilas's book has become a world bestseller? Because, I am afraid, he has never been contaminated by any anti-Communist activity and as a matter of fact has remained the Communist he has always been.

Unlike anti-Fascist fighters, the old anti-Bolshevik fighters are not admired but opposed. Even if they do not happen to be regarded as "reactionaries," at best they are seen as old bores, and not only in leftist circles.

Should, for instance, some writer in exile approach *Figaro Littéraire,* which is regarded as a right-wing publication, with lists of the millions of people murdered by the Communists, the editors would immediately get rid of him along with his worn-out phraseology. But there suddenly appears in the very same editorial office a writer representing the young generation of dissatisfied Communists whose books no one on the editorial staff has read. (I am referring here to Marek Hłasko—*Author's note.*) A lengthy interview with him is arranged immediately, and the new star, with a knowing knitting of his brows, reveals that "there is a shortage of toothbrushes behind the Iron Curtain." This statement appears on the front page of the Paris weekly, as if the lack of toothbrushes, considering all we know about the reality of life under Communism after forty years, were a kind of revelation.

The case of this writer proves to be typical when it comes to making an assessment of the contemporary trend in the West that I would call the political fashion à la Mlle Sagan. Many women have written better about love affairs, but not at the age of eighteen. Similarly, not everybody who writes about Communism is or has been a Communist.

Without comparing literary talents, we can draw an instructive analogy from a juxtaposition of the cases of Hłasko and Pasternak. Soviet trade unionists, factory workers, Komsomol members, and thousands of other people, acting on the orders of the party, called Pasternak a pig and a traitor. How did all these people know that Pasternak was indeed a traitor and a pig if none of them had read his book, since it had not been published in the Soviet Union? In our free part of the world, Hłasko received plenty of good publicity. Hundreds of articles about him and interviews with him appeared before his books were translated into foreign languages. How did people know that he deserved such massive coverage?

The Warsaw *Trybuna Ludu* accused Hłasko of joining the camp of anti-Communist literature. Reacting to the accusation, this leading representative of the latest European fashion replied from Paris with indignation: "This is a slander! This is a denunciation!" And nobody was shocked by his indignation. Can you imagine the reaction should somebody accused of joining the camp of anti-Fascist literature reply publicly, "This is a slander! This is a denunciation!"?

Characteristically, a few dozen years have passed since that time but, as "a new émigré Hłasko" then, so, today, the so-called dissidents from several Communist countries, in particular from the Soviet Union and the People's Poland, diverse "critics of the regime," "defenders of human rights," and "oppositionists" of all kinds protest in exactly the same manner against being called "anti-Communists"! . . . And this applies both to those who are in the West and to those who remain in their own countries, regardless of their intellectual standing, which varies greatly. Whether it is Academician Sakharov or the leader of the "workers' opposition" Wałęsa in Poland, Solzhenitsyn in the United States or Kuroń along with Michnik from the Warsaw "Solidarity"—they will all consider that calling them "anti-Communists" is "slander" and "denunciation." [Addendum of June 27, 1981.]

Such a great moral elevation of Communism over Fascism in the eyes of the world is unquestionably due to Hitler and his criminal methods, which compromised the idea of an anti-Communist crusade.

The Western democracies, on the other hand, which had supported the headquarters of international Communism during the last war not only materially but also morally, found themselves, after the Soviet victory, forced into a position that was easily exploited by Communism.

None of the Western powers has any intention of admitting that mistakes have been committed in this respect. Nobody likes to admit his own mistakes, and this is particularly true of the great powers of this world. After the war, the West introduced a kind of new political chronology in accordance with the division of good and evil; the opening date was June 22, 1941. After this date, everything that was done to help the Soviets was good; anything that was done to put obstacles in the way of their victory over Germany was evil. Those who aided the Soviets during the war, regardless of their personal political convictions, have the right today to speak in the free world, while those who impeded Soviet progress have no say in anything. If one transferred this formula to the attitudes adopted toward the nations enslaved by Communism, it would look as follows:

In the eyes of the West, every nation enslaved by Communism has the right to defend itself or to disappear from the face of the Earth, in which case it can count on sympathy. Since 1941, however, no nation has had the right to resist the Soviets, as they were involved in a war, and, moreover, no nation has had the right to resist them by cooperating with the German army. In such a case, irrespective of its national interests, a nation ipso facto becomes an enemy of democracy. This obligatory formula has forced the exiled representatives of the countries in Eastern Europe that fought the Communists during the last war to develop a political alibi. In order to present to the West extenuating circumstances and to gain its indulgence, it was necessary, in their own interests, to distort the actual course of events to a greater or lesser degree. This is the reason for their frequent assertions that they did indeed revolt against the "Stalinist tyranny" but that they obviously hated the Germans as well. Or, more effectively, they assert that they really "had been fighting on two fronts from the start." Even the members of the Vlasov army tried to "pay for their sins" by exaggerating as much as possible the final episode of the war when, in agreement with the Czech underground in Prague, they turned their arms against the Germans. Of course, this did not help them very much during the first postwar phase, since, together with the Cossacks and other anti-Bolshevik units, they were turned over by the West to the Soviets to face, in many cases, certain death.

In this new chronology, Hitler plays a role similar to that of Lucifer in the Middle Ages. He is Evil by definition, and one is prevented from analyzing this definition more closely by the threat of excommunication from the universal democratic church. The universality of this church has to be taken literally, since it includes not only the non-Bolshevik but also the Bolshevik world. The old liberal right to unlimited comparisons has been limited by a moral prohibition that even purely scientific and scholarly research may not upset. And it is clear that any case of anti-Communism during the last war can easily be related to the person of Hitler through the use of the appropriate prosecution dialectics.

There were never so many compulsory liars in the world after the end of any other war. Many people found themselves in situations that forced them to falsify not only their own biographies but also the histories of their nations. Even a man of such an impeccable past as, for instance, Mannerheim, the Marshal of Finland, found it necessary after the end of the war to give a humiliating and degrading interview in which he almost completely omitted his years of fighting against the Bolsheviks and merely highlighted the moment when the alliance with Germany was broken. I have personally met people from the former Vlasov army who even today instinctively turn around and lower their voices when they admit that they were fighting against the Bolsheviks at that time.

One should not be surprised by this. Immediately after the war, the great American poet (he is also one of the greatest poets in the world) Ezra Pound was placed in an iron cage designed for monkeys and kept in it until he was pardoned and transferred to a lunatic asylum, all because he took the side of Italian Fascism. The eighty-six-year-old Knut Hamsun, one of the greatest novelists of world literature, was also placed in a lunatic asylum, since during the war he favored an alliance with Germany.

On the other hand, Thomas Mann, the great novelist of world fame, who stated that "Anti-Communism is the greatest folly of the world," is not suspected of having lost his reason. Doubtless, rightly so.

Recently, translations of the works of a splendid Soviet writer of the early period, Isaak Babel, have been published in the West. In West Germany, in 1961, three publishing houses rushed to bring out his works. These new editions were received by the critics with great acclaim.

Until the end of his life, Babel was a committed Bolshevik who started his career in the Cheka, which used to induce shudders of fear. The talented writer describes his service in the Cheka with a great deal of gusto; his reminiscences, in keeping with his distinctive style, are engagingly austere and realistic, yet enlivened with passionate romantic touches.

According to calculations, which, of course, like all calculations of mass murders and mass deaths, may be exaggerated, while Babel served in the Bolshevik political police, this same Cheka in one year (1918–19) murdered 1,700,000 people in the territories of Southern Russia alone. In the Kuban area, they amused themselves by hewing to pieces with their sabers prisoners standing on the edges of open graves; in Tsaritsyn (later called Stalingrad, then Volgograd), the prisoners were kept in the holds of old barges; men, women, and children were crowded into confined spaces where they had to endure inhuman conditions and the terrible stench of their own excrement, only to be drowned later in the Volga; in Kharkov, they specialized in the scalping and the pulling off of "gloves" (skinning people's hands), and so on.

If we compare the figures, we can see that the Bolshevik Cheka, together with its successors (GPU, OGPU, NKVD–NKGB, MGB, MVD, and KGB), has, over the course of more than forty years, committed "genocide" on a far greater scale than the Gestapo did during its comparatively short period of existence.

Isaak Babel is quite rightly a literary success in the West. Let us, however, recall the general indignation created by the "unmasking" of the Romanian émigré Constantin Virgil Gheorghiu, author of *The 25th Hour,* or the worldwide scandal that broke out after the Goncourt Academy unfortunately awarded a prize to the émigré writer Vintilă Horia for his book *God Was Born in Exile*. Neither of these writers, however, had served in organizations like the one in which Babel served; they were alleged only to have expressed, in the past, views that could not be reconciled with those that prevail today.

I am interested in Babel, since he can be used as a subject of my comparative method. He is, by the way, an excellent writer. Among other things, he hates everything Polish, and especially Catholicism. His works abound with blasphemy and sacrilege. He describes a Catholic priest who, after the brassieres of his housekeeper have been washed, hangs them on the nails of the crucifix in his church; he writes that Princess Deborah was the mistress of Christ, and so on. The Catholic writer Zofia Starowieyska-Morstinowa writes in the *Tygodnik Powszechny*, which is regarded as truly Catholic, about Babel's work as follows: "This life depicted so realistically, so brutally, at the same time arranges itself into . . . a fascinating Chagall composition. Everything here is ultra-realistic and at the same time visionary. And how beautiful it is! I am simply enchanted by this rich and teeming world. . . . What a writer! He is really worthy of taking his place among the greatest masters of Russian prose. What kind of literary art . . . is able to transfer everything into a stratosphere where there are no longer words like 'nice' and 'ugly' . . . but where there is only the word 'beautiful'?"[4]

I would be the first to protest against the placing of Isaak Babel's books on any kind of index. These personal views, however, would not change the objective fact that not a single Catholic writer in the world before 1941 would have written such a review of this book and that no Catholic paper in the world would have agreed to publish such a review. Superficially, it looks as if there has been a change for the better, as if we had here a case of some definite progress in tolerance and in the acceptance of differing points of view. In reality, such a conclusion would be completely false, since it would be drawn from misleading appearances. It is rather simply a proof of the collective one-sidedness that prevails today, a manifestation of which may be observed in the "opening up to the left" even of the Italian Christian Democrats.

The Nuremberg trial, which was supposed to be a tribunal of world justice, surprised many by its one-sidedness, not so much by its revelations of Nazi crimes as by its unprecedented suppression of objective morality. The representatives of the Soviet Union who should have been tried on every single one of the charges did not sit alongside the accused. On the contrary: they were among the judges! In one particular instance, they accused someone else of a crime they themselves had committed. This was known to all the judges; otherwise, they would not have dropped the case of Katyń so discreetly. And so it came to pass that the mere fact that the Germans were not accused of the Soviet crime, and that the crime itself was shelved, was regarded as a manifestation of justice and of international objectivity. Whatever else could be said about this trial, it is obvious that, in days gone by, its conduct from beginning to end would have been called unfair. Objectivity was out of the question, since any comparative criteria were eliminated from the outset.

This was an unfortunate start for the postwar era. Here we can see the origins of a peculiar supplementary formula that to all intents and purposes is still valid: one may be a victim of "Stalinism," but it won't do to be an open enemy of Communism. This formula was adjusted to the new chronology, and it has endured even through the later period of the Cold War.

In this way, all knowledge about the past of Communism is being, so to speak, officially forgotten. During the peak of the Cold War, one could have compared Stalin to Hitler, but never the other way around. Had one said that Stalin was always worse than Hitler, one would have turned upside down the whole hierarchy of saints and devils in the new chronology, and the whole meaning of the last war and of the postwar arrangements would have been thrown into question. And so one is allowed to blame Stalin for the treaty with Hitler, but it is unthinkable to blame Hitler for the treaty with Stalin; it is permissible to compare Soviet labor camps with Hitler's concentration camps, but the reverse comparison is unthinkable. History tells us something else, however. The decree concerning the establishment of "forced labor camps" was signed by Mikhail Kalinin, chairman of the All-Russian Central Executive Committee (VTsIK), on April 15, 1919. This decree was extended and elaborated in detail in accordance with the resolution of the above-mentioned Committee of May 17, 1919, signed by Varlaam Avanesov; it established the classic organizational structure of these camps, which was later copied by Hitler. During 1919 alone, that is, at a time when Hitler was still a completely unknown vagrant, ninety-seven concentration camps were set up in Soviet Russia. Other historical facts have been presented in the same way. This has made it possible in practice to treat any anti-Communist movement before 1941 as something suspiciously "reactionary" and any such movement between 1941 and 1945 as "high treason." It is as if there were no Bolshevik reality between 1917 and 1945, as if the world learned about Communist reality only after World War Two with the beginning of the "East-West" conflict. The reason for this collective distortion is the need to justify morally the alliance with international Communism during the war. Without such a justification, no argument for this alliance against Hitler would be possible, or, at the very least, it would be more difficult to make.

Against the background of this distortion of historical truth, a number of myths developed that have by now become a permanent fixture. In this group of myths, one finds, in the first place, the myth that the Bolshevik Revolution in Russia was ("despite everything") progressive in comparison with the reactionary tsarist system; then the myth of so-called Stalinism in comparison with the "better" (or perhaps even "good") "Leninism"; and the myth of Nazism as "extremely reactionary."

This last myth in particular is never disputed. Yet, it is well known that the Nazi leaders deep in their hearts hated the conservatives more than the Bolsheviks, despite the tactics they had used to come to power. For some time, Goebbels was even enthusiastic about Bolshevik methods. Himmler stated in 1937 to C. J. Burckhardt, the High Commissioner of the League of Nations in Gdańsk: "I have just ended a visit to the concentration camps in Austria. They contain Jews and aristocrats; the first are too ugly and too agile, the others too beautiful and too impotent."

And Hitler stated in 1939: "Don't forget, as a proletarian, I cannot look at things the way you do, because of my background, my elevation, and my general outlook."[5]

Nazism was based on a system and a terror of a clearly Socialist type, although, in contrast to Bolshevism, it was non-Marxist. The anti-Hitler plot in Germany also had all the specific characteristics of a classic counterrevolution from the right, although, in light of the views that are obligatory nowadays, the Germans try to give it a "democratic" character. Among the 158 participants in the plot who were hanged or murdered or who committed suicide to escape torture, there were twenty-five counts and barons and thirty-one members of the gentry with the surname preceded by "von." This makes fifty-six noblemen altogether, or more than a third of all those executed.

It was necessary to refashion historical truth, since, without this reshaping, the whole boundary line between Nazi crimes and Communist crimes would have to be basically redrawn and even the boundary line between the crimes of Hitler and those of the Western powers would become somewhat blurred. And so, the bombing of Hiroshima, where sixty thousand civilians perished, the bombing of Dresden, where more than two hundred thousand civilians (according to some sources about four hundred thousand) perished, and the handover of people to Soviet executioners after the war could all be subsumed under the moral and legal heading of "genocide," which was exactly what those tried in Nuremberg were hanged for.

The policies of the West during the war were guided by conditions imposed by the alliance with the Soviets; after the war, Western policies were guided by conditions arising from the desire for peaceful coexistence with the Soviets. The disproportion in the treatment of Nazi crimes and Communist crimes has no moral basis, only a political one. It comes from the difference in attitude toward a criminal who has been destroyed and a criminal with whom one wants to coexist, even to the point of engaging in "cultural exchanges." It is clearly the result of a so-called Realpolitik. Unfortunately, any policy, if considered as the art of predicting the future and influencing historical developments, has to be based on a knowledge of the past. Once this past is falsified, once historical facts are replaced by invented facts, once reality is adjusted to the current form of wishful thinking, such a "Realpolitik" may easily become a completely unrealistic policy.

To complain about the extent of this kind of dual morality is fruitless. Dual morality has always existed, in the lives of individuals and in the lives of human communities. At the moment, we wish only to state the objective fact that the post-Nuremberg moral and legal norm still prevails in contemporary collective thinking, despite all the shocks of the past seventeen years.

In Israel, Eichmann was hanged after being convicted of murdering or participating in the murder of six million Jews. The Communist countries took part with a vengeance in the general publicity surrounding this trial. Eichmann defended himself with the argument that he was only executing orders, that he was a small cog in the total apparatus. And so the Warsaw Communist paper *Polityka* wrote on this subject as follows: "This part of the Eichmann confessions is the most appalling. . . . It shows the psychological mechanism of crime—it represents the Eichmann way of thinking. . . . Everything that serves the German nation is good and useful!"[6]

The exclamation marks are meant to show the great moral indignation of the Communist writer. But if we look into the *Politicheskii slovar'*, a political dictionary, we may read on page 362: "MORALITY—The opposite of bourgeois morality is Communist morality. From the standpoint of Communist morality, everything is moral which serves and contributes to the victory and strengthening of the new Communist society."[7]

Were we to replace the phrase "German nation" by the word "Communism," we would have the following sentence: "Everything that serves Communism is good and useful." We have thus arrived at an analogous formula. We know that during the past forty years or so the Soviet Union has carried out the task of exterminating millions of people, and we know that the number of people in Soviet concentration camps averaged between ten and twenty million at any one time. We also know that the Communist system does not allow any kind of insubordination; there is no opposition, there is no power of veto, there are no objections, there are no strikes, there is no diversity of opinion. Blind obedience in the service of Communism always was and continues to be more total, more deaf to any appeal, and more sanctioned by official morality than in any period in any other system.

At the same time, the whole world, on the occasion of the Eichmann trial, while resurrecting the Nazi crimes, said not a word about any Communist crimes. At a ceremony honoring the victims of the Katyń massacre on March 12, 1961, there were only sixty-five Poles gathered in the Soldiers' Home in New York.

Eichmann was accused of annihilating six million Jews. Ukrainian sources assert that three to six million peasants were murdered in the Ukraine during the "purges" and the "anti-kulak" campaigns. While some raise this figure to seven million, others speak of only two million, so it is probable that these figures are exaggerated. Perhaps also the figure of six million Jews is exaggerated, but it is not the precise numbers that are most important in this case. Let us say six million Jews and "only" one million peasants. The central issue remains the same. In the same way, it cannot be denied that the degree of personal responsibility of Nikita Khrushchev, then party secretary in the Ukraine, for the extermination of the kulaks and his later responsibility for the murders in Hungary is far greater than the responsibility of Eichmann for the extermination of Jews. Eichmann did not belong to the leaders of the Nazi Party and did not publish inflammatory statements calling for murder in the *Völkischer Beobachter*. Khrushchev, however, wrote in the Moscow paper *Pravda*, on January 31, 1937, the following words about supposed opponents of the party: "It stinks like the filth of dirty and abominable degenerates. These murderers were aiming at the heart and brain of our party. They raised their hands against Comrade Stalin. . . . By raising their hands against Comrade Stalin, they raised them against everything that is best in humanity. For Stalin represents our hopes and our expectations; he is the beacon that guides all progressive mankind! Stalin is our victory. The vile bandits have received their just punishment. . . . The reptile has been crushed in the Soviet Union."

He glorified the extermination in the Ukraine in the following passage: "Today, after we have unmasked the machinations . . . of the bourgeois Ukrainian nationalists . . . of those scoundrels etc., we know well that you, our Stalin, have contributed most to the unmasking of those scoundrels. We thank you and salute you, Mighty Stalin, and your best student Nikolai Ivanovich Yezhov! You, who have exterminated those vermin."[8]

"Filth, reptiles, scoundrels, vermin," and so on—these words are just as strong as those used by the Nazis against the Jews. The question arises: where, in what book of divine or human law, is it stated that persecution for one's race or nationality is a greater crime than persecution for one's social origin, religion, or views? Why should the murder of people because they are Jews be worse than the murder of people only because they have achieved a certain social status or because they believe in other ideals? At the same time that Eichmann was kidnapped and hanged, in violation of laws obtaining throughout the civilized world, in full view of the world community, and without a word of protest from any organization for the "defense of human rights," Khrushchev, in full view of this same civilized world, was decorated with wreaths like a sacred cow in India, spent a night in France in a former king's bed, and his peace of mind was regarded as so important that some of the émigrés whom he had not managed to kill were deported to an island to ensure that they would not spoil his appetite by arranging a demonstration. The greatest statesmen of the world cordially shook Khrushchev's hand, toasted him at banquets, and wished him a long life.

This obviously did not happen because the whole world loves Jews and does not love Ukrainian peasants. It happened because the world has submitted to psychological pressure, not only the pressure of the obligatory formulas inherited from after the war, not only the pressure of "Realpolitik" and its propaganda, but also the pressure of the dominant intellectual circles that are trying to create a certain tendency, a trend in thinking, an atmosphere that does not favor human individualism and, therefore, also limits the freedom to make comparisons.

The atmosphere prevailing in our times cannot be defined easily by the use, for instance, of old, trite simplifications such as "Jewish Communists," "Popular Fronts," and so forth. Some speak about a "dictatorship of the intellectual left." This, however, is not a precise description, since today the original notions of "left" and "right" are blurred. They no longer mean what they used to and can be interpreted more or less as one likes. The system found in Israel or the social reforms of Nasser in Egypt, for instance, have much in common with Fascism, although it would be regarded as an insult to call them by this name.

Sometimes one has the impression that the intellectual aristocracy, which today acts as a so-called controller of the spirit, is like a group of snobs who conspire to regard the breaking of certain ideological limits as intolerable, as once the infringement of strict rules of etiquette was regarded as unacceptable by certain exclusive circles. "Anti-Communism" produces the same reaction of disgust as using a meat knife to eat fish produces in well-mannered dinner guests.

In reality, this camp finds its representatives among the countless ranks of the "progressives" of our days, although they may be of a different political hue. Obviously, all of them are democrats, but who is not a democrat today?! What they have in common as far as their attitude toward the contemporary situation is concerned is not the fact that they call themselves democrats. We can find, however, a common and characteristic similarity in their attitude to the past, namely their positive, if only to some degree, assessment of the 1917 Bolshevik Revolution in Russia.

In the thirties, a common core was evident in the anti-Fascist front during the Spanish Civil War. We can see this in the anti-Franco stance, which was undoubtedly pro-Communist and even, to some degree, pro-Soviet. A good example of this period is Hemingway, who was not a Communist: "Let us win this and it will all be Republic!" (*For Whom the Bell Tolls,* published, incidentally, in book form as late as 1940.) The disenchantments of the coming years, and especially the Hitler-Soviet Pact of August 1939, forced people to make a certain revision of their previous position. This was done by inventing the happy formula that made it possible to find a way out of this situation without losing face, without losing ideological continuity or the prorevolutionary tradition. This magic formula was "anti-Stalinism," as distinguished from "reactionary" anti-Communism. During World War Two, to be sure, it had to be locked away in a drawer, but it assumed a still greater importance afterward when the Cold War began. From this time on, the hero of the day is the ex-Communist who has become disillusioned because of Stalin. The fashion and the demand for people of the Koestler type were so great that some were found who described themselves as ex-Communists, although they had had no connection with Communism, or even with Socialism, in the past.

The glue that externally bound this group together remained "anti-Fascism" and a negative attitude toward everything reactionary; an ironical attitude, accompanied by an indulgent shrug of the shoulders, toward the monarchical, liberal, nineteenth-century, prerevolutionary epoch and everything connected with it. This attitude also extended to the individualism of that era.

All these, however, are only the visible signs of the intellectual camp that is dominant today. More characteristic, perhaps, are the invisible signs.

La dolce vita of the contemporary "asphalt intellectuals" is not devoid of thorns, however. They are contained in certain fundamental questions:

1. Was life in Russia before the revolution better or worse than life after the revolution? Since everything indicates that it was better, it was decided not to discuss this embarrassing question.
2. Is the Leninist model of the Bolshevik Revolution more closely related to Fascism than to the liberal "reactionariness" of the prerevolutionary era? Since everything indicates that there is a closer affinity between Communism and Fascism than between Fascism and "reaction" of the old type, it was decided not to discuss this embarrassing question.
3. Is it possible to find any inherent differences between Stalinism and classic Leninism? Since everything indicates that no inherent differences can be found, but only differences in method, it has been decided not to discuss this embarrassing question.

These questions are only examples. Perhaps the selection is not even the best possible. The ceaseless evasion of clear answers, however, and the placing of all comparisons outside the parameters of philosophical debate create the situation of inner insincerity that characterizes our intellectual collectivism to a substantial degree today. When the Nobel Prize winner Albert Camus, for instance, wrote in his *The Rebel:* "We are living in the era of premeditation and perfect crimes. Our criminals . . . have a . . . philosophy, which can be used for anything, even for transforming murderers into judges,"[9] one would have thought that to support this statement the author would use the most classic of all examples in this area, the case of the Soviet murderers in Katyń who accused the Germans of this very crime while sitting on the judges' bench. Camus, however, omits such examples and returns to the "Hitler Apocalypse" and so forth—in other words, to the orthodox formula of his circle. Sometimes it seems as though omissions of this kind create a degree of insincerity that leads to doubts about the very sincerity of the condemnation of the crime. The order of things is, as it were, reversed: Hitler's guilt is not a consequence of his crime, but the crime is defined as such because it was committed by Hitler.

A similar reversal may be observed in the way contemporary problems are treated. While Hitler's National Socialism is continuously condemned, National Communism is supported, although the differences between it and Nazism are so blurred that the lack of the obligatory anti-Semitism seems to be the only thing that separates them. Nobody even asks the following question: if totalitarian Communism is negative and nationalism is also negative, why should the combination of these two negative phenomena in the form of National Communism result in a positive phenomenon?

In the so-called good old days, Russia was regarded as the most retrograde and reactionary country. From that country came the common term a "trustworthy" person [*blagonadezhnyi*], contrasted with an "untrustworthy" person, that is, a person who revolted against the existing order of things. At that time, General Spiridovich of the gendarmerie, the chief of the Okhrana (secret police) of Tsar Nicholas II, wrote a book entitled *Partiya Sotsialistov-Revolyutsionerov i yeyo predshestvenniki* [The Socialist Revolutionary Party and Its Predecessors]. He kindly sent a copy of this book to the famous revolutionary Vladimir Burtsev. Burtsev thanked him in the following words: "Your attitude to the problems of the revolutionary liberation movement is of such a nature that it allows for the possibility of discussion. And where discussion is possible, there is always the possibility of finding the truth."

These were times when the space for discussion was wide, like a spread-out fan. Today this space for argument no longer exists; the fan is folded. One no longer debates with those who do not abide by the rules of "trustworthiness." It is a paradox that those who sympathize with a system that regards all fundamental discussion as a crime are now "trustworthy" (and socially acceptable).

The outline presented above is an attempt to describe a certain state of affairs by the use of freely selected examples. Obviously, there are many exceptions that prove the rule. The dictatorship of collective thought in the free world cannot become total, cannot bring about the complete destruction of sovereign thought, if only because of the fact that there are still many countries that guarantee freedom to the individual and that free people who live in those countries are so numerous. By "the sovereignty of thought" I mean a condition in which human thought does not submit blindly to any dogmas imposed from above and does not allow those dogmas to influence and shape it without any questioning. If it is true that a feature of the sovereignty of a state is the unlimited right to select allies, so the unlimited right to select one's own views ought to be a hallmark of the sovereignty of thought.

Poland is not one of the free nations; it is a prisoner of the Communist system. Only émigrés can indulge fully in freedom of thought, a handful in comparison with the numbers of the whole nation, and this handful is obviously to some degree subject to pressures from the atmosphere that surrounds it. Without a description of this atmosphere, as sketched above, a criticism of the stance taken by the Polish émigrés would have been one-sided and perhaps even unjust. On the other hand, we have not detected among Polish émigrés as a whole any effort to liberate themselves from the pressures of collective ways of thinking; rather, to the contrary, we find a nearly complete submission to these ways. And so, for instance, instead of countering the "strangled thought" in Communist Poland with free thought preserved in exile, they counter it with a kind of thought that, although not as narrow as the Communist type, is still considerably restricted in the form of POLREALISM.

There is an affinity between the Communist socialist realism (Socrealism) and the nationalistic Polrealism. Both reject individual judgment in favor of collective judgment. Socrealism teaches that something is real and just only if it serves the interests of the Socialist (Communist) Party; Polrealism teaches that something is real and just only if it serves the interests of the Polish nation. Here the affinity ends, however. Socrealism extends its activities to all nations of the world, while Polrealism is relevant to one nation only. While there are no doubts as to who directs and guides Socrealism, one is never sure who really determines the guidelines of Polrealism, that is, who decides which national interests and which of the constantly changing programs (both on occasion elevated to the rank of sacred dogmas) are right and which are not.

It is obvious that, in comparison with the situation under Communist rule, there is freedom of speech in exile. In practice, however, in every matter that is crucially important, indeed, fundamental, this freedom of speech does not always include the right to express views that are not in keeping with the obligatory Polrealism. It would not be possible to list in one go all the important problems that, in accordance with Polrealism, cannot be criticized but are unanimously accepted.

This unanimity in fundamental matters or, if one prefers, the number of questions that cannot be openly discussed is not a new phenomenon. Even in the current atmosphere of collective thought, we differ in this respect from other societies in the free world. We have always traditionally complained about Polish "brawling" and "Polish discord." In reality, compared with other nations, we have long been one of the most disciplined nations in the world. This is undoubtedly the outcome of 150 years of captivity and of the resulting unidirectional political thought. These are things too well known to be discussed here. Without attempting to scrutinize this issue of discipline, one ought to state objectively, however, that, during the period of partitions, and especially because of the influence of nationalistic ideas on the rise at that time, national thought in Poland became "politicized" and "dehumanized" to a degree. The "individual" was giving way to the "Pole." This process is best illustrated by comparing Polish and Russian literature of the nineteenth century. The hero of Russian literature was the individual, while in Polish literature the individual could often be perceived only as a façade for the real hero—Poland. This great Russian literature, therefore, captivated the whole world, since an individual is always of interest to other individuals. At the same time, Polish literature, despite the existence of great literary talents, has not been met with the same acclaim, since Poland was of interest to only a small number of people in the world.

Obviously, at the time of the great humanistic movements of the nineteenth century, Polish thought still had a relatively wide range in comparison with the totalitarian era of the twentieth century. The collective unanimity reached its peak during and after World War Two. It still exists today, despite appearances to the contrary that signify merely tactical or often only personal differences, and, furthermore, despite the division between the Polish People's Republic and the political émigrés.

During the war, this one-sided Polrealistic totalism assumed an almost ecstatic form. It did not contribute to the recovery of a sovereign state after the war. It contributed substantially only to the degradation of sovereign thought.

This dwindling of free thought almost to the level permitted by the internal discipline of one party seems to be particularly deadly, since it is happening at a time when the dark cloud heralding the destruction of spiritual freedom has already covered more than half the sky above our world.

Part Two **Poland No Longer Between Germany and Russia**

Chapter 2 Does Russia Still Exist?

The concept of today's Polrealism is based upon two fundamental premises: (1) the Polish state still exists, although subjugated by a Communist "régime," and (2) Poland is still situated between Russia and Germany.

Both these premises are, in our opinion, false. They come from an innate lack of understanding of the essence of the 1917 Bolshevik Revolution. This whole concept assumes that the Soviet Union, today the center of the so-called world Socialist (Communist) system, is in essence the old Russia. Since at the same time many other groups in the free world—for different reasons—would like to maintain this identification of the Soviet Union with "Russia," Polrealism not only employs this generally accepted but misleading political perception but contributes to its strengthening and, in this way, to the perpetuation of this gross disinformation. This disinformation concerns the nature of Russia and the nature of the "European East" in general.

OPINIONS

Without wanting to belittle the merits of many scholars, politicians, and writers, one sometimes has the impression that we would know more about the European East had less been written about it. It frequently happens that specialists, even in the exact sciences, show an inclination to arrive too quickly at a diagnosis. This inclination, quite understandable from the human point of view, is all the more pronounced in less exact areas, such as the study of the "European East." We all know the proverb about not being able to see the woods for the trees. The area of the "European East" is so vast and, in the nature of things, has so many "trees" that they can successfully prevent us from seeing the "woods."

One of the most prevalent errors of this type is the theory that Bolshevism is nothing but a historical consequence of old Russia and that it is a typically Eastern creation, since Russia itself was always a creation of the East. This theory clearly does not take into account such simple facts as the nature of prerevolutionary Russia—a country based on belief in God (even in accordance with the law of the land), on Christian morality, on private property, on free competition, on a capitalist economic structure, on human individuality, and so on—which was more closely related, let us say, to Portugal at the western tip of Europe than to the Soviet Union of today, if we want to engage in comparisons. Naturally, one would not deny the specific geographic, climatic, ethnic, and historic differences, as well as the diverse customs and so on. Taken together, however, they do not show intrinsic differences greater than those that one will normally find between two Western European countries. Life in St. Petersburg and Moscow was closer to life in London than life in London was to life on Sicily. In reality, the dividing line between Eastern and Western Europe, which has assumed almost the status of a myth, did not exist at all.

THE THEOLOGICAL DISPUTE

This dividing line, no matter what we say, is very old. It originated in the clash between the Western and the Eastern Churches, between Catholicism and Orthodoxy, and it is clearly a theological dispute. What is now called Western culture is the successor to Latin culture, in short, to Catholicism. Propaganda is not an invention of recent times. Propaganda has always existed, and a classic model is to be found in church propaganda. In the West, many generations remained under the influence of Catholic propaganda, which formed their opinions throughout the centuries. The average European, even today, when asked to describe European history in a nutshell, will say: Rome—the Middle Ages —the Renaissance. In his memory, there is hardly any room for the thousand years of the Byzantine Empire. In reality, however, Byzantium was the center of European culture for many centuries at the very time that its Western counterpart was shrouded in the so-called darkness of the Middle Ages. It so happened that Latin propaganda in its dispute with Orthodoxy was able not only to make people forget the historic role of Byzantium but even to transform this very word into a negative term. We all know what is meant by the term "Byzantine." Not everybody, however, is aware of the fact that at that time this *mot d'ordre* had a purpose identical to that of all the slogans used whenever nationalism was rampant in order to awaken allegedly historic enmities between nations. And so anything bad in Byzantium was called "Byzantine," that is, Eastern, but nothing equally bad in the West was given a permanent sobriquet but was regarded as transient, as a kind of temporary mistake.

In reality, there were no essential qualitative differences, either positive or negative, between the two. In Eastern as well as in Western Europe, murders were committed and eyes were gouged out; the manifestations of barbarity were similar, if not identical. When today one looks in Italy at remnants of Byzantine art that were damaged just because they were not Latin, one cannot escape the impression that such an action would be called typically "Byzantine" had it not been Roman in reality. Similarly, many horrors, wars, religious persecutions, and certainly the procedures of the Inquisition would have been regarded as typically Eastern had they not been carried out in the West.

The territorial dividing line (by the way, this was very close to the current one) was known by the characteristic name of the "bulwark of Christendom." In fact, this bulwark was located not on the borders of Christendom but on the borders of the domain of the Catholic Church. The Teutonic Order fought its greatest battle in 1242 not against pagans but on Lake Peipus against Alexander Nevsky, who was later to become a saint of the Eastern Church. In Polish history, 1386 is the date of the "Baptism" of Lithuania. Actually, the Grand Duchy of Lithuania had a minimal number of pagans at that time, and the vast majority of its inhabitants had already accepted Christianity, but in its Orthodox form. The oldest churches in Wilno (Vilnius) and Grodno belong to that rite. The term "baptism" was, therefore, used only to describe the enthronement of the Catholic Church in Lithuania.

The reverse is also true: on May 29, 1453, when the capital of the thousand-year-old Eastern Christian Empire was captured by the infidels, the Latin West did not provide any assistance apart from the Venetian fleet, but even this meager aid did not get to Constantinople because of adverse winds.

DOUBLE STANDARDS

Out of this traditional mutual antipathy between the two Churches comes the duality of the standards used to assess so-called Eastern and Western Europe, a duality that exists even in our times. I still remember how, in prerevolutionary days, the use of the nonmetric system of weights and measures in Russia was regarded as typically backward. The similar system found in England, which exists even today, is interpreted as adherence to tradition. The fact that the last emperor, Nicholas II, was officially the head of the Church was regarded as "typical Byzantinism"; however, Queen Elizabeth II is today the head of two Churches at the same time, but this merely shows the "popularity of the monarchy." When today in the misery of Bolshevism people quietly queue up in front of shops, one frequently hears words like "slave-like submissiveness" or "the heritage of Ivan the Terrible," and so on. When people in London queue up obediently for much less important purposes, this is cited as an example of social discipline. When a tsarist policeman hit someone in the teeth with his fist, this was an example of the barbaric East. When the French police hit people on their heads with batons, frequently for less compelling reasons, this is not regarded as typically Western. We may be certain that were Switzerland located not in the center of Europe but on its Eastern edges, many experts would have seen the absence of female suffrage as a remnant of Tatar influences and would have managed to prove this scientifically. Similarly, the 1905 pogroms against Jews in Russia, as well as the 1913 trial of Beilis in Kiev on the charge of ritual murder, were regarded at one time as possible only in the benighted East. But it would seem naive to compare those excesses with the terrible forms of persecution of Jews under Hitler. Yet, during World War Two, Jews were persecuted all over Europe by Hungarians, Frenchmen, Dutchmen, Belgians, and many other West Europeans, admittedly under pressure and on Hitler's orders.

How much erudition graced the pages of Western newspapers during the 1937–38 Moscow trials with the aim of proving that the self-incrimination of the accused could be explained only by their inheritance of Byzantine psychology and by centuries of training in servitude! When, however, after 1945, during similar Bolshevik trials, similar confessions were made by a German general, a British attaché, a Catholic bishop, a Roman cardinal, and others, there was no longer any talk about "the Eastern soul" but only about mysterious pills.

DOES "THE EASTERN SOUL" EXIST?

There are many specialists in this field who emphasize the alleged peculiarity of the Eastern soul, especially of the Russian soul, and who try to prove it by using statements by philosophers and great Russian writers such as Herzen, Bakunin, Gogol, Khomyakov, Aksakov, Tyutchev, Dostoevsky, and others: "Listen to what they say about themselves!" We shall not delve so deeply into the polemics of historiosophy, nor will we enter into a discussion about which Church is right, the one that maintains that the Holy Spirit proceeds only from the Father or the one that asserts that It proceeds from the Father and the Son. As is well known, this is the main subject of the dispute. It seems that both these polemics, one from the period between the sixth and eleventh centuries, the other from the nineteenth and twentieth centuries, have something in common in their complex "talmudic" approach. It is, however, difficult to avoid the impression that the problems many experts encounter in their search for "the Russian soul" are based on the fact that they are looking for something that does not exist.

The difference between the Western and Eastern European psyche, if and where it does exist, relates rather to the backwardness of the Eastern parts of Europe and the illiteracy connected with this backwardness. I still remember my first visit to France as a child, in 1911. My attention was drawn to a cabman with the remark: "Look! A cabman on his coach-box reading a newspaper!" The Russian peasant did not read newspapers. He was not interested in which team would win a football match, nor was he interested in many other problems discussed in the newspapers. In his free time, he reflected on more accessible problems: "Does God exist?" and "Where is Truth?" Hence the proverbial, allegedly typically Russian "search for God and the Truth" [*Bogo- i pravdoiskatelstvo*], which also found its reflection in literature. In America, Ernest Hemingway wrote *The Old Man and the Sea,* for which he received the 1954 Nobel Prize. We read that the old fisherman, battling with the ocean and the fish, alone between the sky and the water, finds his thoughts still returning to baseball and to the American League in its competition with the National League.

On the other hand, we have in that same America 118 churches of different denominations; in Western literature, just as in life and in the accounts of crimes, that is, in millions and millions of instances, we find the same themes, the same reactions, motives, dreams, and actions, which would be called examples of the "Eastern psyche" by the expert if only they had been observed in the East. So, also, in the era of nationalisms one readily identifies as typically

French, English, Polish, or German something that in its essence is only typically human.

Before the First World War, one was wont to regard as typically Russian such concepts as "love of humanity" [*chelovekolyubiye*], "nihilism" and "Dostoevskyitis," and so on. Today not much of the "love of man" is left in the Soviet Union, and, as far as "Dostoevskyitis" is concerned, with its reflections of the dark side of the human soul, a reading of some Western European writers creates the impression that they have frequently surpassed the Russian archetype. Jean Anouilh, for instance—if I remember correctly—describes a young girl parading naked around the room and killing time by spitting on the portrait of her mother. Graham Greene's work, such as his story where children destroy a home or the novel *Brighton Rock,* is permeated by instincts of evil, murder, destruction, and radical nihilism. It does not measure up to the descriptive talent of Dostoevsky in *The Devils,* but he surpasses him quantitatively to a substantial degree. In Frankfurt recently, a man was nailed to a tree. The police revealed that he was the leader of a religious sect who could drive the other members into such a state of ecstasy that he was able to order them to crucify him like Christ. Had something similar happened not in the center of contemporary Europe but in the remote Siberian taiga, one can easily imagine the comments by the specialists on the subject of "the Eastern soul."

We treat these comparisons neither as a "reproach" to the West nor as a "defense" of the East. All we want to say is that problems concerning God and Truth are not culturally inferior to those of current politics, sports, or films. A person trampled to death by an ecstatic crowd that stampeded to see a master of rock and roll does not die a more cultural death than a person murdered by the ecstatic members of his religious sect.

Illiteracy, against which all nations of the world rightly battle, played a certain positive role in Eastern European life. In the prerevolutionary period, this illiteracy protected the lower social classes from the pseudo-culture with which the West is swamped today and that finds its recipients in the pseudo-educated masses. In the East, "society" at that time consisted exclusively of people from the upper strata, whose culture was on a par with contemporary Western culture. The self-made man from the bottom of society would come directly into this culture and start reading the classics without passing through the intermediate stage known in German as "Schundliteratur."

THE SOVIET UNION IS NOT A CONTINUATION BUT A NEGATION OF OLD RUSSIA

It was the Bolshevik October Revolution that brought about changes in Russia and reversed the existing order. It abolished the old culture of the higher classes because it was "bourgeois" culture, and it "raised" the masses from illiteracy but only to the level of pseudo-culture. A law dispensed with questions about God and Truth, and these questions were not replaced by others, since all the problems of the world had already been solved by Lenin and it was necessary only to learn the answers by heart. Doubt became punishable, and where there is no doubt there can be no reflection and, therefore, no inquiring minds. And so old Russia, famous—perhaps to an exaggerated degree—for its "hair-splitting," was transformed into a collective, repeating mechanically the verses of the Leninist dogma.

Certainly one has to agree with the statement of I. A. Kurganov that "Russia has not only changed, it has become the USSR; that is, in essence it is a new country almost completely different from old Russia, as well as from any other country of the free world."[1] One could venture to state that the Soviet Union is more than simply a change from old Russia; it is a kind of reversal. This is true in every respect: its political and constitutional system; its economy, philosophy, customs; and especially, perhaps, its psychology. While the external forms of the empire were maintained, its internal substance was transformed.

One could say, with some oversimplification, that nineteenth-century Russia was a country of conspirators and rebels, while the Soviet Union is a country of silent obedience; the symbol of Russia was its domed churches with golden crosses, while the symbol of the Soviet Union is the abolition of the cross; Russian poetry spoke of forests and wide expanses, while Soviet poetry speaks of factory chimneys; Russian literature was guided by the spirit of opposition and criticism, while Soviet literature has been guided by the spirit of submissiveness and praise; in old Russia people gathered to defend the wronged, whereas in the Soviet Union they gather to trample over the wronged; in old Russia the favorite theme was doubt about everything, while in the Soviet Union the only theme is unshaken certainty; in Russia a spy or informer was despised even by those using his services, whereas in the Soviet Union denunciation has been raised to the level of a civic virtue; Russia in the nineteenth century developed a social stratum of "intelligentsia" and a clamorous public opinion, whereas the Soviets abolished society and annihilated public opinion; Russia, after its judicial reforms, was famous for having the most objective courts in the whole of Europe, whereas the Soviet Union is famous for the bloodiest parody of justice in history. Such comparisons could be continued ad infinitum.

We shall end them here with the following anecdote. The well-known Russian politician and historian Pavel Milyukov relates that in Moscow University, in the second half of the nineteenth century, a collection was organized to gather funds for a monument to the assassinated Tsar Alexander II. One of the students ostentatiously put on the plate not a coin but a button, and another student informed university officials about it. They expelled not the one who offered the button but the one who informed on him. Sixty years later, during the Moscow trials, which brought about the greatest degradation of human dignity in all history, *Pionerskaya pravda* published large numbers of letters written by children aged nine through twelve: "We were very glad to read about the death sentence; how nice it would have been even for a moment to be the Chekist who caught those dirty scoundrels.—Our beloved Chekists prevented those wretched bandits from carrying out their dirty plans. We children declare that the verdict of the court is our verdict too!—We gathered every day at the loudspeaker to hear the reports on the trial of the counterrevolutionary murderers. The day before yesterday we heard the verdict. We were overjoyed."

It is not important to know how these letters originated. It is important to notice that such changes had occurred that the publishing of letters of this nature could demonstrate the virtue of the children.

People look at Soviet foreign policy and point out many analogies to the foreign policy of tsarist Russia. The general guidelines of foreign policy, however, arise from geographical position, and should we replace the Italians with the Chinese or the Scandinavians, their foreign policy would still be based on the geographical position of the Appenine Peninsula.

Lenin taught that to reach a goal, literally every tactical maneuver is legitimate. It would certainly be strange had he excluded here the maneuvers used by old Russia. But it is, perhaps, precisely the totality of Soviet foreign policy that constitutes the feature most different from that of old Russia. Soviet policy is not a state policy; rather, it is a policy of conspiracy against other states. It would have been pointless for old Russia to have had diplomatic posts in Chile, Argentina, the Congo, India, Malaya, in fact across the world, if the main aim of those diplomatic posts was to overthrow the governments and political order of the countries in which they were situated. In Soviet policy, however, this is the very purpose of their activities. It is, therefore, not Russian imperialism that uses international Communism but international Communism that uses the methods of Russian imperialism whenever they are convenient.

Sometimes one hears the following argument: "How can it be explained that Communism took root only in Russia?" One could answer with a long treatise, or with some brief counterquestions: how can it be explained that the bloody French Revolution took root only in France and that the monarchy was restored there? How can it be explained that the cradle of European romanticism, the nation of "poets and thinkers," allowed Nazism to come to power? Nazism was a repugnant phenomenon, and so enemies of Germany try to prove that it came from a peculiarly German mentality. Bolshevism is also repugnant, and so enemies of Russia try to prove that it "corrupted the teachings of Marx" by introducing into it certain purely Russian features. But Communist rule in Russia is the result of many circumstances, as was Hitler's rule in Germany, Fascism in Italy, or even Communism in Cuba. Not much would have been needed, as we know, to bring about the victory of Communism even on the western edge of Europe, in Spain.

THE "SECRET" OF COMMUNISM IS IN THE WEST

The mysterious psychological disposition of the Bolsheviks is usually ascribed to Moscow. Wrong. In Moscow, everything is subjected to external compulsion, that is, it is deformed by a mechanical factor. Furthermore, it is difficult to go to Moscow. It seems, therefore, that it would be more sensible to transfer one's research to an area where the Communist phenomenon exists in a nearly pure form, that is, without the addition of the external pressures of the police, and where the subject of inquiry itself is commonly and easily accessible. This could be done, for instance, in Togliatti's Italy or Thorez's France, where up to 30 percent of the population votes Communist out of free, unrestrained choice. It is also difficult to deny that Communism is a product not of Eastern but of Western Europe.

It is commonly held that Bolshevism is a product of the East ("Asia"). This slogan is frequently uttered in Western so-called anti-Soviet (anti-Russian) circles, but it is also voiced by prorevolutionary reformers of Bolshevism, by "revisionists," national Communists, and so on. Deeply rooted in Nazi circles, it was promulgated in the Third Reich by Dr. Alfred Rosenberg. It was he who convinced Hitler, in 1941, that "Bolshevism removed the old ruling class of

Russia and replaced it by a new class of Caucasian-Asiatic descent." This myth is in open conflict with historical truth. In fact, in the Asiatic provinces of Russia, the struggle against Bolshevism lasted longest, up to the year 1927. The only authentic Asians in European Russia, the Buddhist Kalmyks from the southern Volga area, were among the greatest enemies of Bolshevism, and therefore they were used by the counterrevolutionaries to serve in so-called punitive units.

Lenin, it is well known, lived longer in Zürich, Berlin, Paris, and London than in Moscow. He got his ideological inspiration not from Russia but from Western Europe. He was opposed to all the typically Russian, non-Marxist revolutionary parties; thus, Marxism went from the West to the East, not in the other direction. At the end of the nineteenth century, it first filtered through from German Social Democratic circles to Poland and seduced the Polish Socialist Party (PPS). However, it found its most characteristic and radical expression—in a form even then close to Bolshevism—in the Social Democratic Party of the Polish Kingdom and Lithuania (SDKPiL), headed by such subsequently well-known Communists as Rosa Luxemburg, Julian Marchlewski, and the first Soviet chekist, the Pole Felix Dzierżyński [Dzerzhinsky]. They were closely connected to the German Social Democrats through such precursors of world Communism as Karl Liebknecht and Karl Radek, and they received their ideological inspiration from Berlin. Lenin wrote in *Rabochaya pravda* that German Social Democracy was "the only completely progressive and, in the best sense of the word . . . mass workers' party."[2]

Chronologically, Marxism was first accepted by the leaders of the Jewish "Bund" in Wilno (Vilnius), who acted in agreement with the Kiev "Bund." The Russian Social-Democratic Party sprang from these two and was established at a secret convention in Minsk in March 1898. It was only after Lenin had formally joined, during the Second Party Congress in London, in July–August 1903, that the party split into the Mensheviks and the Bolsheviks.

There were hardly any Bolsheviks at all in St. Petersburg [Petrograd] at the beginning of the February 1917 revolution and at the time of the Tsar's abdication. Their leaders were transported from Western Europe in a "sealed train" on the initiative of the imperial German government and General Staff, with helpful cooperation from the governments of Switzerland and Sweden—five hundred people, along with their families. All roads led, as one can see, from the West to the East, not the other way round.

Many people, especially former Communists and pro-Communist Europeans, who became somewhat disenchanted with "Stalinist" methods, persistently contend that "Russian Bolshevism" is not the same as "European Communism." It is difficult to engage in polemics with such a statement, since it is clearly based on a disregard of generally known facts that prove the sameness of ideology, the close connections, and the internal discipline of the whole international Communist movement, regardless of geographic location. Thus, the perception of essential differences is a symptom of wishful thinking, that is, seeing what one wants to see.

THE PHENOMENON OF COMMUNISM

Thousands of books have been written about Communism. Here I would like to point to a phenomenon that, in my opinion, is of the utmost importance, namely robbing words of their original meaning. This phenomenon appears in different guises. Sometimes only a word's meaning is being blurred, but sometimes an exactly opposite meaning is imposed. After the Twentieth Party Congress, and in particular after the Twenty-Second Party Congress and "de-Stalinization," this degradation of words, that is, the most important instruments of human culture, became even more evident than it had been during the times of Lenin and Stalin. For it had never before been admitted by the party so clearly that not only do the billions of words, spoken throughout the decades in the highest political councils, in literature, in theaters, in schools, and at rallies have no relation to reality but also that everyone is absolved of any personal responsibility since everyone utters the same meaningless words.

Since 1956, in the Soviet Union itself as well as in the "people's democracies," the same system has been preserved and most of the principal political actors have remained in the same posts, though for years they spoke and wrote things that are condemned today, as long as they now speak and write only what they are ordered to, using the same vocabulary and, moreover, the same tone. This manipulation of meaning, or rather of lack of meaning, from above is carried out to an extent unknown in the history of verbal juggling. So, the Stalinist purges of 1936–38 and the self-accusations of the old Communists who were, after all, subjected to unknown pressures appear less strange than the leveling of charges against Voroshilov in 1961 before a crowd of five thousand delegates from all over the world while he was still sitting on the platform. What phenomenal psychological pressure must have been exerted to force this old man, who had devoted his whole life to the Revolution, to perform an act of repentance in such a completely absurd way! And not in prison, but while he was free.

This is possible only in a system that uses the material energy of the largest bloc of states in the world to devalue words. This is a situation without precedent, since one is not permitted to defend oneself against this depreciation of words in the Communist system, even by remaining silent. On the contrary, everybody has to say exactly what he is ordered to say.

Communism thus becomes, in the hierarchy of political events, a superior phenomenon that transcends both nations and states. It is not to be identified with Russia, nor is it to be identified with any other nation or state in the world. By depriving words of their original meaning, by calling aggression "liberation," slavery "freedom," lack of toleration "tolerance," nominations "elections," and so on, it intends to force not just a nation but humanity to use language to its own detriment. This means that, in return for renouncing traditional language, culture, and spiritual freedom, it promises total slavery.

POLAND UNDER RUSSIA AND POLAND UNDER COMMUNISM

When we compare Poland's position after 1945 with the situation of Poland under Russian rule before 1914, we must conclude, if we look at things objectively, that these are not analogous but rather reversed historical situations. This reversal flows logically from a similar reversal of the order in Russia.

At the end of the eighteenth century, Poland was attacked by three neighboring states and was partitioned among these states by force. This act of violence, although we may call it "unheard of" in our righteous indignation, in reality was not "unheard of" at all. It was a kind of violence we may describe as conventional in the age-long relations among nations and states. Nearly all human history is composed of wars of conquest, in which the stronger state subdues or occupies the territory of the weaker state. More unusual, perhaps, is the fact that a once-powerful kingdom did not put up much resistance. But even this is not a historical curiosity; even this does not show the Polish nation in a negative light, since nearly all the nations of the world have gone through periods of rise and decline and through internal crises and the psychological changes connected with them. It should rather serve as a warning against coming too quickly to conclusions that generalize about the "intrinsic" characteristics of a nation on the basis of only one or two of its historical periods.

The "Polish Side" and the "Russian Side"

Poland came under Russian influence even before the partitions. Some historians regard the last king, Stanisław August, as docile and accommodating or even as a puppet in the hands of Catherine II; others hold a different view. Without discussing the merits of these historical interpretations, one must state that Stanisław August, despite his tendency to compromise, remained, at any rate, politically opposed to the "Russian side." In other words, in the relations between Poland and Russia, he still represented (quite apart from the question of whether this was done badly or well) the interests of the Polish state and the Polish nation. This also refers to the persons around him, the government and the parliament [Sejm]. Thus, the "Polish side" was forced to oppose or to react in some other way against the pressures and influences of the Russian envoys in Warsaw, for example, Repnin or Stackelberg, who, as Russian power increased and the Polish state weakened, also increased their influence until, in reality, they became dictators, imposing upon Poland the interests of the Russian state. This is a course of action that does not differ from typical forms of pressure exerted by one state on another.

The "Communist Side"

The moment Poland found itself under Communist rule, it was not an analogous situation that arose but exactly the opposite. The highest official of the "People's Poland," the leader of the Communist Party, represents in so-called international Polish-Soviet relations not the Polish side but, on the contrary, the Soviet side. The same applies to the people around him, the members of the governing party, the government itself, the parliament, the whole state apparatus without exception, and all other institutions imposed upon the country. The so-called Polish People's Republic is the antithesis not of the Soviet state but of the Polish nation. This is a state that does not defend the interests of the Polish nation in its relations with the Soviet state but, on the contrary, imposes upon the Polish nation the interests of international Communism represented by the Soviet state.

In the same way, the role of the Soviet envoys in Warsaw was changed. If we omit minor tasks connected with monitoring and espionage, the role of the Soviet representative is limited to that of a figurehead. In the hierarchy of international Communism, the standing of the leader of the Polish Communist Party (whatever its official name) is higher than that of the Soviet ambassador. Thus, if the need arose, the Soviet envoy would not tell Gomułka what to do, but Gomułka would tell him what to do.

Konstantin Pavlovich and Konstanty Rokossowski

A characteristic illustration of this situation, the reverse of the period of Russian occupation and, at the same time, a good illustration of the stubbornness of Polrealism that does not want to see the real situation and prefers to maintain the charade, may be provided by contrasting the role of the Russian Grand Duke Konstantin Pavlovich and that of the Soviet Marshal Konstanty Rokossowski.

The 1815 Congress of Vienna created the Polish ("Congress") Kingdom under the rule of Alexander I, the Emperor of Russia, but with its own government and parliament. General Józef Zajączek became regent of the Kingdom, but military command was not left in Polish hands; it was placed in the hands of a Russian, the Grand Duke Konstantin Pavlovich, a brother of the Emperor, who soon became the most important person in Warsaw.

When Konstanty Rokossowski, a Soviet Marshal, became the Commander-in-Chief of the Polish People's Army in 1949 and, at the same time, a member of the Politburo of the Polish Communist Party, the adherents of the Polrealistic interpretation of history saw here an analogy and attributed to Rokossowski the role of Grand Duke Konstantin. Since this occurred during the Cold War and at a time when anti-Soviet radio propaganda was permitted by the Western powers, the Polish sections of all the American, British, and French radio stations started to attack Rokossowski. Much was made of the fact that the first names were identical. Jibes and jokes on this theme abounded; the name was Russified into "Konstantin," or even "Kostia," and his surname was pronounced with a Russian accent, "Ra-ka-ssov-skiy." All this was supposed to underscore the "Russian character" of Rokossowski as a factor influencing his appointment.

Rokossowski is in reality an authentic Pole. His appointment as "Marshal of Poland" was influenced not by his nationality, however, and not by his rank of Soviet Marshal but by the fact that there was no one among the Polish generals at that time who had similar party standing. The criterion that Moscow applied was not "Pole or Russian" but "trustworthy or untrustworthy Communist."

This persistent comparing of Konstanty Rokossowski to Grand Duke Konstantin clearly illustrates the tendency to emphasize that the People's Poland was "sinking" somehow to the position of Congress Poland, to emphasize the analogy with the Russian-ruled part of the country after 1815. No analogy was actually justified. Rokossowski did not have any influence on the course of events in Warsaw, since it was not he who gave orders to the party but the party that gave orders to him. He did not have and, just like any other professional soldier in the Communist system, could not have any greater importance in Moscow than the Polish party dignitaries. He did not play any major part in the scheme of things, and, as later events have shown, his recall did not change the situation in the least. An analogy is impossible, since the degree of submission under Communist rule is much greater than under Russian rule, and the quality of this submission is incomparable. This is demonstrated below by the presentation of the "Polish content" under Russian rule and the "Polish form" under Communist rule.

The Political Gist Upside Down

Under Russian rule, even the extreme conciliators represented Polish interests to the end, as opposed to Russian interests. The circles working toward an accord with Russia, beginning with the policies of Count Aleksander Wielopolski in the middle of the nineteenth century and including later political groups prior to World War One, distinguished Polish interests from Russian interests, despite their willingness to compromise. The borderline between these two opposing interests was quite clear. The defense of Polish interests against attempts at Russification was directed toward the achievement of such concessions and rights as would make Polish national activities possible: schools with Polish as the language of instruction; books, newspapers, and theaters in the Polish language; Polish associations; courses of higher education in Polish, and so on. The defense of Polish "content" from the menace of Russification constituted the core of Polish interests at that time, and so "concessions" were extracted from the Russians.

Under Communist rule, Polish "content" was actually transformed into Polish "form," since "Socialism" (Communism) became the real content. As a result of this, "concessions" of the previous type lost their meaning, since the essence of these concessions was transformed into its opposite; they were no longer concessions for the Polish nation but a tool by which the hostile government could exert influence on the nation. Schools, universities, books, newspapers, theaters, the cinema, radio, associations, organizations, clubs, even the pure sciences, even music and painting—all of these, directly or indirectly, to a lesser or greater extent, served the Communists as effective tools for transforming a free nation, a free society, into a Communist collective. These tools are especially effective if used in the language of the given nation. And so a seemingly paradoxical phenomenon emerged: the main instrument for the enslavement of the Polish nation is not, as previously, Russification, but Polonization. The paradox disappears when one realizes that this is Polonization in form only; in essence, however, it is Bolshevization, Sovietization, and Communization.

Polrealism practiced in exile has been trying to divert attention from the real state of affairs and to maintain its thesis that the Soviet Union is really "Russia." Although it has frequently endeavored to distort the truth and to suggest that Russification is being carried out in Poland, such attempts belong to the same category of myths as the comparison between the "two Konstantins." It is suggested, for instance, that a Pushkin celebration in Warsaw signifies Russification but a Mickiewicz celebration in Moscow does not signify Polonization. Similarly, tours of Warsaw theaters not only in Moscow but also in Lithuania, Byelorussia, and the Ukraine are not regarded as Polonization. This problem belongs to the general nationality policy of the Communist system, and its discussion would take up too much space here. Let us only mention marginally that one can dance and sing the "Krakowiak" [the Cracowian] in Moscow and buy records of it in shops there; at the same time, "Chubchik," "Sten'ka Razin," "The Volga Boatmen," and other prerevolutionary Russian songs are largely banned; such records are produced clandestinely and sold surreptitiously at markets. One has to admit, however, that the stories about alleged Russification, so devoid of any basis in reality, have recently been almost completely discontinued as a tool of Polrealist disinformation.

The Comparison: "Man"

Tsarist Russia was a class state. It was not so much a state of social injustice—compared with the present, it was frequently easier to get justice there than it is in the democracies of later eras—as a state of social inequality. As far as daily life in Poland was concerned, the real master of the land was still the Polish nobleman, not the Russian official or policeman who would bow to him with respect. It is worth remembering that, despite Russification, on occasion implemented by draconian methods, the state was based not on the idea of nationality but on that of class. If we take a look at the yearbooks of prerevolutionary nominations to officers' rank, we find the greatest number of Polish gentry names in the (Russian) Corps of Pages, in the cavalry guard regiments, in the Cuirassier Guards and in other (Russian) guards units. The percentage declines rapidly in the regular army infantry, where we find almost exclusively Russian names. This is only a marginal illustration, but it is still an indication that the "national persecution" of that time should not be identified with the persecutions of the twentieth century. The term "persecution" today is somewhat automatically connected with the underdog. In those times, since about 80 percent of the Poles who fought for freedom came from the privileged gentry, the situation was such that 80 percent of the Russian nation, who did not enjoy the rights of the gentry, might rather have been envious of the fate of the "persecuted" Poles.

The attitude toward so-called political crimes was also different. Professor Władysław Studnicki, a great enemy of Russia but a righteous man who loathed any kind of lie, told me about his prerevolutionary deportation to the district of Minusinsk, in Siberia. While listening as an émigré myself to his account of the conditions of his deportation, I had the impression that I would gladly have exchanged my current situation for that of a political deportee of that time. Professor Studnicki's life in exile was not only the result of his privileged social position but was also the result of his having committed a rather "privileged" crime. Political crimes belonged to a somewhat "honorable" category, and, quite contrary to Communist norms today, they were treated not as something "worse" but as something "better" than other kinds of crime.

It seems to me that the basis of this different treatment can be sought in a different attitude toward the individual, to the person as an entity generally protected by divine, human, and state law (in conformity with the atmosphere then prevailing throughout the world). Today, none of these laws protects a human being in a Communist system.

A well-known lawyer in prerevolutionary Russia, O. O. Gruzenberg, a Russian Jew by origin, published his memoirs after he emigrated. It is clear that he hated the tsarist regime. He describes the famous Kiev trial of Beilis, a Jew accused of a ritual murder. Gruzenberg cites with indignation and anger all the tricks used by the police to influence the peasants on the jury to bring about the conviction of Beilis. After many such attempts—as he says—the balance turned in favor of acquittal when one of the jurors, a peasant, suddenly got up during the proceedings, crossed himself in front of an icon, and said, "I cannot sin against my conscience by voting for the conviction of an innocent man." While talking about the conduct of this trial with deep revulsion, Gruzenberg does not make any comparisons. Had he done so, perhaps he would have been astonished at how naive and anachronistic this whole method of exerting pressure by the police looks today. The great expenditure of energy on the part of the police apparatus, completely wasted in the end because of one peasant's crossing himself in front of an icon, indicates that the individual was still taken into consideration. Today, the masses in the Soviet Union can be addressed by pushing a button, and the individual is not taken into account at all. In response to a single movement of the finger, not only all the judges of the Communist bloc but all the millions of people living there too would pass any sentence and take any decision demanded by the Party.

Although political life in Poland under Russian rule was subject to official control, there was, generally speaking, no official interference with private life. In his memoirs, Professor Fedor Stepun rightly remarks: "What a huge difference there is between Tsarism and Bolshevism. . . . Obviously State despotism is terrible, but not so much because of its political prohibitions as because of its cultural and pedagogical projects and its designs for a new man and a new humanity. Despite all its despotism, Tsarist Russia did not try to educate anyone spiritually or order people around in spiritual and cultural matters. And it didn't have the power to do so, anyway. The odd story to the contrary would be irrelevant."[3]

Unquestionably, the difference between a mere prohibition and a general command is the most essential difference between Russian rule and Communist rule.

One should not forget that democracy is not freedom. Democracy is only equality, while freedom results only from liberalism. The combination of equality and freedom constitutes the ideal we would all like to achieve. Tsarist Russia was not a democratic country, but at the end of its existence it was a liberal country. The Communist system, however, regards liberalism as its greatest enemy.

Not the Rule of a State, but the Rule of a Party

We see that the rulers of Poland after 1945, the Polish Communists, are zealous spokesmen not for Polish interests but for Soviet political interests. The question arises, therefore, as to what is their real function, not as regards their ideological convictions but in their relationship to Poland. Are they officials of the Soviet state? Were this so, Poland would certainly have been made subject to the internal apparatus of the Soviet state. Actually, the People's Poland is not formally, or even in practice, a part of the internal Soviet state structure. We are dealing here with a completely new phenomenon resulting from the specific structure of the Soviet Union and different from the rest of the world. In keeping with this structure, the current rulers of Poland belong not to the Soviet state bodies but to the party hierarchy. Thus, Poland is not subordinated to the Soviet state per se, but it is directly subordinated to the Communist Party, which rules the Soviet state.

Party interests come before state interests, be they of the Soviet Union, the People's Poland, or other members of the Communist bloc. So, Poland as a state, in its relationship with Russia as a state, is not in a subordinate position; rather, the two states are "comrades" in their common subordination to the same party. One could say that they are united in the misfortune that overtook both countries and the nations living in them.

Poland did not become the seventeenth republic of the Soviet Union; although this could have been in the interests of the Soviet state, it was not in accord with the worldwide interests of party policy. It is in the interests of the "world socialist system" to maintain the fiction of Polish sovereignty, as well as that of the sovereignty of other "people's" republics. This fiction is total and, as we can see, also rather effective.

The present situation of Poland (a country subordinated not to the Soviet state but to the Communist world center) obviously does not mean that Poland has greater weight than the Ukrainian Soviet Republic or any other republics within the Soviet Union. This is a different question. Poland's situation means only that it, in accordance with the plans of international Communism, has been deployed on another level and that on this level it plays a role qualitatively different from that of the Soviet Union's republics. At the same time, this means that Poland is in greater—to use the common term—bondage than at any other time in its history. It is subject to a monstrous form of oppression that not only takes away its independence but paralyzes the essence of its organic existence, threatening, therefore, the transformation of the whole nation into a different "socialist nation" in accordance with Communist plans.

Whether this will actually happen, we do not know. At this point we wish to ask how it has come to pass that many Poles regard this terrible enslavement of thought and spirit that has been imposed upon Poland as a continuation of the Polish state or, at worst, as something comparable to the "Russian" oppression, that is, to something so much milder and of quite a different nature. To answer this question, it is not enough to acquaint oneself with the world political atmosphere outlined in the previous chapter. One has to look into the primary source of the false diagnosis where today's disinformation originated. This means that we have to go back to the historical factors that brought about the transformation of Eastern Europe and that developed into a menace for the contemporary world.

Chapter 3 Between Bolshevism and Nationalism

There is nothing stable in the world, and there is nothing unstable. History may repeat itself, or it may not. Sometimes one has the impression that those who assert that "history never repeats itself" do so because they are too lazy to acquaint themselves with it. In the history of Communism, from the beginning to our own day, the central elements repeat themselves as on an often-exposed negative. Was it only an accident, or was it that Lenin, like a genius, foresaw the role that nationalism would play in helping Bolshevism to achieve stability?

Lenin based the Bolshevik Revolution on two decrees: the "Decree on Peace" and the "Decree on Land," published the day after the beginning of the Revolution, that is, November 8, 1917. After about a week, on November 15, he added the famous "Declaration of Rights of Peoples of Russia," which proclaimed the right of all the nations of the former empire to self-determination and independence, including separation from Russia and the creation of an independent state. Seemingly, this decree could have resulted in the complete dispersal of revolutionary forces, and thus it could have led to the destruction of the Bolshevik Revolution, which, in view of the small number of its adherents, could base any hope of success only on a mighty centralized base of power. Was it the knowledge of the nationalistic mentality or simply of human psychology that suggested to Lenin that in this way he would be able to destroy the solidarity of all the anti-Bolshevik forces? In essence, this "Declaration" was only an empty phrase, since the decision as to what the "real expression of a nation's will" was had been given not to the people but to Bolshevik cells. Still, it proved very convincingly the correctness of Lenin's tactics. Though the obvious falsehood became evident nearly at once, the absolute majority of nationalistic leaders came to the conclusion that independence might be achieved through certain compromises and cooperation with the Bolsheviks, rather than through cooperation with the counterrevolutionary forces.

WITH OTHER NATIONALISMS AGAINST THE BOLSHEVIKS? OR WITH THE BOLSHEVIKS AGAINST OTHER NATIONALISMS?

When confronted with this kind of question, the several nationalistic movements (today we might call them "national realisms") as a rule chose the second option. None of the nations involved, including the Russian, took into account the transnational, purely human side of the problem and discerned the real nature of Bolshevism-Communism, the new content that constituted an overwhelming transnational danger. The leaders of those nations that fought for independence and freedom from Russian imperial rule saw in Bolshevism rather a sign of the weakening of this empire, that is, a "lesser evil," and they saw the victory of the counterrevolution and, soon, even the demands of other neighboring nations as the greater evil. At the same time, the leaders of the Russian counterrevolution treated the independence or "separatist" movements of the individual nations as a greater danger for Russia in many cases than Bolshevism itself.

These views led to historic events that should be recalled today not only because they seem relevant but primarily because of the analogy between the outlook then and now, which, in this light, appears to have remained unchanged. Sometimes, when listening to current disputes, one would simply like to cry out: "But all this has happened before!" I am of the opinion, therefore, that people who would like to assess the present situation objectively must become acquainted with what has been there before.

Finland left the anti-Bolshevik front at the very time when the fate of the Bolshevik Revolution was in the balance. Some Russian forces, the so-called

Northern Army led by General Yudenich, broke through the lines of the Seventh Bolshevik Army at Yamburg on October 10, 1919. It took up positions on the Pulkovo hills on the southern outskirts of Petrograd on October 21. Anti-Bolshevik riots started in Petrograd. Lenin cried out: "At no time has the Soviet Republic faced such a mortal danger." The official Soviet history, *Kratkaya istoriya grazhdanskoi voiny v SSSR* [A Short History of the Civil War in the USSR], writes about this period: "Fortunately, at the most crucial moment of the struggle the small bourgeois states refused to render assistance to Yudenich. The first to declare its refusal of assistance was Finland. The attempt to use the small bourgeois states in the struggle against Soviet Russia did not succeed. . . . Finland did not engage in open warfare against the Bolsheviks."[1]

Finland preferred to maintain a position of "armed neutrality." Only once, in May 1919, on the personal initiative of Mannerheim, did a Finnish partisan unit under Elwengrein advance in the direction of Karelia, but this was an episode without significance.

Estonia initially did not have any army with which to defend itself against the Bolsheviks, and so, with British aid, it even paid the units of the Northern Army of Yudenich, which protected it against the Bolsheviks. But, on July 28, 1919, the British general March sent him an ultimatum demanding the recognition of Estonia's independence within . . . forty minutes; otherwise, he threatened to hold back all aid for the continuation of the fight against the Bolsheviks, which had just started to show some successes. (How well do we know such gestures!) This recognition was granted, but it was delayed until August 18. By then, however, the Estonians, who in the meantime had tried to begin negotiations with the Bolsheviks, did not want to offer any further assistance to the Whites. They not only refused to help but, immediately after Yudenich's defeat, began to disarm the White Russian units on their territory. Estonia signed a peace treaty with the Bolsheviks on February 2, 1920, while the fight against the Bolshevik Revolution was still continuing on other fronts. This was the first peace treaty and the first example of "coexistence" between the Soviet Union and a capitalist state. Ivan Maysky, later the Soviet ambassador in London, said that for the second time in history a window to Europe had been opened.

Lithuania from the start assumed a friendlier attitude toward the Bolsheviks than toward Poland, mainly because of the dispute over Wilno (Vilnius). In December 1918, the Polish government proposed to the Lithuanian government a compact to fight the Bolsheviks. The Lithuanian government made its agreement conditional on the recognition by Poland of Wilno as Lithuania's capital. The Polish government refused. Meanwhile, Soviet troops were approaching Wilno. In Wilno, a Polish Committee improvised a kind of "self-defense" and proposed to the Lithuanian government that they defend the city jointly. The Lithuanian government not only rejected this proposal but in addition solemnly protested against the establishment of the anti-Bolshevik Polish self-defense organization. The government left the city on January 1, 1919, and settled in Kowno [Kaunas] under the protection of the German army, which was still in control of that city. The weak Polish "self-defense" unit was smashed by the Bolsheviks, who advanced as far as the line Szawle—Możejki—Kowno—Olita—Grodno—Prużany—Kobryń. In February 1919, when Poland began to liberate the area from the Bolsheviks, the Lithuanian government and the government of the "National Byelorussian Republic," though neither possessed sufficient forces to drive the Bolsheviks out from the occupied territories, formally protested against this Polish offensive, which reached Wilno on April 19 and Minsk on August 8.

The dispute over territorial boundaries and conflicting national demands completely obscured any awareness of the common danger of Bolshevism. On July 12, 1920, during the great retreat of the Polish army, Lithuania signed a peace treaty with Soviet Russia, which contained a secret clause concerning the right of Bolshevik troops to march through Lithuania against Poland. And this despite the formal existence of the Communist government of the Bolshevik "Lithuanian-Byelorussian Republic," which had claims to these same territories. But Lithuania stuck to a policy that it regarded as "realistic" and that regarded Poland as a greater danger than the Communists. Even a minimal understanding of the nature of Bolshevism would have shown how completely unwarranted such a policy was. It was only the Polish victory in the battle of Warsaw that saved Lithuania from being incorporated into the Soviet Union in 1920.

After Piłudski broke the Polish-Lithuanian Treaty of Suwałki signed on October 7, 1920, and after General Żeligowski occupied Wilno, Lithuania, as far as its relations with Poland were concerned, notoriously cooperated with the Soviets. It did not take part in the anti-Bolshevik cordon sanitaire promoted for some time by the West, mainly because Poland was the central link of this chain. This state of affairs persisted until World War Two, when, after the fall of Poland, Lithuania and the other Baltic states were taken over by the Soviets.

Byelorussia took a still more unequivocal stance by choosing to side with the Bolsheviks against Russian and Polish nationalism. The decisive influence here came from the social radicalism characteristic of the Byelorussian national movement. After the Bolshevik Revolution, the slogans of the Byelorussian "Hramada" differed little in fact from the slogans of the Bolsheviks. The "Hramada" regarded the "Polish reactionary forces and the Russian counterrevolution" as its main enemies. A "Byelorussian Congress" convened on December 28, 1917, in Minsk and, referring to Lenin's declaration, demanded Byelorussian independence. The independence of the "National Byelorussian Republic" was actually declared on March 9, 1918. This declaration did not produce much excitement in the country, both because of the lack of a power base and because of the national indifference of the Byelorussian masses. After the withdrawal of the Germans, the Bolsheviks occupied Minsk, without meeting any resistance, on December 7, 1918. The Council of the "National Byelorussian Republic" escaped to Kowno.

On December 30, 1918, the so-called Sixth Congress of the Communist Party of the Northwestern Area changed its name to the First Congress of the Communist Party of Byelorussia and proclaimed the establishment of the Byelorussian Socialist Republic with borders from the Smolensk area to Augustów (the official proclamation was issued on January 1, 1919). A large number of the leaders of the Byelorussian national movement officially switched to the Bolshevik side, and some even joined the party. The Byelorussian historian Josef Mienski explains this event as follows: "For a long time they had been members of nationalist organizations aiming at the transformation of Byelorussia into a national state. In this case the nationalist factor was decisive for them. ... The Byelorussian Communists also gave priority to the national cause. They tried, however, to coordinate national liberation with Communist ideology."[2]

Here we find not only the first germ of classical "National Communism" but also the same apologia as is used today to argue for the "coordination of Communism with the national interest" or for the "placing of the national cause above ideology."

A similar tactic was also used by Lenin vis-à-vis the Byelorussian emigration. Through the Latvian government he established secret contacts with the Byelorussian Council in Kowno in June 1920, and confidentially invited its representatives to Moscow. This invitation was accepted. Delegates of the Council participated in secret discussions that centered around the establishment of an "independent" Byelorussia under the protectorate of Communist Moscow. From this moment onward we find in Byelorussian circles the predominance of a so-called realistic approach to national matters; this was crowned very soon by the greatest achievement of Leninist tactics in the form of the first national New Economic Policy (NEP).

The Ukraine. We omit the period of Hetman Skoropadski, which was closely connected with the German occupation. After the collapse of Germany in November 1918, Skoropadski signed a "Hramota," declaring a Federation of the Ukraine and Russia on November 14, 1918. He tried in this way to win support among the anti-Bolshevik Russian forces in his struggle against the Bolsheviks. Two days later, on November 16, he was overthrown by Ukrainian left-wing opposition parties. On December 19, 1918, the so-called Directorate, headed by Vinnichenko along with Petlyura, was established. But by then Bolshevik forces were already entering the Ukraine in the name of the "Ukrainian Soviet Socialist Republic." The Directorate escaped to Równe in Wołyń [Volhynia]. A chaotic situation developed, with the Ukraine being represented simultaneously by three governments: the Directorate, the Soviet puppet government, and the provisional government of the West Ukrainian National Republic (involved especially in the struggle with Poland over Lwów and Galicia).

In this situation, the Directorate asked such basic questions as: with whom should we side? On whom should we rely? On the Western powers, which, for the time being, support anti-Bolshevik Russia and Poland, or on the Bolsheviks against Russia and Poland? The chairman of the Directorate, Vinnichenko, was in favor of the Bolsheviks. His reasoning was not devoid of "National Communist" arguments or, if one prefers, of "national realist" arguments similar to the ones used by the Byelorussian leaders. Vinnichenko argued as follows: the Entente supports counterrevolutionary Russia and reactionary Poland. As a result, Russia and Poland will again divide the Ukraine, as they did centuries ago. It is better to have a Ukraine, even if it is a Bolshevik one, that is not under the rule of Poland or Russia. National interests were put above ideological interests.

A majority of the Directorate declared itself against "all kinds of intervention," that is, in practice, for a compromise with the Bolsheviks. Only Petlyura spoke for an alliance with Poland against the Bolsheviks. A split occurred, as a result of which Petlyura declared himself the "chief ataman" of the Ukraine.

The government of the West Ukrainian National Republic, meanwhile, entered into a temporary agreement with Denikin in Ziótkowicze on November 6, 1919, and subordinated its Ukrainian Army of Galicia to him. But, on January 12, 1920, this entire army went over completely to the Bolshevik side by means of simply changing its name to the Red Ukrainian Army of Galicia.

It was at this time that the Directorate chairman, Vinnichenko, openly joined the Bolsheviks. He declared Poland to be the main enemy, and he assumed the position of vice chairman of the Ukrainian Sovnarkom. (The chairman at that time was Christian Rakovsky, an old Bolshevik, who later, until 1928, was the Soviet ambassador in Paris.)

In reality, only Petlyura was left on the anti-Bolshevik side. On April 22, 1920, he and Piłsudski signed the so-called Warsaw Treaty, which set out details of their intended joint action against the Bolsheviks and of the future boundary between Poland and the Ukraine. The expectation that the Ukrainian people would spontaneously support Petlyura did not materialize, however. Petlyura started to form two divisions that were to fight as parts of the Polish Third and Sixth armies, but they played only a minor role. Piłsudski did not remain true to the Warsaw Treaty, in which both sides solemnly undertook not to sign separate peace treaties. After the unsuccessful Kiev Expedition, as is well known, he signed a separate treaty with the Bolsheviks in Riga. This was followed by the disarming and internment of Ukrainian units in Poland, similar to what happened to the Yudenich army in Estonia. Petlyura's protest in the name of the Ukrainian National Republic was left unanswered.

Piłsudski. None of the parties involved describes the course of events as we do above. Each shows a tendency to blame somebody else for what happened. The young nationalisms arising in areas that had once belonged to the historic Polish-Lithuanian state direct their charges especially against Poland, and in particular against the Polish leader of the time, Piłsudski. There is much injustice in these charges, but there is also some truth. History knows Piłsudski as a political "romantic." This myth is firmly established not only in Poland but also in the West. As is the case with many legends, it seems beyond criticism. In reality, things were quite different.

There was not too much, but too little, of the romantic in Piłsudski. His adherents and apologists admit that nobody knew the details of his plans, since it was not customary for him to share them even with his closest associates. This happened not because, once recognized as a genius, he did not have to reckon with the people around him and could demand blind obedience from all those who believed in him. It happened, rather, because, throughout his life, he had accustomed himself to act in an atmosphere of conspiracy. Once elevated to the pedestal of a man of destiny, he certainly believed deeply in his own mission. And so he was not reluctant to be caustic, sharp, and slighting in his relations with people, frequently irritating and repelling those whom he should have won over to himself. This was especially true of his behavior toward representatives of the young nationalisms who, because of a social class complex, were especially sensitive to any sign of condescension. Piłsudski was too sure that everything could be achieved simply by means of a fait accompli—"with a gun in hand," as he wrote to Leon Wasilewski in a letter of April 4, 1919. This excessive "realism" of his revealed, at the same time, a deep lack of knowledge of human psychology. This, in turn, led to the inability to understand the phenomenon of Bolshevism, which is based on mass psychology.

Piłsudski tried to solve the Lithuanian problem through the underground Polish Military Organization (POW) and thereby contributed to poisoning the atmosphere of Polish-Lithuanian relations. In a single year, 1920, he broke two treaties: the "Suwałki" treaty with Lithuania and the "Warsaw" treaty with the Ukraine. The breaking of the Suwałki treaty was completely unnecessary, and it can be explained only by his attachment to old conspiratorial methods. The "Żeligowski rebellion," had he wanted, could have been brought about by the same means and at the same time, without endangering Poland's honor by signing a treaty with the clear intention of later breaking it—and here we have a treaty with a "brotherly" nation. This extremely unpleasant Suwałki affair, covered up in Poland partially by deceit and partially by saber rattling, would be sufficient in itself to prove a lack of "romanticism" in Piłsudski's actions. It ended in a strange way. Piłsudski, who, contrary to the Polish national democrats, had extended an apparently brotherly hand to the Lithuanians, Byelorussians, and Ukrainians and who wanted to live with them in a federated state, came to be hated by them and became more a symbol of "evil Poland" than the most fanatical Polish nationalist.

These elements of Piłsudski's policy did not substantially influence the fate of Eastern Europe. Looking at things objectively, we may assume that, even had Piłsudski's "internal" policy toward the Lithuanians, Byelorussians, and Ukrainians been different, it would have influenced the "external" attitude of these nations toward the Bolsheviks only to a very small degree. Infatuation with national interests and a combination of national radicalism and social radicalism produced the attitude that regarded Bolshevism as a "lesser evil" that could be employed in the fight against a neighboring nationalism. Not only did Piłsudski fail to develop a different view on this most important subject, but, on the contrary, he was a leading exponent of the "lesser evil" concept and one of the precursors of the views on Bolshevism that have prevailed up to our own times.

Out of his faulty diagnosis came the naive idea that it would be enough to pronounce national slogans and thereby unite the Ukraine and the peoples of the former Lithuanian Grand Duchy "against Russia." Not only did the nationalistic Lithuanian leaders prefer the Russians to the Poles (their first task was to "depolonize" Lithuania!), but also the leaders of the Ukraine and Byelorussia, appealing to social radicalism, tried to outdo the Bolsheviks in their struggle against their erstwhile "Polish masters." At the same time, the Bolsheviks employed the slogans of national independence much more successfully than did Piłsudski.

The peasant rebellions and anti-Bolshevik riots of this period clearly had a counterrevolutionary character. They arose from the simple, human hatred of the new system. They were not able to bring about an ideological synthesis, however, because the national leaders involved tried to impose on them a nationalistic character that they actually lacked. The Bolsheviks, using the same slogans, took the wind out of their sails. Formulas that had become ossified in the struggle against the old Russian empire did not apply in the fight against the Bolsheviks. They were anachronistic.

"One and undivided." In this false diagnosis of the essence of Bolshevism, Russian nationalism was not an exception, either. The Russian counterrevolution was not able to oppose Bolshevism with anything but the criterion of state interest alone. The slogan of the "one and undivided" Russia removed any possibility of discerning reality to such a degree that the leaders of the White movement were more willing to refuse the assistance of anti-Bolshevik "separatists" than to recognize their demands in any way. "For assistance in the fight against Bolshevism," wrote Denikin, "not an inch of Russian soil!"

Sazonov, a cabinet minister, presented a memorandum to representatives of the Western governments in Ekaterinodar, late in 1918, in which he said: "The ephemeral states which at the moment have some appearances of independence cannot take part in the process of liberating Russia [from the Bolsheviks] until they give up their demands for an independent existence. The demands of the Ukraine, the Don, Lithuania, the Baltic countries, and the Caucasus have to be approached with a great deal of caution."

The Russians recognized without question only the independence of Poland ("in its ethnic boundaries"). They had, however, fundamental reservations with regard to Finland. Denikin wrote in May 1919, after Finland's independence was recognized by Great Britain and the United States: "Russia favors independence for Finland . . . but this decision, taken without Russia's consent, is not acceptable to the Russian nation."

In order to gain assistance in his fight against the Bolsheviks, General Yudenich worked toward the unconditional recognition of Finland. Maklakov, a cabinet minister, reacted thus: "We cannot restrain him in his intentions, but we cannot support him, either." The declaration of the "supreme ruler of Russia," Admiral Kolchak, presented to the Entente powers on June 4, 1919, contained the following points: "3. The recognition of Poland and even of Finland; the designation of their final borders will have to be decided, however, by the Constituent Assembly. 4. Estonia, Latvia, Lithuania, and the Caucasus should get autonomy, to be approved by the Constituent Assembly."

When Brătianu approached Denikin in August 1919 with the proposal that Romania would give all possible assistance in the fight against the Bolsheviks in return for the cession of Bessarabia to Romania, the answer was negative, as Denikin recalls with pride: "I did not sign the bill!" Similarly, he rejected in advance a proposal made by Colonel Stryżewski, in the name of some fairly unreliable Ukrainian forces, through General Gerua in Bucharest, to engage in a struggle against the Bolsheviks without settling any political questions beforehand. Denikin answered that he was "fighting for one, indivisible Russia. Within its boundaries the Ukraine can expect to receive only autonomy. Should it intend to break away, it would become an enemy similar to the Bolsheviks."

Although, in contrast to the other nationalities of the former empire, all Russian parties apart from the extreme left regarded the Bolsheviks as a "gang of murderers and bandits," declined any kind of compromise with them, and, despite the threat to end Western assistance if there were a refusal, categorically rejected the proposal of Wilson and Lloyd George put forward on January 12, 1919, for talks with the Bolsheviks (even Lord Curzon's "One can talk with robbers, but this does not mean one recognizes the robbery" did not persuade them), they did, however, support the principle of the primacy of national interests over the interests of a common struggle against the "Bolshevik pestilence" in a manner similar to that of the other nationalities. They held on like grim death to the program for the "complete reestablishment of the status quo . . . with the exception of the areas which were to become Polish."

Denikin wrote in his émigré memoirs, "Even if we had recognized the claims for independence of all these nations, would this recognition have induced them to make sacrifices for the liberation of Russia? (Let us put it more concretely: for the destruction of the center of the common threat.) Later events tell us something different."

Denikin's skepticism actually seems to be well founded, and, had he lived to the present day, he would have been even more justified in expressing it.

AN AGE-OLD THEORY ABOUT THE "EVOLUTION OF COMMUNISM"!

We have not considered, in this brief outline, the attitudes of the Entente, now known as the Western powers. The analogies would be excessively stereotypical. The policies of Lloyd George and the policies of Great Britain today; the policies of Roosevelt in his later years and then those of Kennedy; the policies of Bevin at that time and in later days ("Hands off Russia!"); the tendency to scent "reaction" in anti-Communism then, just like "Fascism" today; these are banal analogies.

One cannot resist, however, mentioning an episode that could be of some interest to the Polrealists of our day who unanimously support American aid to the People's Republic of Poland under the guise of "aid for the Polish nation." This also has happened before! It was accompanied by nearly identical slogans and nearly identical political speculations.

At the end of 1919—that is, when the war against the Bolsheviks was still going on—Lloyd George suddenly lifted the blockade against Soviet Russia and decided to enter into commercial relations with the Communists and to give them economic aid on the pretense of opening contacts with the "Russian people" and of "aiding the Russian nation." This most certainly was a grave blow to the anti-Bolshevik forces in their difficult fight for freedom. Maklakov wrote to Denikin from London with regard to these decisions: "What is more important, many Russians regard it as a crime not to support Lloyd George's decision. They assert that a blockade could have been maintained only as long as the liberation of Russia seemed to be imminent. Since this liberation has not yet been achieved, a further blockade would only be a crime against the Russian nation. . . . As far as Western political circles are concerned, they are of the opinion that the opening of relations with the Soviets, by the mere fact of contacts with the West, may contribute to a change in the essence of Bolshevism, may contribute to its transformation."[3]

We see here that the contemporary theory about the "evolution of Communism" and of the impact that Western economic aid, along with the opening of contacts and "cultural exchanges"—now regarded by some as the latest political fashion—may have on this evolution, is in reality nearly as old as Bolshevism itself. This theory consists merely of reheated clichés that originated nearly half a century ago.

There were obviously many reasons for the ultimate victory of Bolshevism. Nothing in this world happens as a result of a single cause; there is always a multitude of causes. We showed the reader the role played in this chain of cause and effect by purely nationalistic interests. Below we shall attempt to demonstrate the most important factor in this chain of causes. Not only did it largely contribute to the salvation of international Communism at its most critical moment, but, despite the passage of many years, it also directly influenced the development of the views of today's Polrealism.

Chapter 4 Mikaszewicze

The course of events described below is not generally known to Polish readers, since traditionally it was explained exclusively from the standpoint perceived at that time as the Polish "raison d'état" and the "Polish national interest." This is what actually happened.

KOLCHAK

Admiral Kolchak, who at the end of 1918 and in early 1919 had at his disposal the greatest military force, which was concentrated in Western Siberia, had been recognized as the leader of all the anti-Bolshevik forces in Russia. In the spring of 1919, he began a great offensive toward the Volga. After crossing it, he intended to march toward Moscow. At that time, anti-Bolshevik revolts were in progress in Gomel, Simbirsk, and Samara. On March 14, Kolchak entered Ufa. Soviet sources (*Kratkaya istoriya grazhdanskoi voiny*) admit: "The situation of our forces was complicated by the kulak rebellions in our rear which cut communications and destroyed railways."

The Bolsheviks used all their forces to stop Kolchak's offensive and to push him back behind the Urals. On May 29, 1919, Lenin wired to the Revvoensoviet [Revolutionary Military Council] of the Western Front: "If we do not capture the Urals by winter, I regard the defeat of the revolution as unavoidable!"[1]

Meanwhile, more and more anti-Bolshevik insurrections were occurring. Conspiracies and secret counterrevolutionary organizations became more and more numerous. Strikes, assassinations, and revolts became common. Desertions from the Red Army increased; some units switched in their entirety to the side of the Whites. On May 31, 1919, Lenin and Dzerzhinsky signed a proclamation calling on the people to be "vigilant," to report on others, and so on. The terror began, in dimensions hitherto unknown. On the night of June 14, the Cheka carried out mass arrests in Petrograd; allegedly, large amounts of hidden arms and munitions had been found. Mass executions of people suspected of sympathizing with the counterrevolution followed. Despite this atmosphere of fear and terror, an anti-Bolshevik organization, the so-called National Center under Lieutenant Nekhlyudov, started an open fight and occupied the main fort on the outskirts of Petrograd, Krasnaya Gorka. A large part of the Soviet garrison of this fort (and, before long, the forts of Seraya Loshad' and Obruchev) joined the insurrectionists. Anti-Bolshevik riots developed in the Seventh Soviet Army. Kronstadt was under attack by the three rebellious garrisons. The insurrectionists were expecting at any minute the intervention of the British Navy and aid from Finland, Estonia, and General Yudenich, but no help came from anywhere apart from General Yudenich, who, himself in difficulties, arrived too late. The Bolsheviks were able to suppress the insurrection and to direct all their forces against Kolchak.

UNDER THE RESTRAINT OF DOCTRINE

The man who had devoted all his life to the struggle against tsarist Russia, Piłsudski, because of his stubbornness, so characteristic of politicians with "single issue" experience, was not in the least inclined to revise the old doctrine. He did not understand the phenomenon of the Bolshevik Revolution. He treated it simply as a weakening of Russia, and he considered the possible overthrow of Bolshevism by the counterrevolution as a potential strengthening of Russia. He therefore placed his bet on the "weaker" Russia, which would be a lesser danger to Poland. Emotional considerations certainly played some role here. He must have felt some aversion to the thought of assisting former tsarist generals against revolutionaries, a group to which he had himself belonged all his life.

He was also closely connected with the Polish Socialist Party, a socialist movement with a national emphasis, which was in some way similar to the left-wing radical nationalistic movements of Poland's neighbors.

In the middle of May 1919, Julian Marchlewski, the leading Polish Communist at that time, arrived in Warsaw on a secret mission from Lenin. He was well received in the circles of the Polish Socialist Party and also among the people close to Piłsudski. He conferred with Józef Beck, then deputy minister of internal affairs, and with Tadeusz Hołówko and others. It cannot be doubted today that at that time the final decision must already have been made as to which one of the "two Russias" Poland should hope would win. Piłsudski placed his money on "Red Russia," on the Bolsheviks. At the time when Lenin began his decisive counteroffensive against Kolchak, *Robotnik,* the leading organ of the Socialist Party, published a long series of important articles with headings like the following: "Kolchak not recognized by the Coalition!"; "Kolchak and Denikin combine"; "More about Kolchak"; "America does not recognize Kolchak"; "Kolchak acts," and "About Kolchak."[2]

Nearly every day there was an article. More articles appeared on June 11, 12, 15, and 16, and finally there appeared a programmatic article by Tadeusz Hołówko on June 17, entitled "The Spectre of Tsardom."

A contemporary Polish Communist, Józef Sieradzki, writes about all these and later articles: "This matter is never absent from the pages of the leading socialist paper, which is proof of the publicity campaign which was at least inspired by Julian Marchlewski. . . . Without doubt we can discover here threads of the discussions conducted by Marchlewski in Warsaw with various people. . . . Anyhow, in the newly arisen Poland the specter of a counterrevolutionary Russia and the logic of his arguments were enough to induce Piłsudski to 'allow them to continue his [Marchlewski's] work,' and after some time the Polish authorities assigned an officer to accompany Marchlewski when he left to discuss these matters further with Lenin."[3]

At this time, the Polish forces were at a standstill on the Berezina line. Military actions were nearly nonexistent. A pamphlet, *Polska a "kapitalistyczna interwencja" w stosunku do ZSSR, 1918–1920* [Poland and the "Capitalist Intervention" in the USSR], published in 1945 by the Second Polish Corps in Rome, supported this decision of Piłsudski's: "Despite conditions favoring a further offensive, the Polish forces stopped. The main reason for this halt was the strong feeling of the Polish government . . . that a further offensive could contribute in a large degree to a victory of the Russian counterrevolution."[4]

As documents show, Poland did a lot to facilitate the situation of the Russian revolutionaries in their fight against the reactionary counterrevolution and to ensure victory for those political circles that she regarded as progressive.

In May and June 1919, the Bolsheviks indeed succeeded in stopping the Kolchak offensive and in pushing his armies to the east of the Volga, but a few weeks later a new and terrible danger arose for the Bolsheviks in the south. One can say that the existence of today's center of international Communism really hung by a thread. It would have been enough to cut this thread to end it forever.

"THE MOST CRITICAL MOMENT FOR THE SOCIALIST REVOLUTION"

"The most critical moment for the socialist revolution" was the description given by Lenin of the situation at that time.[5]

In June 1919, Denikin took Kharkov, Tsaritsyn [Stalingrad, Volgograd], and Ekaterinoslav. The Don Cossacks took up arms. Nearly everywhere behind the Soviet front, peasant revolts occurred. In the Ukraine, the bands of Makhno, Grigoryev, and others were active. On July 4, 1919, Denikin started his great offensive in the general direction of Kursk—Orel—Tula—Moscow. On July 9, Lenin made his famous appeal: "Everybody to arms against Denikin! All the forces of workers and peasants, all the forces of the Soviet republic should be directed against Denikin!"[6]

Denikin took Poltava on July 29; in August, he liberated Nikolaev, Kherson, and Odessa from the Bolsheviks; on August 10, the cavalry corps of General Mamontov broke through the front and took Tambov; on August 31, Denikin took Kiev. In the Soviet cavalry corps of Mironov at Saransk, an anti-Bolshevik rebellion broke out. On September 12, Denikin ordered his men to march on Moscow and took Kursk; on October 6, Voronezh; on October 13, Orel. At the same time, Yudenich was renewing his attack on Petrograd. Lenin wrote: "At no other time was the enemy so close to Moscow, so close to Petrograd."[7]

Numerous anti-Bolshevik conspiracies were organized in Petrograd, Penza, Saratov, and Moscow itself. On September 25, bombs exploded at the meeting of the Moscow Party Committee, killing twelve leading party members. Lenin and Dzerzhinsky replied with bloody terror, worse than ever before. By October 1919, Denikin had liberated eighteen gubernias and districts from the Bolsheviks, comprising an area of about 810,000 square versts and about forty-two million people.

But, after September 25, the Bolsheviks removed from the Polish front first the Latvian Division, then the Pavlov brigade and the newly formed cavalry of the Red Cossacks. These units were sent to the most endangered sections of the front. And the Polish army, on Piłsudski's orders, stood by without intervening.

INSTEAD OF "MOZYRZ," "MIKASZEWICZE"

In the strategic situation that had developed, Denikin proposed to Piłsudski that the latter mount an offensive in the general direction of Mozyrz and reaching the right bank of the River Dnieper. We shall not describe the proposed operation in detail. It is enough to look at a map of the fronts as they then existed to see that this would have been a mortal blow to the right flank of the main Soviet forces. Thus, the whole Twelfth Soviet Army, maintaining a front against Poland from Byelorussia to Wołyń [Volhynia], would have found itself in a trap and been destroyed. At the same time, the Polish forces of the southern front would have been freed and the whole left flank of Denikin's army protected. The final defeat of the Bolsheviks would have been ensured.

Piłsudski was clearly aware of this fact and wrote: "An attack on the Bolsheviks in the direction of Mozyrz could undoubtedly have been a decisive factor. . . . On its Polesie front Poland had enough forces to carry out such an attack."[8]

Why did this offensive not take place? Piłsudski himself explains it in the following passage: "Cooperation with Denikin in his fight against the Bolsheviks is not in the Polish state interest. . . . The basis of the policy of the head of the Polish State is the fact that he does not want to contribute to a victory of the Russian reactionary forces in Russia. He will, therefore, do everything in order not to allow this to happen."[9]

Instead of destroying the main Bolshevik forces, just the opposite happened; the Polish forces stayed put and the Bolsheviks withdrew forty-three thousand soldiers and the entire Twelfth Army from the Polish front. The latter simply made a U-turn and threw its whole weight into an attack on the left flank of the Russian anti-Bolshevik forces. And this happened for the following reasons.

Piłsudski was in permanent contact with Lenin through Marchlewski. This was kept completely secret, in line with the conspiratorial inclinations of Piłsudski. In the first days of July 1919, Marchlewski went to Poland again. In Białowieża, he met Count Kossakowski, Piłsudski's plenipotentiary. The details of their discussions are unknown. Most certainly, a fundamental agreement was reached by which Poland promised not to support the Russian anti-Bolshevik forces. Marchlewski returned to Moscow. In October 1919, he again arrived in Poland, this time as an official, although secret, emissary of the Soviet government. His plenipotentiary powers were issued by the "People's Commissariat of Foreign Affairs of the Russian Socialist Federated Soviet Republic," carried the number 11/853, and were signed by People's Commissar Chicherin on October 4, 1919. Piłsudski was represented by Captain Ignacy Boerner, and some part was also played by the journalist M. Birnbaum, a lieutenant in the army. The place of the secret negotiations was a small town in Polesie, Mikaszewicze. Marchlewski himself later wrote about these negotiations: "During the Mikaszewicze talks the situation of Soviet Russia improved considerably. . . . Yudenich was defeated, and so was Denikin; Kolchak was pushed away far to the east."[10]

Thanks to the friendly neutrality of Piłsudski, the Bolsheviks were indeed able to mass all their forces against Denikin. They regained Orel by the end of October; in November, Kursk and Chernigov; and in December, they pushed the White forces out of Kharkov and Kiev. Meanwhile, Marchlewski, having received directives from Piłsudski, returned to Moscow. On November 21, 1919, he was again in Mikaszewicze with an answer from Lenin "detailing the Soviet attitude in all the matters contained in the Piłsudski statement."

Piłsudski would not have been a born conspirator had he not at the same time sent a Polish mission to Denikin. The delegation, which arrived in Taganrog on September 13, 1919, was composed of General Karnicki, Mr. Iwanicki, and Major Przeździecki. The purpose of this mission is unclear. Perhaps it was supposed to find out the real intentions and political plans of Denikin. Its real purpose, however, was to lull any suspicions and also to divert the attention of those Western circles that supported Denikin. It is certain that Karnicki indulged in delaying tactics. When asked why Piłsudski was not starting an offensive, he gave evasive answers. Meanwhile, the situation of the anti-Bolshevik Russian forces was deteriorating catastrophically.

On November 26, 1919, Denikin sent a personal letter to Piłsudski asking for help in the name of the common cause, the struggle against the Bolshevik threat. This was the same day that Captain Boerner presented to Piłsudski his report on the Mikaszewicze talks, along with the text of Lenin's answer. To the enquiry of Western representatives, Piłsudski answered that "there is nobody to talk to, since Kolchak and Denikin are reactionaries and imperialists." And the Bolsheviks were winning on all the fronts of the civil war. How well this conspiracy was kept secret and how great was the disorientation of the Russian anti-Bolshevik leaders of the so-called Volunteer Army is shown by a memorandum of General Wrangel dated December 25, 1919, in which he proposed relying completely on Poland and terminating his earlier arrangements with the Cossacks (since, under the influence of nationalistic "separatist" propaganda, they were more and more frequently refusing to fight outside their own territory). Answering renewed pleas for assistance, Piłsudski stated in January 1920 that he might be able to give aid in the spring. This answer has a mocking ring to it, since all the anti-Bolshevik "forces of Southern Russia" were already on the point of collapse. The remnants found refuge in the Crimea.

THE MOST CRITICAL MOMENT FOR POLAND

Piłsudski had made a choice. The catastrophic results of this choice are well known. After crushing the White armies, the Bolsheviks turned all their forces against Poland, and six months later the very existence of Poland was in question. On Lenin's orders, the same Julian Marchlewski who only yesterday had been an intermediary in the secret Piłsudski-Lenin negotiations led the first Communist government in Poland (the Provisional Revolutionary Committee), among the other members of which were Felix Dzerzhinsky, Felix Kon, and Edward Pruchniak. They waited in Białystok for the capture of Warsaw to transform Poland into what it was to become in 1945, twenty-five years later.

What neither Piłsudski nor Denikin nor other national leaders of that time (like their modern successors who support "Realpolitik") understood, and what they were never able to perceive, is the fact that Bolshevism and Russia, or any other country in the world, are really located on different planes and that therefore a choice on one level, that is, a choice between a "White Russia" and a "Red Russia," was in reality excluded. A contest or an agreement with Communism always pertains to different planes. The essence of one's attitude to Bolshevism cannot be the problem of one territory or the other, of one boundary or the other. Lenin did not aim to incorporate Poland into the Soviet state; he wanted control of Poland so as to be able to march through it to capture other countries for the Bolshevik Revolution. The immediate goal of the 1920 campaign was not Warsaw but Berlin. Lenin made the famous statement that "Berlin is the key to Europe. He who possesses Berlin possesses Europe. He who has Europe has the world."

On June 20, 1920, plans were already being discussed in Moscow regarding the organization of "Soviet Poland," "Soviet Germany," "Soviet Hungary," and "Soviet Finland." At the beginning of the great offensive on July 2, 1920, Tukhachevsky issued his remarkable order to the twenty divisions under his command: "The fate of the World Revolution will be decided in the West!

Over the corpse of Poland we shall march toward a general world conflagration! Forward to Minsk—Wilno—Warsaw!"

The order of the Revolutionary Military Council No. L. 1847 of July 20, 1920, states: "Soldiers of the Red Army, remember that the Western Front is the front of the world revolution!"

On August 19, 1920, the Central Committee of the Bolshevik Party issued a proclamation signed by Lenin, Krestinsky, Trotsky, Stalin, and Bukharin: "Due to the worldwide historic importance of the Polish front, the Central Committee regards itself as entitled to summon all Communists of the world to a heroic effort!"

Poland was now on the edge of a precipice. Piłsudski, who a short time earlier had accused Denikin and Kolchak of "imperialism and reaction" in order to win the sympathy of the Western European leftists, now became the target of the attacks of the European "progressives." On August 6, 1920, the Secretary of the British Labour Party, Henderson, emphatically warned people against giving any assistance to Poland; on August 10, Ernest Bevin, leader of the British Union of Transport Workers, protested against the sending of arms and munitions to Poland; Germany and Czechoslovakia, ruled by left-wing parties, refused to allow military equipment transit; dockers in Gdańsk refused to unload munitions; the Czech government in Prague prevented thirty thousand Hungarian cavalrymen from going through the country to assist Poland, and so on.

It is well known that the Bolshevik onslaught was halted and destroyed in the battle of Warsaw as if by a "miracle." The origins of the future drama, however, lay not in this "miracle"—as Karl Radek wrote jeeringly in *Izvestiya*: "It is not good to rely on miracles, since all miracles have the characteristic that they do not repeat themselves on order"—but in the fact that no one drew the proper conclusions from this great experience. The victorious battle of Warsaw saved Poland and Europe; it delayed the deluge of Communism by more than twenty years. So Lord d'Abernon was certainly right when he counted the battle of Warsaw among the "eighteen decisive battles in the history of the world." But did Piłsudski himself, who at that time was in command of the victorious Polish armies, appreciate the real meaning of Lord d'Abernon's statement? It seems that he did not.

THE "SECRET" OF THE RIGA TREATY

Lord d'Abernon in *The Eighteenth Decisive Battle of the World* writes about the goals of Soviet policy in 1920 as follows: "The enemies of the Poles had no ambition but to set class against class, no creed but destruction of the existent order, no policy but to annihilate all that stands for our conception of religion, justice and good faith. . . . It is difficult to estimate the relative importance of these events in the tenth and seventeenth centuries as compared with the Battle of Warsaw in our own time, but the surmise is justifiable . . . had the Soviet forces overcome Polish resistance and captured Warsaw, Bolshevism would have spread throughout Central Europe, and might well have penetrated the whole continent."[11]

Piłsudski could not see this. What a difference between his and Lenin's comprehension of the goals of this war!

Piłsudski attempted to give the war against the Bolsheviks, in defiance of the facts, a national, clearly bilateral character and to base it on a difference in state interests; he felt that he was fighting in defense of Polish, and only Polish, interests. Therefore, he denied its ideological character as an integral battle against the "Bolshevik pestilence." Lenin understood the war dialectically. For him, it was not a national or state war but a revolutionary war. The relationship to Poland was a subordinate question, remaining on a secondary plane. This was not a conflict between states but an integral battle against the system of all other capitalist states in the world. It was not a bilateral but a global contest. We find an identical interpretation in all the statements of other Bolshevik leaders—not just Lenin, but also Trotsky, Zinoviev, Stalin, Kamenev, and so on. They are not concerned with Poland; they are interested in the expansion of the revolution to the whole of Europe. Tukhachevsky openly admits in his book *March Beyond the Vistula* that the Soviet-Polish war was treated as a means for bringing about the revolutionary conquest of all Western Europe. L. Degtiarev writes: "The impact of our Warsaw campaign in 1920 on the international revolutionary movement was especially important. It brought about a political crisis in Europe and contributed to the development of the revolutionary movement. As a result of the successes of the Red Army, 'Action Committees' sprang up in England, workers started to take over factories and other industrial estates in Italy, the whole of Germany was reduced to turmoil. There was hardly a single country in which workers and peasants did not follow in hope and suspense the military achievements of the Red Army. The opposite is also true: the defeat of the Red Army in Warsaw brought about a defeat of the working class in a great number of states."[12]

Marchlewski (whom we may describe with objective accuracy as the abortive predecessor of Bierut and Gomułka) wrote, quite logically, from the Bolshevik point of view, as follows: "When war is waged between two states of the same social and political type, between two capitalist states, for instance, the army which enters the enemy's territory sets up a government of 'occupation' to administer this territory.... It is quite different when a war takes place between two states with different systems. In this case the armies entering the enemy's territory... have to destroy the existing social system in the occupied country out of necessity. The Red Army of the proletarian state entering bourgeois Poland had to destroy the bourgeois system and sweep away the capitalist rubbish; it had to destroy property rights and introduce the Soviet system."[13]

Against this criterion of global change, Piłsudski tried to set the particularism of Polish interests, asserting emphatically that these interests had no connection whatsoever with the interests of an international, anti-Bolshevik intervention. The analogy with today's Polrealism is quite obvious. A similar analogy can also be found in his optimistic belittling of the Soviet danger. In an interview with the London *Times,* Piłsudski declared: "I don't think that the propaganda of the Bolshevists is a danger for those who know them."[14]

He should have said: "The danger of Bolshevist propaganda can be understood properly only by those who know the Bolshevists." We see that the stubbornness with which Piłsudski represented these anachronistic views had not been changed even by his recent experiences.

It was in such circumstances and in such an atmosphere, following the Warsaw victory, that the peace treaty with the Bolsheviks was signed in Riga. This treaty was a negation of the "federal idea of Piłsudski." Everyone was astonished. Why should Piłsudski, the head of state, who did what he wanted and who, without taking into account the views of most of his opponents, decided the fate of the war and of Poland, have suddenly capitulated before these opponents just at the moment when his authority as a victorious leader was at its zenith? This question remains a mystery that bothers his adherents and apologists. Attempts to blame the "intrigues of the opposition" and the "immaturity of society" explain nothing, since "immaturity" and "intrigues" had existed before. An unquestioning admirer of Piłsudski wrote a few years ago: "It seems that not one of Piłsudski's biographers has been able to solve this secret; to find the explanation of his psychological reserve."

It is important to note that the Bolshevik armies were not only defeated at Warsaw but almost completely dispersed during the retreat. The road for the victorious Polish army was open. And here we again find a mysterious second halt after only a quarter of the campaign trail had been covered. Piłsudski himself spoke about this only once, during a lecture in Wilno on April 24, 1923: "The Bolshevik army was then so completely destroyed on the whole front line that there was no obstacle to prevent me from going as far as I would have liked to. What stopped me was the lack of moral power in the nation."

This rather nebulous reference to an obstacle of a very nonspecific nature can only with great difficulty be related to the haste with which Piłsudski came to a "provisional peace" with those tattered remnants of the Bolsheviks and halted the march of his troops on October 12, 1920. This "provisional peace," later signed formally in Riga on March 18, 1921, seems to be the real key to the mystery. To a substantial degree, the defeat of the Bolsheviks by Poland in the autumn of 1920 restored the situation that had existed in the autumn of 1919.

Now General Wrangel, who became the chief commander of the remnants of the White armies in the Crimea in April 1920, started an offensive. He had only limited forces, but the defeat of the Bolsheviks in Poland could have been of advantage. In addition, his small army had been reorganized and had received substantial supplies, especially from the French. Taking advantage of the general chaos on the Bolshevik side, the Wrangel offensive quickly went beyond the borders of the Crimea. Soon, a representative of Wrangel, General Makhrov, arrived in Warsaw and, with energetic French support, pressed for the coordination of actions against the Bolsheviks to bring about their final destruction. General Wrangel stated in an interview published in *Volya Rossii* on October 14, 1920, that "Poland should enter into an agreement with us and tie down the largest possible number of Bolshevik troops on its front; should this be accomplished, then by the spring of 1921 we may count on the final downfall of Communism."

General Weygand, who, as a representative of France, participated in the elaboration of plans for the battle of Warsaw, was of a similar opinion. In an interview published in the *Paris L'Information,* he stated on August 21, 1920: "If the Polish commanders are able to exploit this victory fully, I am certain that the Bolshevik armies in the near future will cease to count."

Petr Struve, the foreign affairs minister of the government in the Crimea, stated in an interview with the Paris *Matin:* "The major problem is the Polish question . . . the future depends on it. If the Poles stop the war and sign a peace treaty with Moscow, the whole Red Army will be concentrated against us and will crush us by virtue of their numerical superiority."

Maklakov, then a representative of Wrangel in Paris, did his best to persuade the French government to impede the Riga negotiations. The Russian politician and historian Pavel Milyukov wrote in his history of the Russian revolution: "The attempt by Wrangel, taken up by Struve in Paris, to keep the Polish armies at the front and send them toward Kiev did not bring the desired result.

The Poles did not want to fight and, especially, they did not want to help Wrangel."[15]

Details about Piłsudski's refusal to aid Wrangel in his struggle against the Bolsheviks can also be found in Grigory Rakovsky's *Konets Belykh* [The End of the Whites] and in Aleksandr Valentinov's *Krymskaya epopeya* [Crimean Epic].[16] It was impossible to win Piłsudski away from his doctrine that the "Bolsheviks are the lesser evil" either by arguments or by pointing to past experiences. The pamphlet published by the Second Corps in Rome, already mentioned above, makes the following statement: "Just as earlier in the case of Denikin, in its relations with Wrangel in 1920 the Polish government and the Polish command avoided the least sign of any kind of cooperation. The government press and the press of the parties supporting the government, while backing the Polish war effort, did not suppress their joy that the Russian revolution was strangling the White Russian reactionaries so hated by the Poles."[17]

It seems therefore that the "mystery of the Riga treaty" and its provisional predecessor signed in October 1920 are to be explained by Piłsudski's fear that these "White reactionaries" could have defeated the Bolsheviks even at this late date. He therefore held his armies back in order to enable the Bolsheviks to defeat this "reactionary movement" for the second time, even though this meant leaving them the eastern parts of Byelorussia and the Ukraine. The anti-Bolshevik forces of Russia were definitively strangled and crushed.

We have lingered on the details of events that happened forty-three years ago since they mark the real beginnings of today's situation. They are also the genesis of the "bilateral" policy with regard to the global problem of the Soviet Union.

General Denikin, who himself, some time earlier, had solemnly stated, "Not an inch of Russian soil in return for assistance" (against the Bolsheviks), as an émigré wrote the following prophetic words about Piłsudski's policy, which had brought Poland to the brink of catastrophe in 1920: "Has the Nemesis of history, through this catastrophe, already given her verdict against the leaders of this innocent nation, or was this only the thunder before the storm?"[18] We know today that it was only the thunder of warning; the "tempest" came in 1945, and a second "miracle" did not occur to halt it. And the whole of Poland was subjected to Communist slavery, just as twenty-five years earlier the whole of Russia had been subdued.

Polish historiography has adopted the position that Piłsudski's decisions were the only just and possible ones, since Kolchak, Denikin, and other leaders of anti-Bolshevik Russia did not want to recognize Poland in any form except within its "ethnic" boundaries. This is true, but the same historiography neglects the fact that Lenin and all the other Bolshevik leaders did not recognize even an "ethnic" Poland. This was certainly not because they represented a "better" or "worse," "stronger" or "weaker" Russia but only because, from their doctrinal standpoint, from the standpoint of global revolution, they could not recognize any Poland but that which was at that time represented by the "Revolutionary Committee" of Marchlewski and Dzerzhinsky in Białystok and that today is represented by Gomułka in Warsaw: a Communist Poland. The problem of state boundaries is, in this context, secondary for the Communists, or one brought into play only for tactical purposes. Piłsudski, on the other hand, while supporting the Bolsheviks against the "White" Russians because the latter did not want to recognize Polish claims in the East, reduced his policy to a "defense of the Eastern frontiers." Today, the claims to those frontiers seem to many to be anachronistic, but contemporary Polish realists support, in their turn, the Communists against the Germans "in the defense of the Western frontiers" of Poland.

Piłsudski undoubtedly helped decisively to establish this type of Polish political thought, which still assumes that Poland is located "between Germany and Russia," although the Eastern neighbor is no longer national Russia but the center of the "international socialist system." In this case, Piłsudski's view was close to that of his greatest opponent, Roman Dmowski, although the reasons for their views were different. The National Democrats, who tried to divert attention from the East and direct it to the West (to Germany, which they regarded as the major opponent), obviously could not simultaneously take the stance that in the East, that is, in the rear of the front that they wished to direct toward the West, a super-enemy had emerged, endangering not only Poland and all of Europe but the whole world. Therefore, they consistently maintained the thesis about the continuity of "the same old Russia" (Stanisław Stroński: "Nothing other than Russia!"). The result of this, during the twenty years of independence, is described well, although with some bias, by the Communist journalist Mieczysław F. Rakowski: "The whole propaganda machinery was aimed at implementing an educational program based on the thesis that there are no differences between tsarist and Soviet Russia."[19]

As we have seen before, this view, in its general outline, is identical (for the reasons described above) with the attitudes of all Eastern European nationalisms (with the slight amendment that Soviet Russia is really better than tsarist Russia)—and this obviously could not but influence the attitudes of Western Europe toward the newly established Soviet Union.

Chapter 5 "Gomułkaism" (National Communism) of the Twenties

Obviously, the title of this chapter is tendentious. It should be "Lenin's National NEP [New Economic Policy]," because that is what we are going to talk about. The tendentiousness lies in drawing attention to the identical nature of the Communist tactics involved, which many have either forgotten or, ignorant of history, have never even heard of. It dispels the currently fashionable illusion about the so-called evolution of Communism, which is said to be finding its expression in a transition to "National Communism."

In actual fact, "National Communism" is a very old invention; conceived by Lenin, it was, at the inception of the revolution, the basic starting point for Bolshevik tactics. It also brought identical results in the form of what was then called "poputnichestvo" [fellow-traveling] on the part of "realistically minded," non-Communist nationalist circles.

NATIONAL COMMUNISM—BY MEANS OF NEWSPAPER ADVERTISING

Soviet Byelorussia can serve as a classic example of the creation of National Communism during the first years of the Bolshevik Revolution. I do not think that my Byelorussian friends will resent the fact that I mention these details. For there can be nothing offensive in stating that during that period the Byelorussian national movement was in its embryonic stage. Every movement has to start at some point in time. The number of enlightened Byelorussians was totally disproportionate to the ethnographically extensive Byelorussian territories, unified, as from December 30, 1922, in the Byelorussian Soviet Socialist Republic, or the BSSR. Consequently, Lenin's Byelorussian experiment may be regarded as a textbook example in this field, in the same way that the whole of the "national NEP" experiment became the model for future People's Republics, including the Polish People's Republic. This, incidentally, is stated in the official Soviet explanation: "The experiments of NEP had international significance.... At the present time the same basic principles which constituted the foundations of NEP in the USSR are being applied in the various peoples' democracies in accordance with their individual characteristics, historical development, and the actual conditions prevailing in the country in question."[1]

In Byelorussia, as in other Soviet republics, the government embarked not on a program of Russification but, on the contrary, on a program of de-Russification. However, it became clear that there were not enough members of the intelligentsia with a command of Byelorussian, and, as a result, in February 1921, the Central Executive Committee in Minsk approved a resolution calling on anyone who could read and write Byelorussian to return to Byelorussian territory. This appeal was sent out to Soviet newspapers in the form of an advertisement: "It does not even matter if your command of your own language is not quite perfect! Here, among your fellow countrymen, it will all come back and you will master it again."

In April 1923, the Twelfth Party Congress condemned tsarist Russia's policies of Russification and approved a resolution on the practical promotion of the language and culture of Byelorussia. In July 1924, the Central Committee [CC] plenum of the BSSR formally decided to make Byelorussian compulsory in all Party, State, and public institutions and organizations. Employees who did not learn Byelorussian within a prescribed period of time were to be sacked. Compulsory Byelorussian language courses were introduced. In October 1925, the authorities responsible for not implementing this policy enthusiastically enough were reprimanded and ordered to redouble their efforts. In October 1926, a CC plenum decided that "the whole of the Communist (Bolshevik) Party of Byelorussia must speak Byelorussian." By 1927, there were already thousands of elementary schools, four Byelorussian universities, four workers' institutes, thirty technical colleges, thirty vocational schools, and fifteen schools for artisans, all with Byelorussian as the language of instruction. At the same time, numerous institutes of art and science, museums, theaters, libraries, and so on were established, with "The Institute of Byelorussian Culture" (INBYELKULT) at their head. Newspapers, periodicals, books, and other printed works in Byelorussian were published on a massive scale.

It must be admitted that the pace of this experiment is staggering if one considers that it started literally from nothing. The Ukrainization of Soviet Ukraine proceeded along similar lines. *Entsyklopediya ukrayinoznavstva* [Encyclopaedia of Knowledge About Ukraine], published by émigrés, states: "In those years (1922–1933) Ukrainian literature, art, theatre, etc., flourished in a hitherto unprecedented manner."[2]

This was only a tactical move on the part of the Communists, calculated to bring about the Communization of the masses all the more effectively. It followed the classical formula: "national in form, but socialist in content."

THE BIRTH OF THE FIRST "FELLOW TRAVELERS"

Despite the fact that the tactics then, as now, were basically quite clear and, at times, even naively obvious, Lenin was not mistaken as to their effects in a "milieu blinded by the desire to make the slogans it promoted a reality." This was the birth of the first great "poputnichestvo" [fellow-traveler] movement, which years later was to reach its zenith in "Gomułkaism," even though its original name was no longer in common use.

Even then, the leading national "realists" put forward the slogan that what was happening was taking place not because of Communist tactics but "under the pressure of the national masses," despite the fact that precisely in the classic instance of Byelorussia there could have been no question of any "pressure from below, pressure of the masses," because a mass national consciousness hardly existed. In spite of this, the thesis of the "influence of public opinion" being decisive at that time is obligatory to this day for Byelorussian nationalists, just as the thesis about the "Polish October" is obligatory for Polrealists. The argumentation is also similar: "We should exploit the opportunity for legally promoting our national culture and developing the awareness of our own nationhood," as a Byelorussian historian, Uladzimer Hlybinny, put it.

Most Byelorussian and a considerable proportion of Ukrainian national activists declared themselves in favor of cooperation with the Communists. Many émigrés decided to return "to the homeland" in order to undertake "organic groundwork" for the good of the nation. Those Ukrainians who returned included such eminent politicians and activists as Prof. Mykhailo Khrushevsky, A. Nikovsky, M. Chechel, P. Kristyuk, M. Shrug, and others. There were also a substantial number of officers from the former Ukrainian National Army.

In making his decision to collaborate with the Communists, the Byelorussian nationalist Dr. S. Trampovich made this appeal to his fellow countrymen: "The Byelorussian intelligentsia must take the initiative and prove that they wish to be responsible for the work and fate of the nation."

Vsevolod Ignatovsky, the doyen of Byelorussian historians and a literary critic, appealed for every opening to be utilized to the advantage of the Byelorussian movement: "Since the system has come to be run by the Communist Party, this Communist Party must be exploited." He joined the party himself, maintaining that this was the only way one could in fact work for the good of the Byelorussian cause. Nor did the tactics of what we have called Byelorussian "Gomułkaism" of the time fail to influence the Byelorussian Catholic clergy as well. In 1926, the Rev. Adam Stankevich, at that time a Deputy to the Polish Sejm in Warsaw, launched an indictment of the Polish administration, describing with approval the contrasting situation which obtained under the Soviets: "The fact remains that there . . . the life of the Byelorussian people is making rapid progress, that thousands of Byelorussian schools have been created in the BSSR!"

In 1925, Zhilunovich, a Byelorussian activist, traveled from Minsk to Prague and Berlin on a clandestine mission entrusted to him by the Communist government to establish secret contacts with the then government-in-exile of the "National Byelorussian Republic." He succeeded in persuading two of that government's successive prime ministers, Tsvikevich and Lastovsky, to return. (Strangely enough, this coincides exactly with the case of two prime ministers of the Polish government-in-exile who, thirty years later, allowed themselves to be persuaded in the same way to go back to their country.) This caused the temporary disintegration and even the official "liquidation of the government-in-exile." The resolution adopted states that "the national NEP has realized the hopes of transforming the BSSR into a truly national state." A protocol of liquidation was signed on October 15, 1925, stating, among other things, that, "In recognition of the fact that the People's Government now in office in Minsk, the capital of Soviet Byelorussia, is truly seeking to awaken the aspirations of the Byelorussian people for their own state and culture, and that today Soviet Byelorussia is the only real force capable of liberating Western Byelorussia from the Polish yoke . . . we have decided to liquidate the Government of the Byelorussian National Republic and recognize Minsk as the sole legitimate center of Byelorussia's revival as a nation and state."

We may observe two significant points in this resolution: first, the recognition of the BSSR, despite some reservations ("*seeking* to awaken"), as a Byelorussian State; second, a common interest with the Communists in the form of a joint anti-Polish front.

I have called these points "significant," as it is really hard to resist the striking analogy between them and the current attitude of the Polrealists: the recognition, despite reservations, of the People's Poland as a Polish State and the presence of a joint anti-German front with the Communists. (Cf. Juliusz Mieroszewski: "We reject the principle of the primacy of any kind of ideology above national interests. We stand with the Communists wherever they incontrovertibly serve Polish interests."[3] Also cf. other similar examples of this attitude quoted in later chapters of the present book.)

ANTI-POLISH NATIONAL COMMUNIST FRONT

Communists know from as far back as their civil war experience that nothing attracts and consolidates nationalism as effectively as supporting its hatred for another nation. On the other hand, the homogeneity required by Communism demands the erosion of national differences. Thus, by skillfully stifling national animosities within the USSR's boundaries, the Communists were able deliberately to channel the dynamism of those animosities outward, in exactly the direction they wanted. And so, under the slogan of "regaining" Western Byelorussia and Western Ukraine, hatred toward Poland was consistently and systematically cultivated in both the Byelorussian and the Ukrainian Republics. Thus, for instance, the "Communist Party of Western Byelorussia" (KPZB), created as early as December 1923, united in 1924 with the "Byelorussian Revolutionary Organization" and shortly afterward amalgamated both Communist and nationalist anti-Polish elements into the Byelorussian "Hramada." The "Hramada" was run directly from Minsk and nourished via Stockholm by funds from Moscow.

Identical anti-Polish activities conducted in the Ukraine are described inter alia by Stepan Vytvytsky and Stepan Baran in the article "Ukrainski zemli pid Polshcheyu" [Ukrainian Territories Under Polish Rule], which states: "Among the various Ukrainian groupings, pro-Soviet attitudes were aroused both by Poland's imprudent policies and by Soviet policies in the years 1924–29 . . . because the latter gave rise to hopes that, under the Soviets, Ukrainian national culture had been given a chance to develop not only in form but in content too. . . . This conclusion was reached even by those circles which hitherto had nothing in common with the Communist world view."[4]

Increasingly close contacts developed on the basis of this "common interest" between Communists and a number of prominent Ukrainian nationalists. Such nationalists as A. Krushelnitsky, V. Bobinsky, M. Lozinsky, S. Rudnitsky, M. Chaikovsky, F. Samora, M. Gavrilov, I. Kossak, and many others adopted a clearly pro-Soviet attitude. SELROB [Ukrainian Peasants' and Workers' Socialist Alliance], which in Lwów had two papers at its disposal, *Vola Narodu* and *Nove Slovo* [The Nation's Will and New Word], took up an extremely anti-Polish and pro-Soviet position. In 1927, following the split in UNDO [Ukrainian National Democratic Party], there came into being the pro-Soviet "Ukrainian Workers' Party," which published the weekly *Rada*. A. Krushelnitsky's *Nowi Szlachi* [New Ways] and V. Bobinsky's *Wikna* [Outlook] were published in Lwów with money provided by Soviet Kiev. Parallel to these developments, the Communist Party of the Western Ukraine (KPZU) intensified its activities, publishing, among other things, *Nowa Kultura* [New Culture], which was even published legally. These are only some examples.

There is no doubt that Polish policy with regard to the so-called national minorities was deplorable, especially where it affected Ukrainians and Byelorussians living in compact, historic territories. However, had it been any different, would it have been capable of changing the anti-Polish attitudes of those people? Attitudes that in time assumed the character of a mandatory hatred and that to this day often stigmatize every effort made at the time to reach some kind of consensus with no less passion than Poles condemn "collaboration" with the Germans? Most probably it would not, for the simple reason that at the time the Communists' experiment of "Gomułkaism," that is, the national NEP, was extremely successful. Since the majority of the Byelorussian and Ukrainian activists recognized, or were inclined to recognize, the BSSR and UkSSR as their "states," Poland was brilliantly outbid by Communist tactics in the matter of solving the Byelorussian-Ukrainian problem within an internal Polish framework.

WHY "RUSSIA"?

In order not to admit the thesis of a common, supra-national threat.

The Destruction of "Natsdemshchina"

Lenin's national NEP came to an end in the early thirties with the destruction of the so-called *Natsdemshchina,* that is, "bourgeois-nationalist deviation from the Party line." At that time, Communists concluded that the tactics of National Communism had achieved sufficient results, had done what they were supposed to do, and should therefore be terminated so as to proceed to the next stage of the plan. At the same time, Stalin embarked on forcible collectivization, while on the other hand National Communists were inclined (naively, as it turned out) toward maintaining individual peasant farming ["khutornoye khozyaistvo"]. It is obvious that the national democrats ["nats-dems"] could not be excluded from the large-scale purge of all internal opposition and punishment for every deviation from the party line. All the "liberties" and national (National Communist) privileges that were too abundant for the Communist system were its first victim.

It must be noted that at that time there was not and there could not have been any question of any kind of Russification, because "Great Power Russian Chauvinism" [*velikoderzhavnyi russkii shovinizm*] continued to be regarded as internal enemy number one. In the earlier Soviet period, "Russian-ness" was not only in disfavor but in practice enjoyed even fewer privileges than other "national forms." Now all these privileges were revoked and equalization came to pass: a uniform norm for all. And so this was a typical process of strengthening Communism, with the accompanying terror, impoverishment of towns and cities, penury, and famine leading to cannibalism in the rural areas, especially following the "de-kulakization" of villages. In short, there came yet another pestilence, terrible in its hopelessness, that struck human life under Communist rule and tormented everyone regardless of age, sex, race, or nationality.

What happened in the meantime was that many National Communists and fellow-travelers who were no longer useful were arrested, deported, or shot; a considerable majority, often including the most prominent national poets and so on, joined the new trend and began to deify Stalin. On the other hand, those who then managed to flee abroad and those who had emigrated at the very beginning of the Revolution unexpectedly put forward a "Russian thesis." That is, they put the blame for ending NEP not on the party, not on Communism, but on "Russian chauvinism," which had allegedly seized control of the top echelons of the party and reverted to the traditional policy of an "eternal Russia" that persecuted other nations. From then on, this "Russian thesis" began to identify the Soviets with the old Russia, and this identification became the slogan of the leaders of nations made captive by the Communists and remains so to this day. This thesis proclaims that world Communism is merely a by-product, a tool in the hands of Russian imperialism. Why did this happen?

For several reasons: for instance, for the Byelorussian and Ukrainian nationalists to reveal what the Soviet tactics really were would have been tantamount to revealing their own illusions and their own naiveté, that is, to compromising definitively the policy of fellow-traveling, which, until recently, they had so warmly advocated. By putting the blame on "Russia," however, they presented matters in such a way as to show that Communism was really not so bad; they had, therefore, been right in wanting to collaborate with it, and they would have continued to do so had it not been taken over by "Russian imperialism." Yet, the main reason for developing this theory was something else, something not everyone was aware of, either then or now.

The "Russian" Thesis Equals the "Anti-Polish" Thesis

Although this sounds paradoxical, it is not a paradox, because the whole point was not so much to awaken antagonism toward Russia as to disallow the thesis that the Soviets could be a hierarchically superior enemy, because the moment this attitude was adopted, that is, with the recognition of the Soviets as the main source of danger to the world, Poland automatically became the lesser enemy and might even be regarded as an ally in the face of a common foe. And that is exactly what Byelorussian and Ukrainian nationalisms, under the influence of rampantly anti-Polish propaganda, wanted at all costs to avoid. On the other hand, the reduction of international Communism to the level of Russian nationalism created values of equal gravity, of Russia and Poland as enemies of the same kind. And in practice, in any case, especially among certain groups of Ukrainians, there remained the belief that Poland was the greater enemy, with whom no compromise was possible.

And just as the national NEP was coming to its sorry end in the Soviet Union, a congress of the Ukrainian OUN [Organization of Ukrainian Nationalists] was called in Vienna, where, on July 29, 1930, it was suggested that people engage in armed anti-Polish operations, which, as we know, entailed, as a consequence, the "pacification of Galicia," of which there are such unhappy memories.

The "Russian" Thesis Is an "Anti-German" Thesis

As we noted in the introduction, the method pursued in this work is the method of comparison. By comparing the anti-Russian attitude of present-day Polrealists to the anti-Russian attitude of the Byelorussian and Ukrainian nationalists in the early thirties, we shall perceive a historical analogy.

There commonly exists in Germany, especially among those circles seeking a rapprochement with the Poles, a view that those Poles who are anti-Russian for nationalistic reasons will find it all the easier to adopt a pro-German stance. This view stems from an anachronistic opinion, mostly based on experiences from the First World War (Władysław Studnicki). Nowadays it is none other than Germany's greatest enemies who present to all and sundry the "anti-Russian" thesis, namely that the Soviets are basically "the same old Russia" and that international Communism is nothing more than a tool of the old Russian imperialism. Because, for the very same reasons that the most anti-Polish Byelorussian and Ukrainian circles brought the Soviets down to the hierarchically equal level of "Russia—Poland," the Polish anti-German groups reduce "Russia—Germany" to the same status, in other words, they want to obscure the view that the Soviets might represent a qualitatively more dangerous enemy. By establishing the thesis that Communism is a threat to the whole of humanity rather than to individual nations, one would automatically reduce Germany to a hierarchically lesser enemy or even to a potential ally in the struggle against a universal danger. Thus, this would turn upside down the concept of the Polrealists, who consider the recognition of the Oder-Neisse frontier to be a more important issue than the recovery of freedom and who view the Germans as enemy number one.

It is hard to say whether many people realize the role that the reduction of the Soviet Union ("Russia") to the same category as Germany plays in distracting attention from the international threat posed by Communism. Certainly, the most prominent figures in the Polrealistic camp do; otherwise, a formulation like the following, "Membership of the anti-Communist bloc would mean having to accept German hegemony,"[5] might seem surprising or even incomprehensible. No doubt the Communists, too, realize this, since, for many years now, by openly propagating world revolution on the one hand, they have been quietly profiting from the "Russian state" thesis on the other and, as we shall presently see, even promoting similar disinformation themselves.

Chapter 6 The First Great Provocation About the Alleged "Evolution of Communism"

THE GPU "TRUST" AFFAIR

We have been pointing to those historic facts that worked in favor of Communism. In the first decade after the Bolshevik Revolution, there still remained in the West some powerful elements that looked upon Bolshevism with genuine revulsion, despite the fellow-traveling nationalists and the pro-Communist attitudes of European "progressives." (In Poland itself, ordinary people regarded the word "Bolshevik" for a long time as a term of abuse!) Many states refused to recognize the Bolshevik government. Attempts were made to create out of the Baltic states, Poland, and Romania a cordon sanitaire against the "Bolshevik pestilence."

It is therefore understandable that, parallel to the revolutionary undermining of Europe and America, Soviet efforts were aimed simultaneously at breaking down this negative attitude. We mentioned that as far back as the period of the Civil War, certain Western groups were putting their money on a gradual mellowing of Communism, on its evolution. Such hopes sprang up not only in the head of Lloyd George. Within barely two years of the Bolshevik Revolution, even the separatism of the Don and Kuban Cossacks, tired of the war and refusing to fight outside their own regions, was justified by the optimistic argument: "Ah, these Bolsheviks are not the same as they were. . . . They've grown tired, they've grown wiser." Optimism, as we know, is a powerful factor in the life both of individuals and of communities. The Bolsheviks decided to exploit this human inclination toward optimism, and for this purpose they mounted one of the greatest provocations ever, known by the name of the "Trust."

I cannot present the affair better than the greatest expert on the subject, so I will let Ryszard Wraga, a brilliant publicist and authority, speak. Below are printed excerpts from his article published in the London *Wiadomości* [The News].

> The "Trust" is one of the most interesting cases in the history of provocation to date. The point of it was that as early as 1922 the GPU began to take over the most militant Russian anti-Bolshevik organizations and all the active Western intelligence services by setting up as a decoy an organization of its own. *The basic idea of the provocation was to make the West believe that Bolshevism was gradually turning into . . . capitalism and that the Soviet Union was becoming a "normal state"; that any outside interference would only entail the rebirth of militant Bolshevism at a time when "peaceful co-existence" was helping to strengthen the forces of national reconstruction.* [All the marks of emphasis are mine—*J.M.*] It can be said without exaggeration that the period when the "Trust's" influence reached its culmination (it even included the United States) was the years 1925–26, when Soviet provocation scored an incredibly brilliant goal: Shulgin, one of the most irreconcilable Russian reactionaries, was "secretly" taken to Russia and was so thrilled by Russia's reconstruction that on his return he published his famous *Three Capitals*, in which at the dictation of the GPU he faithfully expounded all those theories that were most *helpful in disarming not only the émigrés but the West as well.*
>
> The "Trust" had dozens of branches, including some strictly intellectual ones such as the Eurasian branch, the Masonic, the aristocratic, the literary, etc. This provocation was by no means produced solely by Moscow. Russians in the GPU did not play a major role in the "Trust's" establishment. The "Trust" was the work of Poles, Jews, Latvians and various rootless wanderers, red mercenaries and fanatics; during that period such Bolshevik institutions as the Narkomindel, Vneshtorg, the offices of the Comintern, and, above all, the GPU were packed to capacity with such activists. A number of circumstances combined to produce this phenomenon: the peculiarities of NEP; the lack of experience of the European intelligence services in matters related to Communism; the post-Versailles conflicts and contradictions in Europe; and, above all, the fact that *even then the fundamental principle of all Western policies toward Bolshevism was an all-powerful wishful thinking.*

Today, after nearly forty years, reading books and articles written by Russian emigrants, one feels like suing present-day Polish publicists and journalists in London, Paris, or Munich for plagiarism. The only difference is that the former staked their money on Stalin's "State" and "anti-Comintern" ambitions, and on Trotsky's "anti-Stalinism," while the latter place their bets on Gomułka's "patriotism" and "hostility to Russia" and on the revisionists' "anti-Stalinism."

There were many reasons why, in 1927, the GPU halted its very fruitful little game. . . . The fact that the "Trust" was no longer treated as secret by its creators did not preclude its continued functioning. The idea of the "Trust" was too deeply embedded, and not only in émigré attitudes. . . . It was too deeply ingrained in the defeatist fat-headedness of "peaceful coexistence" for it to be liquidated even after the GPU revealed the truth. The "Trust" was immediately reborn in a multiplicity of forms among various émigré groups; it penetrated everywhere from the nooks and crannies of espionage to ministerial and editorial offices. After the Second World War, "Trusts" became something indispensable in international life, and today no one can say where and when they are organized by Communists and where they are the result of "private enterprise."

Next, Wraga mentions other Soviet provocations, including the myth of the alleged Tukhachevsky plot, which was actually created by the joint efforts of the GPU and the Gestapo,

"later taken up by those Russian exiles who for various reasons befuddle the West with visions . . . of palace revolutions. However, let us not be too hasty in mocking the Russians. These stupid but noxious myths are of exactly the same kind as our Polish ramblings about Gomułka's threatening Khrushchev with a gun; about the concentration of "Polish forces" under the command of the "good Pole," General Komar, against the "bad Muscovite," Rokossovsky; our trying to persuade foreigners that in Poland "there are no Communists," only "agents"; and similar canards about the "Polish October Revolution."[1]

Thus Ryszard Wraga.

Another expert in Soviet affairs, Charles Malamuth, an American of Jewish descent, writes in the September 1961 issue of the paper *Nashe Obshcheye Delo* [Our Common Cause], published in Munich: "Then as now the tempting but mendacious doctrine of the 'evolution of Communism' forms the basis of all the intrigues of Soviet intelligence, from the 'Trust' to the 'Committee for the Return to the Homeland and the Development of Cultural Relations with Fellow Countrymen.' Much has changed in the Soviet Union (sometimes for better, sometimes for worse) in recent years, but the essence of the dictatorship remains what it always was: a totalitarian police régime. And this régime cannot change because it is rooted in the premise of a conspiracy directed against the whole of mankind."

LENIN'S THEORY OF "DEAF AND DUMB BLIND MEN"

In 1921, Yu. Annenkov, the Russian artist, son of a famous revolutionary in the People's Will Movement, painted Lenin's portrait. After Lenin's death, Annenkov was invited to the "Lenin Institute" in Moscow to see the materials for illustrating books dedicated to Lenin that were planned for publication. At the Institute, Annenkov copied down certain notes by Lenin that had hitherto never been published. He has now published them for the first time in the Russian quarterly *Novyi Zhurnal* [New Journal]. Here are the most important excerpts from Lenin's private thoughts and remarks:

> As a result of my observations . . . I have concluded that the so-called cultured classes of Western Europe and America are incapable of comprehending the current situation and the real balance of forces; these classes should be regarded as *deaf and dumb* and treated accordingly. A special maneuver must be used. . . .
>
> (a) In order to reassure the deaf and dumb, a (fictitious) separation should be declared between our Government, etc. . . . and the Politburo and, above all, the Comintern; they shall be presented as independent organizations, tolerated on USSR territory. *The deaf and dumb will believe it.*
> (b) Express the desire to establish relations with capitalist countries on the basis of noninterference in their internal affairs. *The deaf and dumb will believe it.*
>
> Telling the truth is a bourgeois superstition. On the contrary, it is the end that sanctifies the lie. While chasing profits in the Soviet market, the world's capitalists will close their eyes to reality and thus change into *deaf and dumb blind men*. They will give us credits that will help us to maintain Communist Parties in their countries and, by supplying us with essential materials, will rebuild the war industry we need for our future victorious attacks on our suppliers. In other words, they will be working toward their own suicide.[2]

It seems, nevertheless, that despite his reasonably correct prognoses, Lenin failed to appreciate the extent of his capitalist opponents' "deaf-and-dumbness," since subsequent practice has shown that they can remain deaf and dumb even when the Bolsheviks stop lying or even when, either as a result of their own excessive self-assurance or plain stupidity, the Bolsheviks reveal their cards without concealing their aims.

This is how the great evolution began, not the evolution of Communism but the evolution of the free world's attitude toward Communism. This explains why every present-day machination in the Soviet bloc involving the so-called dissidents and opposition movements has enjoyed a success in the West. [Addendum of June 27, 1981.]

RAPALLO: FROM WHITE ST. PETERSBURG TO RED MOSCOW

In time, as a result of the "evolution of the attitude toward Bolshevism," one Western state followed another in beginning to establish diplomatic relations with the Soviet Union and to recognize the Bolsheviks as the rightful representatives of "Russia," until we reach the summit of Roosevelt's alliance and policy of friendship.

Germany made the first step in that direction. On April 17, 1922, barely two years after the Soviets' abortive march on Berlin "across Poland's dead body," a historic treaty was signed in Rapallo. It was actually a treaty between Germany and the Soviet Union, and its business end was clearly directed against Poland. Undoubtedly, this occurred not because of the influence of the above-mentioned disinformation "Trust." At the time, that particular Soviet provocation was still at the construction stage. Even more, perhaps, than Piłsudski's "Mikaszewicze," Germany's "Rapallo" is a characteristic example of the ossification of an anachronistic political doctrine.

The Treaty of Rapallo laid the foundation of Soviet-German cooperation in both the political and the military fields, as well as in the sphere of the economy. Among other things, Germany supplied machinery for the feverish construction of Soviet heavy industry, largely planned for armament purposes. Count Brockdorff-Rantzau (as we know, one of those who sent Lenin off in the "sealed railway carriage") was a precursor of many of today's Western statesmen who cherish similar optimistic theories. He expressed the view that, through contacts and rapprochement, the Soviet Union could be led into a mood "more favorable to peace" and that trade relations would prevent the compressed atmosphere of the Soviet Union from "seeking a safety valve outside." Four years later, on April 24, 1926, came the signing of the so-called Berlin Agreement, which unambiguously tightened the ring encircling Poland. Stresemann openly discussed with Chicherin the possibility of jointly revising the frontiers at Poland's expense. During this time, the Reichswehr was vigorously helping the development of the Red Army, making a considerable contribution to the armed potential of international Communism. After Stresemann's death, through the good offices of Curtius and Treviranus, German aid in the development of Soviet military strength reached its peak in the years 1929–30. General von Seeckt wrote: "Russia and Germany within their 1914 frontiers—this should be the basis of an agreement between them."

As we know, the concept of Rapallo was invented by German politicians and generals not only as a first step toward breaking free of the constraints imposed by the Versailles settlement and as an attempt to emerge from the desperate situation that had arisen in the wake of their defeat in the war but also as a kind of return to the Bismarckian concept. In actual fact, it was not a return to Bismarck's concept but a reversal of it. There was a world of difference between Bismarck's wishes for rapprochement with "White" St. Petersburg and Stresemann's rapprochement with "Red" Moscow. Obviously, from the Polish point of view, neither the old agreement between Germany and Russia nor the new one between Germany and the Soviet Union could be in Poland's interests. But, from the German point of view, Bismarck's policy of securing Germany's eastern flank by means of rapprochement with Russia (at, let us put it quite dispassionately, Poland's expense) was undoubtedly in Germany's interests. Until 1914, Russia laid no territorial claims to Germany and, moreover, entertained no dreams of occupying Berlin. On the other hand, the support that the Treaty of Rapallo lent to the center of international Communism not only did not protect Germany from the east but, on the contrary, increased the danger from that quarter for the whole of Germany, if not the whole of Europe (and this was the work of German hands!). In Bismarck's time, Polish territories could have served as a bridge between Germany and Russia. In Stresemann's time, Polish territories could have served only as an effective barrier protecting Germany. And it was the Rapallo policy that strove to destroy the very barrier that barely two years earlier had halted the Red flood by destroying, in the vicinity of Warsaw, the Bolshevik armies marching on Berlin! One could rightly ask whether *Pravda* no. 92, published in Moscow on April 30, 1920, had ever reached the hands of German politicians. It contained Lenin's speech: "Poland started the war with us in order to reinforce the barrier separating us from Germany's proletariat!" Could German generals and politicians have been ignorant of Lenin's description of Berlin as "the key"? Could they have been ignorant of Tukhachevsky's orders quoted above and of the Central Committee's appeals two years earlier? Of course not: they must have known. But objective knowledge was blurred by political wishful thinking.

So the error of Stresemann and the German generals could not have lain in their overlooking this contrast with Bismarck's policy, because in that form the error would have been noticeable to everyone. The error was simply their denial of the existence of the contrast because of their unrealistic, doctrinaire attribution to the Soviet Union of its old biological substance, that is, the substance of the Russia of Bismarck's time. And, in fact, the contrast disappears when the substance of international Communism is replaced by the substance of "Russia." Thus, this was a repetition of Piłsudski's mistake, but in a different context. Inasmuch as it would be almost totally justified to speak of "Mikaszewicze" as having saved the Bolsheviks from destruction, one could also speak of Rapallo as having substantially strengthened their position in the world.

Rapallo is not a symbol of cooperation with Moscow, as is commonly maintained. Rapallo is a symbol of cooperation with *Communist* Moscow. So, today, when listening to the plans of German politicians to establish closer contacts with Communist Warsaw, one can hardly resist the impression that these plans too must be rooted either in an identical lack of orientation or in deliberate insincerity, because the talk is of contacts with "Poland," when what is really meant are contacts with the "People's Poland," that is, the repetition of the same kind of initiative as Rapallo. For there is no fundamental difference between the headquarters in Moscow and their agency in Warsaw, either in their substance or in their political or ideological content.

It would seem that after its experiences with East Berlin and with the DDR (German Democratic Republic), which for quite a long time it rightly regarded simply as a Soviet "zone" and which is merely the German equivalent of Communist Poland, Germany should be the last to have any illusions on that score. It would seem that, having lost their freedom and independence to the Communists, Poles, too, should have no illusions on that account. That is why it would seem logical for people of good will representing both nations to lend their best efforts toward preventing that kind of political initiative. Yet we are witnessing the reverse: it is precisely those who are lending the most support to this initiative who are regarded as expressing the greatest good will; and sometimes they really are. . . . Moreover, to increase the paradox, it is they who are nominated as the representatives of "Realpolitik." In this sphere, there is such a confusion of ideas that those Germans who would like to renew the treaty of Rapallo with Communist Moscow in order to direct it against Communist Warsaw also regard themselves as "realistic politicians."

Doubtless, one of the characteristics of the modern world is the great divide between so-called Realpolitik and actual reality.

Part Three **Between the Quality of Life and the Boredom of Communism**

Chapter 7 The Second Phase of National Communism

BEFORE THE NEW WORLD WAR

There is a generally accepted opinion that world politics are conducted by people good or bad, wise or foolish—but at any rate of a cut superior to that of the average "café politician." There is a large element of exaggeration in this generally held view. Here, for instance, Count Jan Szembek, Under-Secretary of State in the Polish Ministry of Foreign Affairs, quotes the U.S. Ambassador in Warsaw, George Biddle, from a conversation on January 6, 1939, that is, a few months before the outbreak of the Second World War: "Biddle does not believe that Germany will decide to attack Soviet Russia in the near future. Militarily, they are not sufficiently prepared. In the first place, they do not have enough cavalry and, in particular, they lack the small horses necessary for operations in western Russia. The appropriate German military authorities have tried to fill this important gap by purchasing horses in England, but the horses have turned out to be useless."[1]

And here is Patrick Hurley, Roosevelt's emissary sent to Chung-King to reconcile Chiang Kai-shek with Mao Tse-tung, in a conversation of September 6, 1944: "In my opinion, Marshal Stalin is nowadays deeply convinced that Communism can succeed only in Russia and he is not trying to enforce it on the rest of the world. Today, Russia does not subsidize or direct Communist activities among other nations. I understand that Communist Parties exist in other countries too, but they are no longer supported by Russia."

While on his return to America in November 1945, he states at the National Press Club in Washington: "The only difference between the Chinese Communists and Oklahoma Republicans is that the latter are not armed."[2]

Naturally, even an old diplomat of the Austrian school like Count Szembek, whom we have quoted above, is capable of saying, in a conversation with Carl Jacob Burckhardt, Secretary-General of the League of Nations, on March 4, 1937: "The present Nazi system in Germany is more favorable for Poland compared with the former inclinations of Prussian conservatives or with the Center parties, constantly bothering us with their demands and claims."[3]

However, one should never generalize, and this also applies where the ignorance of professional politicians is concerned. Leaving aside a detailed analysis of events and political judgments prior to World War Two, one can nevertheless venture to state that, when dealing with a countless number of problems, they devote the least attention to the matter that is the most vital for the world's future.

As far as Poland is concerned, the lack of judgment and proper evaluation of actual reality can be illustrated by the restrictions placed on the Orthodox population and by the destruction (burning!) of Christian Orthodox churches right along the eastern frontier at a time when all belief in God was being persecuted on the Soviet side of that frontier. However, although these are obviously not the most important events of 1938, they can nevertheless symbolize Poland's total loss of awareness as to its situation in time and space. In contrast, the decision by the Minister for Foreign Affairs, Józef Beck, who, despite a clear threat from Germany and pressure brought to bear by the Western powers, categorically refused Soviet "assistance" in the form of passage through Poland's territory, might be regarded as having had a partial flash of perception at the very last moment. In this instance, Beck rightly perceived that this "assistance" would put paid to Poland's existence not only in this case but in all other cases as well, in that, even if the war against Germany were won, Poland would be integrated into the international Communist bloc. And this is just what happened six years later.

Where Germany is concerned, Hitler's sudden shift toward the policy of Rapallo, his attack on Poland, and the destruction, with Soviet aid, of the cordon sanitaire in which Poland was the central link in Eastern Europe can be regarded as the ultimate in lack of perception. But it should also be noted that Hitler's decisions bore only the semblance of state policy. In fact, they were a concatenation of irresponsible personal whims. In this respect, the Communists use a more precise terminology, such as "Hitler's policy" and "Hitler's invasion," though they do it for their own purposes, rather than for a better definition of objective truth. Hitler simply scrapped the "Anti-Comintern Pact" he had put together and, in a speech, said that "Germany only once waged war on Russia and she will never do so again." In this unexpected transformation of the concept of the "Comintern" into the concept of "Russia," one could perceive a certain allusion to Stresemann's policy. However, the ridiculous slogan of "Jewish Bolshevism," which accompanied yet another volte-face in 1941, proves how totally arbitrary Hitler's fancies were.

POLAND'S EASTERN FRONTIER—A FRONTIER BETWEEN TWO WORLDS

If, when speaking about Hitler and his methods, I use terms such as "madness," "crime," and so on, I do so not to abuse nor yet to follow the prevailing fashion that forbids a writer to omit these epithets. Let fashion be. I have lived long enough in this world to know the vagaries of fashion. It is simply because I am convinced of the objective accuracy of these words. Of course, there is crime and madness in every war. There always was, and there always will be. That is inherent in war. Most frequently, however, these crimes strike at one of the warring parties and eventually profit the other. Then the victorious party puts its criminality into question. And so the crime, from being unequivocal, becomes equivocal. Hitler's acts of madness and his crimes are unquestionable, if only by dint of the fact that they were seen practically from the outset not to benefit but to harm the very side that was committing them. It is this and not their number that made them "worse" than the crimes of the Bolsheviks. The Bolsheviks committed more crimes, but they made them "equivocal" because they were committed in their own interests. Hitler's crimes were in nobody's interests; on the contrary, they became the direct cause of Germany's defeat.

The fact that, despite such criminal methods, at least half the population of Eastern Europe still wished the Soviets to be defeated can serve as an eloquent example of the extent of people's hatred of the Communist system. But in this, there was a characteristic division: by declaring themselves for Germany, the

Lithuanians, other Balts, Byelorussians, and Ukrainians on this side of the frontier delineated by the Treaty of Riga did so, at least according to their outward slogans, because of national, anti-Russian, and anti-Polish sentiments. In contrast, all those who rose against the Soviets or who sided with the Germans on the Soviet side of this frontier, regardless of their national origin, did so out of a simple anti-Communist reflex, that is, for purely human reasons. The explanation often given by uneducated people who lack fluency in sociopolitical definitions, in reply to the question about why they hate the Communist system, is characteristic: "Oh, life's boring." This statement includes not only boredom in the literal sense but also the boredom of poverty, the boredom of fear, the boredom of lack of prospects, the boredom of monotony, the hopelessness of a life not worth living.

Naturally, as far as the rule was concerned, there were numerous exceptions on both sides of the frontier. As Hitler's methods became more and more unbearable and disillusionment grew, there followed considerable changes, to the Germans' disadvantage.

STALIN'S NEP

As we know, Lenin resorted to his NEP [New Economic Policy] and to the National Communism associated with it as a means of extracting Bolshevism from serious internal difficulties. Stalin adopted this model when, in consequence of German conquests and of popular attitudes, the Soviet Union was nearly at the edge of the abyss. Hitler himself was creating a situation more favorable toward Communism by his methods, which, instead of driving a wedge between the party and the people, significantly neutralized internal antagonisms; nevertheless, the Communists also undertook some serious tactical moves with the same aim.

The formal dissolution of the Comintern and of the Communist Youth International happened only in May 1943 and made the alliance between the Western democracies and the Soviet Union much more palatable. The whole world was swept by a new wave of optimism that proclaimed fundamental changes and "internal evolution" in the Soviet Union. General Kopański, Polish Chief-of-Staff in Exile, quotes a conversation he had with Lord Selborne, Minister of Economic Warfare, in London: "I remember how in December 1943 I was invited to dinner by Lord Selborne and had to listen to his views on the evolution of Russia towards true democratization, a return to former patriotism (as proved by the Orders of Suvorov and Kutuzov), to religion, etc."[4]

Such views have become universal in the West, especially because Stalin, even before actually dissolving the Comintern, brought out of storage the Leninist formula of National Communism. There is a somewhat simplified explanation, which states that Stalin appealed to Russian national patriotism and thus saved the situation. In reality, it was the classic "national NEP" method that was applied, the only difference being that this time it related to the Russian people as well. Because of their overwhelming numbers, the proportional contribution of relevant slogans turned out to be suitably effective and thus able to create the impression that everything was unilaterally staked on "Russian patriotism." There are several reasons why this myth has survived to this day in the West:

1. The propaganda of the Western powers profited from the occasion to endow their Soviet ally with a "patriotic-nationalist-Russian" character.
2. The anti-Russian nationalists of Eastern Europe exploited it to confirm their "Russian" thesis.
3. Anti-Communist Russian émigrés in the West profited from it in their own way in order to stress the thin veneer of Communist convention beneath which "there beats the heart of the Russian people," capable of heroic deeds the moment their national-patriotic feelings are invoked.
4. Finally, the "Wunschtraum" [wishful thinking] of all those who wanted to see in the Soviet Union a return to the old Russia contributed to the popularity of this myth more than other factors.

In reality, Stalin's national NEP included all the nations of the Soviet Union, with the exception, naturally, of those that were in the process of liquidation for having "collaborated" with the Germans (Crimean Tatars, Ingushes, Kalmyks, et al.). Russian, Byelorussian, and Ukrainian national heroes formerly, after the destruction of "Natsdemshchina," declared reactionaries were swiftly rehabilitated. This applied not only to Kutuzov, Suvorov, and others, but even, for example, to Frantsysk Skoryna, a sixteenth-century printer, who was restored to the status of a "great Byelorussian humanist"; Konstanty Kalinowski, leader of the 1863 uprising in Lithuania, was again declared a "Byelorussian national hero," and so on. The Soviet government appealed to Byelorussian and Ukrainian writers, including many who had hurriedly been released from concentration camps and prisons, and told them to resume creative work; in this instance, the socialist element was ignored and there were even confidential enjoiners that it could be temporarily withdrawn from circulation so that the main emphasis could be laid on the topical subject of patriotism, which should be as anti-German as possible. Byelorussian poets such as K. Bayla, Maxim Tank, Anton Byalevich, Arkadi Kuliashov, and many others were restored to favor. The same applied to the Ukrainians. Uladzimer Hlybinny writes: "This definite swing in the direction of historic patriotism awakened great hopes for a new national policy in the Party. Some of the intelligentsia began in all sincerity to believe that with the end of the war a new era would begin for the development of national culture."

And so history begins da capo. The 1920 models were applied once more, especially in relation to Poland. Just as then the "Revolutionary Committee" of Marchlewski-Dzerzhinsky came into being, so now, on May 8, 1943, the Union of Polish Patriots was created; within a year, on July 22, 1944, it would be transformed into the Polish Committee of National Liberation and then, on January 1, 1945, into the Provisional Polish Government. The Kościuszko Division was organized in the likeness of the Polish Communist units of 1920. Władysław Gomułka was sent to Warsaw by the Soviet government to organize the Polish Workers' Party (PPR), which, as Gomułka himself would admit in his jubilee speech on January 20, 1962, "always considered itself to be one of the branches of the international Communist movement." Obviously, it is immaterial how the party saw itself; what is meaningful is Stalin's directive whereby, under the provisional cover-name of the PPR, Gomułka was to rebuild as soon as possible the Polish Communist Party, completely destroyed in a previous purge.

There is nothing new in this entire operation. There is hardly a detail that is original. Everything is old, tried, and tested, déja vu and clear to anyone willing to apply common sense rather than succumb to illusion.

But lo and behold, it now turned out that the majority of national leaders and professional ("realistic") politicians had an obvious inclination to succumb to illusions. And so, in this instance, too, Stalin was not mistaken in his calculations, just as years earlier Lenin was not mistaken when speaking about the tactics to be adopted toward "the deaf and dumb."

Chapter 8 Alliance or Collaboration with the Soviet Invader?

In the Second World War, the great Western powers could be Soviet allies both de jure and de facto. Poland, however, because of its weakness and its geographical position, could be only an ally de jure. However, through this alliance, it became de facto "a collaborator with the Soviet invader."

Well-brought-up people usually avoid embarrassing comparisons that are offensive to others. However, it is impossible to avoid embarrassing comparisons when applying the method of comparative research. No doubt General Sikorski, along with many other Polish politicians and generals, acted and wanted to act in good faith and with the best of intentions. But all these activities bore the appearance of being in the interests of Poland only for as long as they were conducted under the illusion that beneath the guise of the Soviet Union there was, if only approximately, the same kind of state ("Russia"). Hence the enormous outlay of energy by the Polish government and its propaganda apparatus in order deliberately or unwittingly to maintain and even develop the fiction that things were other than they were in reality. This had to succeed because it was also important for the

Western powers, on which the Polish government-in-exile depended, to maintain this fiction for the purpose of war propaganda. But the Western powers could afford to do so because they were sufficiently strong and sufficiently distant from the direct Communist threat. Poland was helpless, bordering directly on the Soviet Union and in practice left to its tender mercies.

There developed an extraordinary situation: the German armies in the East were de facto Poland's only defense against the Bolshevik flood. However, there could be no question of any agreement or understanding on this basis, or even of stating this fact, because on the one hand there was the obstacle of Hitler's insane policies and on the other the obstacle of the blind policies of Poland. Of course, there were people sufficiently enlightened to understand that in this situation the only hope was for the Germans to halt the Soviet impetus until the Western powers attained absolute superiority in the West. "What will happen? What will happen if all the German counteroffensives fail and the Soviet army, even perhaps in the course of this year, begins to overwhelm Poland? . . . This was news that had the effect of a soothing balm . . . the Germans had retaken Kharkov!"[1]

These are private notes, written in a diary in 1943. But, first, there were not many people who thought like this, and, second, to express such views out loud was impossible at that time because they were regarded as heresy, maybe no less dangerous than the heresies for which at one time people were burned at the stake by the Holy Inquisition. Wishful thinking was regarded in this period as Poland's main salvation. In far-away London, false appearances could be preserved with a certain amount of unctuousness. However, under German occupation in the country itself, matters had to be in accord with the actual state of affairs.

THE THEORY OF "THE TWO ENEMIES" WAS NEVER PUT INTO PRACTICE

It is well-nigh impossible to recreate an authentic history of that period in Poland, because it belongs to that part of its history that has perhaps been most thoroughly falsified by conformity for the benefit either of the Communists or of the Polrealists. Naturally, matters could not have been as lacking in depth as they are presented. On the contrary, the pressure of all kinds of passions made that part of history multifaceted, one might say even extremely colourful, if only the terribly gloomy background allowed such a description. Unfortunately, we shall never learn most of the details. The spirit of the Underground censorship penetrated so deep that it led to a hitherto unprecedented degree of self-discipline. Who, remembering those times, can fail to recall those most widespread whispers: "but one shouldn't talk about this"; "but one must not speak of this aloud"; "but this is a great secret"; and so on? And, anyway, this is understandable. It was all happening in an atmosphere of terror and counter-terror, in conditions of conspiracy, deeply underground activity, influenced at times by unbridled personal ambitions, thus, in circumstances in the highest degree abnormal, where it is extremely hard to unravel a ball of thread lost in secrecy; and so, in practice, one hardly ever succeeds. For these reasons, one cannot be resentful that things happened the way they did. But one can rightly resent the fact that the atmosphere of those times has become a norm in a monopolized mendacity of the present day.

In order to represent Poland's official interests in the Homeland, the Underground authorities felt obliged to adopt some kind of a stance with regard to the Communist threat, despite their strictly compulsory solidarity with the anti-German coalition. In this way there developed the alleged double-dealing, that is, "the theory of the two enemies," which Communist propaganda reviles to this day. However, this theory was never put into practice, because the Underground authorities were scrupulous in seeing to it that, whatever happened, the Polish people should never regard those "two enemies" as being of equal status. Thus, insofar as anti-Germanism was obligatory for everyone, anti-Communism was permissible only as a concession granted by the Underground authorities by way of exception, and even then it had to be kept within certain limits and expressed in a manner prescribed from above. On the other hand, any individual or spontaneous manifestations of anti-Communism were on the whole treated as an infringement of national discipline, as troublemaking, or even as collaboration with the Germans.

In rough outline, the picture was as follows: everyone had to be anti-German out of national duty, but only those who had been granted prior permission by the Underground authorities could be anti-Communist. Obviously, this somewhat anecdotal reduction, transferred into practice, defeated the theory of the "two enemies" and not infrequently made anti-Communist activities look ludicrous. Thus, for instance, after the crime of Katyń was discovered and Soviet responsibility for it established, it became compulsory to pronounce the quaint formula that "the Germans also added (to the Katyń graves) some bodies of people they themselves had murdered." Every anti-Soviet statement published by the Underground press had to be redeemed by a long introductory treatise denouncing the Germans. One uncomplimentary word about Stalin required a standard quota of uncomplimentary words about Hitler, and so on. This more or less standard pattern of national censorship was an enormous burden weighing down all Underground journalism, and I do not hesitate to say that it was a largely stultifying influence on all that was written, particularly in view of the not always very high level of political and intellectual sophistication on the part of the Underground "censors."

All this, taken together, meant that the fundamentally correct theory of the "two enemies" could never assume real shape. At any rate, the theory was at variance with the official opinions about Soviet "treason" during the Warsaw Uprising, at the time of the arrest of the sixteen leaders of the Underground, and so forth. As we know, one does not use the term "treason" when speaking of enemies. Only someone close, a friend or an ally, but never an enemy, can commit treason. With an enemy, one fights, but one does not accept invitations from him to conferences over tea. Finally, we all know that after the break in diplomatic relations between the Polish government-in-exile and Moscow, an obligatory practice began whereby the Soviets were treated as "the ally of our allies," a term that could also hardly be included in the definition of "enemy."

WHO IS TO BE BLAMED FOR THE DISINFORMATION?

In writing about the Home Army and the work of the Underground, I avoid clichés in order to mitigate the bad impression that my writing might give. For the sake of popularity, conventional tactical civilities have become the general rule in everything we publish. I do not strive for such popularity. When writing about the Home Army (AK), authors in general use the adjective "heroic." Of course, this is a great exaggeration. As far as ordinary members of the AK were concerned, they were privates, soldiers fighting in the Underground movement, carrying out their soldierly duty in conditions sometimes more difficult and sometimes easier than those that obtained for soldiers on active service on all the world's fronts. It does not seem that they were worse, nor does it seem that they were better, than the soldiers of many other nationalities who participated in the Second World War. As always and everywhere in a war, heroism and cowardice, nobility and knavery, magnificent feats of valor and disgraceful retreats are marching side by side. Our war literature suffers from the one-sidedness of propaganda. If, however, we apply the comparative method and examine the war literature of all the parties involved, we must conclude that we are considerably outdistanced in the number of heroic deeds. Not percentage-wise, I think, but definitely in absolute figures. A larger number of forces on land and sea and in the air provides more opportunities for extraordinary military feats, and a smaller number provides appropriately fewer such opportunities. There is nothing disgraceful in that.

Nonetheless, the embellishment of these opportunities by the AK command and their multiplication, using false statistics, might be regarded as somewhat disgraceful. True, others also did this during the war (Japan and the Soviet Union especially used to provide fantastically exaggerated figures). But this does not alter the fact that the data that pertain to Poland regarding our own losses and those of the enemy, the number of railway lines blown up, assassinations, the number of AK soldiers under arms and, especially, of victims among the civilian population were sometimes exaggerated tenfold. As long as the war continued, this could be explained by the exigencies of propaganda. What is worse is that, after the war, these figures have been recognized as authentic. However, it is not this kind of disinformation that has affected our country's fate.

There is a generally prevalent belief that it is the government-in-exile in London, rather than the Underground authorities in Poland, that is solely to blame for wartime errors. But it seems that exactly the opposite was the case. The policy of the Polish government-in-exile could not influence international events. Still, it could have and should have influenced events in Poland, at least within the limits of the margin for action that still remained. However, the first condition for this to happen had to be honest and dependable information. But the information sent from Poland may perhaps have corresponded with wishful thinking, but it did not correspond with the truth. The huge and dangerous growth of pro-Soviet sympathies was simply not mentioned. Colonel Jan Rzepecki, chief of the Information and Propaganda Office (BIP)—incidentally, one of quite a number of AK commanders who subsequently went over to the Communist side—quotes the alleged words of General Rowecki, the first Commander of the Home Army: "The Poland of the future must be a Red Poland, a home for peasants and workers." Whether or not this was actually true, we do not know. What was undoubtedly true, however, was what Rzepecki wrote in his evaluation of the situation: "A far-reaching radicalization has occurred . . . a general move to the left. . . . The C-in-C is quite inadequately informed about conditions in the country. I consider it absolutely necessary that he be thoroughly and extensively informed of the situation in Poland . . . and that his eyes be opened to the true reality."[2]

Of course, today, Rzepecki has different reasons for wanting those eyes to be opened, but the fact remains that the eyes of the government in London were closed. But the dangerous situation that had arisen was the result of completely natural causes. Before the war, Poland had defended itself from Bolshevik infiltration by barbed-wire entanglements and by its Frontier Defense Corps, counterintelligence, and political police, a very considerable apparatus focused on repelling Bolshevik infiltration. But the infiltration continued, and there was constant evidence of it in the armed forces, in the administration, in public organizations, and so on. So it is easy to imagine its extent when the frontiers were suddenly wide open, the state structure upset, and the gates left unlocked for Soviet agents. And, as if that were not enough, the Polish government signed a pact of friendship with Moscow, so that the former extremely dangerous infiltrator was transformed into an ally. And the Western powers, the sole hope of the Polish nation, were broadcasting pro-Soviet information and propaganda through every radio network. But all this seems still negligible when compared with the pro-Soviet propaganda generated by the terror and other methods of operation introduced by the Nazis!

Those who then emphasized the concentration camps, the prisons, and the murders, that is, only the side pertaining to physical extermination, were moving the center of gravity in the wrong direction. Hitler's terror was dreadful, but with regard to the Poles it did not exceed wartime terror already known in history. In employing our method of comparative analysis, where would we in that case place his treatment of Jews, which exceeded those limits? Anyone living in Poland at the time will well remember that a Jew who managed to obtain documents describing him as Polish-Aryan considered himself to have been virtually saved. Thus, there was a chasm between the fate of the Poles and the fate of the Jews. Therefore, it was not the physical terror employed against Poles that marked the acme of Hitler's mad policy, because it affected only a certain percentage of the population. His policy reached its acme in the fact of the entire population, without exception, being subjected to an insane method of rule whereby its dignity was trampled on at every step: in the tram, on the park bench, in the train, in the restaurant, on the pavement. And this was done by the very oppressor who was simultaneously engaged in a war against the Bolsheviks. Hatred for the invader causes a reflex endowing popularity on everything and everyone opposed to him. Polish hatred of the German occupying powers, resulting from the wrongs suffered, became something of a national idée fixe. In this way, Polish anti-German propaganda no longer required any effort; all the work was done by Hitler's own methods of occupation. With regard to the Nazi occupation, therefore, every Pole was psychologically armed a hundredfold, while becoming more and more disarmed in the area of anti-Sovietism. It would thus seem logical that it was there that the maximum political effort should have been directed. But even when Germany's defeat was imminent and the Germans' retreat from Poland and their replacement by the Soviets had become merely a matter of time, the Underground authorities continued to add fuel to the fire, increasing anti-German agitation practically to the level of frenzy, despite the fact that the cup had already long been filled to the brim. The result in politics is the same as in physics: the enormous potential of anti-German propaganda simply overflowed, and, as nothing is lost in nature, so these floods of energy that had been channelled in one direction were no longer able to feed hatred toward the Germans but fed friendly feelings toward the Soviets.

The fact that under this intense pressure the pro-Soviet sentiments in Poland grew only so much and not more, that, basically, people yielded more to pressure from London than to pressure from Moscow (Radio London, spring 1944: "Remember that any anti-Soviet activities arise solely from German sources!"); that Gomułka's PPR exerted only a minimum of direct influence, so that his current boasting is ridiculous nonsense; all this still testifies to the sound instinct of the majority of the nation.

The government in London should have been informed of the actual state of affairs and the extent of this indirect Communist infiltration. But it was not. Anyway, how could the government be properly informed if the majority of those constituting the Underground authorities were people openly in favor of the most far-reaching compromises with the Soviets; if General Tatar, Deputy Chief of Staff of the Home Army, who himself went over to the Communists at the very first opportunity, had been appointed Director for Home Affairs in the C-in-C's office?!

COLLABORATION WITH THE COMMUNIST ENEMY

On January 20, 1962, in a speech marking the twentieth anniversary of the creation of the PPR, Władysław Gomułka took a retrospective look at the war and the occupation. He mentioned, among other things, that, as early as the beginning of 1943, two meetings between representatives of the PPR leadership and those of the Government Delegate's Office had already taken place for the purpose of establishing cooperation. Although Gomułka deplored the fact that this cooperation did not materialize at that time, we nevertheless do know from other sources that later there were some unofficial contacts and that, beginning in 1944, there was overt collaboration with the Soviet authorities and the Red Army.

We use the term "collaboration" not in order to level some kind of charge but for the purpose of strictly defining the actual state of affairs—because to cooperate with the armed forces and authorities of neighboring governments in one's own territory is to collaborate. One could say that to act in a way that is approved, nay enjoined, by the legal government and its bodies is not consistent with the definition of "collaborating with the enemy." Quite right, of course, but only in regard to those who do not consider international Communism to be an enemy, since the fact of obedience to the legal authorities does not constitute the ultimate decisive factor. In France, it was precisely Pétain's legal government that was declared to be a "collaborator with the enemy," while the disobedient, initially tiny group of people led by De Gaulle was recognized as expressing national aspirations. The pronouncements of the Nuremberg Tribunal also have, at the very least, called into question, as the obligatory norm of behavior, unconditional obedience to the demands of the legal authorities.

Polrealist postwar literature has attempted to reverse the situation by emphasizing the repressive measures, arrests, and the liquidation of AK units after those units lent their support to the Red Army. This is intended to shift the center of gravity to "Soviet treason" and to provide an adequate political alibi. However, this kind of commentary seems particularly unfortunate. First of all, Communists do not "betray" anyone so long as they are liquidating non-Communists. They would be betraying their doctrine only if they transformed their temporary tactics toward non-Communists into an honest and honorable compromise with the latter. Second, the mere fact of Communist repression of somebody is not determined by that person's political stance. Hundreds of thousands of the party's most faithful members also fell victim to repression. Third and finally, Communists are usually in the habit of liquidating all those whom they no longer need and who might become an obstacle in the future. Repression applied to the AK was part of the classic pattern, referred to earlier, of liquidating fellow-travelers who were no longer needed. The Russian word for "fellow-traveler," *poputchik,* comes from the phrase *po puti*—along the way, toward the goal, of course. And, once the goal has been reached or has been proclaimed as having been reached by the Communists, the *poputchik* is no longer needed and can be dispensed with, just like "the Moor who has done his duty." The whole history of Communist tactics leaves no illusions on that score. And if someone does not want to acquaint himself with that history or stubbornly clings to his illusions, so much the better for the Communists. It allows them endlessly to repeat the same tactics, and, as we have seen, in case of dire need, it even allows them to "rehabilitate" those they once liquidated, so as to begin all over again. They acted no differently with regard to the AK. They occupied Poland, they achieved their goal, and they would have betrayed their doctrine if they had then wanted to share their spoils with their non-Communist collaborators. On the contrary, in liquidating them, they acted consistently, and, when a new tactical requirement arose in 1956, they speedily brought about their "rehabilitation." They acted in a similar manner in a later instance of the manipulation of "dissidents"—in Poland, in the years 1980–81, in particular. [Addendum of June 27, 1981.]

So the young Communists' publication *Po prostu* [Plain Speaking] expressed a logical indignation in 1957, when the AK was accused of being "reactionary":

> It is common knowledge that in the years 1943–44 the Twenty-Seventh Division of the AK was fighting in the Wołyń [Volhynia] area, while the units of Major "Tama" and Captain "Trzcianicki" were active in Podolia. Both the Twenty-Seventh Division of the AK, which comprised 6,500 officers and men, and the Podolian units closely collaborated with Soviet partisan groups and subsequently with the Red Army. This can be proved, among other things, by a Radio Moscow communiqué of March 19, 1944, describing the cooperation between AK groups and Red Army units in the liberation of the town of Równe. In the first ten days of April 1944, units of the Twenty-Seventh Division established close contact with the Red Army in the districts of Ostróg and Zdołbunów. "Soviet commanders state that they were given assistance everywhere and express their recognition for the leadership and fighting spirit of the AK"—wrote *Biuletyn Informacyjny* [Information Bulletin], a publication of the AK High Command Information and Propaganda Office, on April 13, 1944. At the same time, other units from the Volhynian Division took the railway station of Stare Koszary, on the Kowel-Luboml line. A Soviet unit whose commander approached the AK commander with a proposal for cooperation also took part in the battle of Stare Koszary. Józef Czerwiński, a former soldier of the Twenty-Seventh Division, now a Major of the Polish Armed Forces, writes in his memoirs (see *Za Wolność i Lud,* 1956, no. 6) about other, earlier instances of cooperation between the Twenty-Seventh Division and the Soviet partisans. The forest unit of Major Satanowski, active in Volhynia and Polesie, also cooperated with the Soviet Army and partisans. Later on, Satanowski's unit, together with most of the officers and men of the Twenty-Seventh Division, would join the Polish Armed Forces. . . . History is being cynically distorted by the Polish Partisans' being described as reactionary. . . . The time has come to end once and for all the distortions in the history of World War Two.[3]

I admit that in this instance I fully agree with the final sentence of the young Communists' article.

Probably the most intensive collaboration between the AK and the Bolsheviks developed in the region of the aforementioned Kowel, as well as around Lublin, where, according to some accounts, the AK assisted the Bolsheviks in taking eighteen localities, and according to others it even contributed to weakening the German front beyond the Bug River, for which a number of AK men received Soviet decorations.

A British officer by the name of Solly-Flood, describing the British Mission's stay with the AK in the winter of 1944–45, in an article published in *Blackwood's Magazine,* quoted General Okulicki's words, that "the Poles gave the Russian Army as much support as they could." Colonel Leon Mitkiewicz, Deputy Chief-of-Staff of the Allied Command, emphasizes "the loyal and active assistance which the AK gave and is still giving to the Soviet troops," in issue no. 1 of the *Zeszyty Historyczne* [Historical Notebooks], published by the Paris *Kultura* in 1961. Anyway, this is a fact confirmed by all the historical sources.

Most noteworthy, perhaps, is the show of deference in the recollecting of the AK's joint action with the Red Army in the taking of Wilno and Lwów. (Incidentally, the military significance of this collaboration is greatly exaggerated.) These are cities to which the Soviets never gave up their formal claims and that, after the "liberation," remained outside the borders even of the People's Poland. The attack on Wilno began on July 7, 1944; it was preceded by an agreement concluded in the village of Praciaty between the AK and the Soviet command. "Even the Soviet commander admits in his memoirs that shortly afterwards the AK attacked the German garrison in Żodziszki. . . . The Red Army benefited from the AK's assistance in the heavy fighting in Wilno, but, as soon as the Germans were defeated, Soviet divisions surrounded the AK units, disarmed them, and deported to concentration camps all those who did not manage to flee."—"On July 7, 1944, AK units attacked Wilno and played a decisive role in the taking of the city, for which they received the highest praise from the Soviet Army."—"Wilk-Krzyżanowski . . . had at his disposal considerable AK forces that cooperated with the Soviet troops. This cooperation included giving them a great deal of help in the capture of Wilno."[4]

The prominent Communist Jerzy Putrament, who entered Wilno with a unit of Berling's Army in July 1944, described his meeting with the AK men thus: "The street is dead quiet. We and they speak simultaneously: 'Aka?

(AK?)'—'Berlingers?'—'First Army!'—we correct them.—'Once again in silence, we shake hands.'"⁵

The battle of Lwów began on July 23, 1944. AK units (of the Fifth Infantry Division and the Fourteenth Lancers) fought in support of Soviet armored action and helped to take the city. Subsequently, the Soviet authorities ordered them to join Berling's Army. In the London *Dziennik Polski* [The Polish Daily] of July 31, 1961, we find the following statement by one of the former AK men in a polemic on the subject of attitudes toward Berling's Army: "If we are to consider former soldiers of Berling's Army as traitors to our country, then I would be interested to know how Mr. . . . would punish those among us who helped the 'traitors' with all our might?"

One could quote whole pages in this fashion. Only the so-called National Armed Forces [NSZ—Narodowe Siły Zbrojne], independent of the AK, broke out of this collaborative attitude toward the Soviets. *Wieś* [The Village], the Underground press agency of the Peasant Party, wrote about this in April 1944: "Calling for a ban on cooperation with the Soviet forces is contrary to the orders of the Commander of the armed forces in our country, and it is clearly harmful."

At the same time, the Underground publication of the Peasant Party, *Żywią i bronią* [They Who Feed and Defend], wrote: "We repeat that those fratricidal crimes perpetrated on units of the PPR's People's Army will be the most shameful blot on the history of our nation's struggle for freedom. . . . Never were the weapons of the Peasant Battalions and of the Home Army turned against the soldiers of the Communist fighting units!"

Nothing changed in this consistent attitude even in the wake of the Warsaw Uprising of August 1944, out of which Soviet propaganda manufactured the ultimate example of an allegedly anti-Soviet act. For the Warsaw Uprising, basically intended for the very proper purpose of preempting the Soviet Army in occupying Poland's capital, was supposed not to defend it from the Bolsheviks but, on the contrary, to welcome them as allies in accordance with the instructions of the AK Command of November 1943, relating to "identifying oneself and playing host to the entering Russian Army." And it was merely this statement of intent, in no way repudiating the spirit of collaboration, that sufficed for the Soviets to declare the Uprising "treasonable." This attitude of the Soviets was confirmed by Gomułka in the aforementioned speech, where he ridiculed the AK Command for having dared to claim the role of "host"! What this meant was that only the Communists could act as hosts in Poland. The AK's duty was to help the Communists to achieve this, without itself striving for power. One could hardly ask, either then or now, for a clearer show of Communist cards.

"LEGIONNAIRES" IN REVERSE . . .

No sensible person is going to say that, after the First World War, Poland rose again thanks to Piłsudski and his Legions. It obviously rose again thanks to the fact that all three partitioning powers simultaneously suffered a defeat. Piłsudski's apologists suggest that he allegedly foresaw this extraordinary juncture of events. Whether he did or he didn't, one must agree that his political camp and his Legions staked everything on what eventually proved to be a winning card and became de facto the corner-stone of Poland's revival as a state and the core of its armed forces. Hence the humanly understandable phenomenon whereby the "Legionnaires" laid claim to the most important positions of state. Nonetheless, freedom of critical thought was still at a high enough level for an enormous portion of public opinion decidedly to oppose the "Piłsudski legend" and the hegemony of his Legionnaires.

After the Second World War, no one in the Polish community that still remained free would dare to oppose the "legend of the Home Army," despite the AK card having proved to be not only a loser but also having been staked on the invader that occupies Poland to this day.

Formally, the AK was controlled by the (special) Sixth Department of the C-in-C Staff in London and was meant to carry out its instructions. Yet, this was a purely formal control. In practice, it was not the government that imposed its will on the country but the country that imposed its will on the government, even in a matter of such supreme importance as the attitude toward the Soviets. This is already apparent, for example, in the story of the "Instructions for the country" issued by the C-in-C (Sosnkowski) in London on October 27, 1943. They include, among others, the order that the moment the Red Army enters Polish territory, "Poland will not collaborate with the Soviet Union"; the AK must remain a secret organization. In reply, on January 1, 1944, there comes a cable dated November 26, 1943, from General Komorowski, the AK Commander, stating that he had issued a precisely opposite order, which was "at variance on this point with the Government's instruction," namely that "the local Polish (AK) commander should report to the commander of the Soviet forces." Moreover, this instruction had also been issued to representatives of the civil Underground authorities. General Sosnkowski, one of the few people who at that time realized the ominous effects of collaboration with the Bolsheviks, was de facto powerless in face of the "Homeland's" decision, and in his letters to the Prime Minister dated January 4 and 9, 1944, he expressed his negative attitude with regard to the decisions made in Poland. But, in February, the government changed his "Instructions," as demanded by the AK command. The President expressed his confidence "in the political wisdom of the authorities in the Homeland." Finally, in July 1944, the government (under Mikołajczyk's leadership) transferred to the "Homeland" the right and duty of making decisions "without prior consultation with the Government." Thus, all power was handed over on July 26, 1944. All General Sosnkowski's protests and attempts to countermand this decision, especially as regards joint operations with the Soviets, were repudiated by his government. The AK was given carte blanche not only in military but also in political actions.

So the responsibility for these actions rests solely with the AK itself. What kind of actions they were in the field of military cooperation with the Soviet Union we have briefly shown in the preceding section. To this must be added the somewhat unambivalent political attitude of the civilian Underground authorities. *Jutro Polski* [Poland's Morrow], the paper of the principal (Peasant) party in the government in London, writes: "The Underground Council of National Unity in the homeland, and thus a representative body of the whole of democratic Poland, has unanimously approved the Yalta agreements. . . . In accepting the Yalta decisions, Prime Minister Mikołajczyk first and foremost obeyed the decisions of the homeland, its express wishes, formulated in the resolutions of the Council of National Unity."[6]

When, in the wake of Mikołajczyk's policy of capitulation, a crisis developed in the government-in-exile in London and the government of Tomasz Arciszewski was appointed, the Council of National Unity in Poland passed a resolution demanding that Mikołajczyk be brought back and his compromise with the Soviet Union confirmed. Finally, when, on May 3, 1945, a motion of no confidence in the London government was defeated at a session of the Central Commission of the Council of National Unity, Stefan Korboński, a representative of the majority (Peasant) party, declared himself unilaterally "the last Government Delegate to the Homeland" and, on behalf of the Underground authorities, recognized Bierut's Communist government.

We all know how it ended. Just as the regaining of independence was not due to Piłsudski's Legions, so the loss of independence was not the fault of the AK and the Underground. In both cases, higher forces were the deciding factor. However, the AK overwhelmingly influenced the shaping of the moods and the direction of the nation's thoughts at home. This influence stemmed from earlier, blinkered reasoning, where the right course of action was seen not in opposing the Bolsheviks but in joining them to finish off an earlier invader who was already leaving Poland's territory. Only thus could the ideological "base" be built on which the Communists developed their dogma of "Poland's liberation," which, though not without certain reservations, was accepted by the majority of the nation, despite the fact that Poland had been struck by the greatest disaster any country can suffer. For the German occupation was only an external occupation, whereas the Soviet occupation has been both external and internal: the German occupation was only physical, the Soviet one both physical and psychological. The former was only temporary, lasting for the duration of the war; the latter has continued in peacetime. The former was not accepted by the world as a whole; the latter was. The entire nation was in a state of war under the former; under the latter—largely because of the AK—the nation has been in a state of capitulation.

Politicians and generals who represent ideas that, even through no fault of their own, result in disaster, are usually removed from positions of influence. This was the consequence of the 1939 disaster for Piłsudski's camp, even though at the time it was not yet a final defeat. Today, however, those who gave armed support to the enemy occupying the country at present not only have not been prevented from influencing the thinking of those Poles who are free but have in many instances gained a monopoly hold over political values and over the making of decisions as to what is or what was right and proper, moral or immoral, consistent or inconsistent with the national interest.

As already mentioned, a considerable number of AK and Underground leaders joined in the trend of capitulating to and further collaborating with Communism. Nevertheless, this did not subsequently prevent some of them from again occupying leading political positions in exile and becoming something akin to shining lights in the life of the nation. It suffices to cite as an example the person of Stefan Korboński, the aforementioned "last Government Delegate to the Homeland." Here is what *Myśl Państwowa* [Thoughts of the State], published in London, wrote in an article entitled "Trzy rodzaje uchodźców" [Three Kinds of Refugee], signed by HAK, the pseudonym of the well-known Polish journalist Henryk Kleinert (who died on June 18, 1958):

> The last Government Delegate to the Homeland ceased to recognize the Government and the President of the Polish Republic and granted his recognition to Bierut. When . . . the Government delegate was requested to turn over his Government money and his instruments of communication with London for the disposal of those who intended to continue their resistance, Mr. Korboński refused to do so. . . . At

any rate, the last Government Delegate to the Homeland turned everything over to the Bezpieka [Secret Service].

Mr. Korboński loyally cooperated with the régime. He became a deputy and voted for the approval of whatever had to be approved. The breakup occurred neither through his wishes nor through his fault, but simply because the régime no longer attached any importance to continued cooperation with Mr. Korboński and his political friends. They had played their part and were no longer needed. . . .

Once the man who had been the last Government Delegate to the Homeland found himself abroad, he did not admit that his decision in 1945 had been a mistake. . . . He continued to recognize Yalta and Bierut. He had only one grudge against Bierut, that is, that the latter did not carry out the Yalta decisions in Poland's internal policy and that he rejected the cooperation of Mr. Korboński and his friends. . . .

Recently Mr. Korboński won considerable publicity with his book *W imieniu Rzeczypospolitej* [In the name of the Republic]. He borrowed the title from the first words of verdicts pronounced by tribunals in the name of the Polish Republic Mr. Korboński betrayed by going over to Bierut. At the moment, basking in the aura of an author's fame, Mr. Korboński feels entitled to pass judgment on people in exile. He published in the press a low and unworthy attack on the person of the President of the Republic. . . . The test of the man's worth is in his words and his acts, committed in the certainty of his total impunity. And yet Mr. Korboński piously instructs everyone what to do and how to behave. . . . Perhaps in a few months or years we shall see former Comrade Światło beginning to instruct us and to pass judgment on members of the exile community who are carrying on the struggle.[7]

At present, Mr. Korboński occupies a high-ranking position in some organization for international understanding, in which he represents Poland. Such phenomena can be explained not only by the line of contemporary Polrealism but also by subordinate—technical is the term that comes to mind—considerations. For it is a fact that many leaders of the former Underground who found themselves in exile managed to obtain easier access to the political nerve centers of the Western powers as a result of the favorable climate prevailing in the West for politicians free of any suspicion of "counterrevolutionary" tendencies. The criterion of loyalty with regard to these Western powers in the past was the involvement in anti-German resistance. Thus was it possible to gain overwhelming predominance, both material and in the sphere of influence, over all the rest of the exiles, generally deprived of the resources needed to disseminate their political views.

Another characteristic point is the fact that the reverent attitude of Polrealism toward the fighting Underground relates only to the anti-German Underground. The moment the matter arises of soldiers fighting for freedom without the aid of an organization or directives, without solid gold coins and "soft" dollars, without arms and ammunition drops, that is, in conditions demanding the greatest possible personal sacrifice but against the Communists, the pathos and the belles-lettres are finished and the punishment of silence or, more frequently, condemnation comes to the fore. This happens with the anti-Communist partisan movement in Poland, which continued after the war to fight for years. This fate is especially common with regard to organizations that broke free from the AK directives during the war. However, it is significant that the same people who once broke away from this moral pressure now tend to conform to the generally prevailing mood. Thus, for instance, a few years ago, I read (I believe it was in the Paris *Kultura*) some accusations leveled by the AK at the National Armed Forces (NSZ) and summed up in the slogan "When the whole of Poland fought the Germans, you were the only ones to collaborate with them!" To which accusation, instead of replying with the counterslogan "When the whole of Poland collaborated with the Bolsheviks, we were the only ones to fight against them!" the NSZ replied with detailed explanations as to where and how they had killed Germans and which ones. Moreover, confrontation with the fact that Poland, our country, our home, remains under the Soviet and not the German yoke suddenly becomes irrelevant. There follows the emotional return to criteria from the last war, no longer objectively important but subjectively significant for those people for whom these criteria represent the sum total of their political achievement and who, having profited thereby, would most likely wish to continue to do so. In this context, it is nowadays still possible to broadcast on the American Radio Free Europe (where the Polish department is managed by former AK people) talks like the one that stated that "Vlasov was a traitor and paid for it with his ignominious death" (October 12, 1961, 18.45 hrs.). It is understood that, naturally, he "betrayed" his "country" (not Bolshevism, against which he actually fought) and that he was justly hanged by the Bolsheviks.

And, because today Communists are most eager to bring about a reconstruction and an emotional revival of the wartime "anti-Fascist front," it seems that Gomułka, not without reason, has effected a partial "rehabilitation" of the AK. And he did so probably not just because of the role it played during the war but also because of the influence it has enjoyed after the war in Poland and among Polish exiles.

This was the beginning of a new era. Since then, under his successors in Poland—and likewise in other countries of the Communist bloc—only a legal, open "opposition," in the manner of "dissidents," has been widely recognized in the Western world; any conspiracy has been ruled out and any form of violence against Communists condemned. In accordance with Solzhenitsyn's prescription: "Neither with a knife, nor with a sword, nor with a gun!" . . . The incident of Lenin's leg being broken off his monument in the vicinity of Cracow is considered an act of "provocation"! The old maxim "one can be a victim of Communism, but one must not be its enemy" has been fully endorsed by Amnesty International and by the celebrated Sakharov Hearings. "Evolution" is permitted, but (counter-)Revolution is not. The Soviet bloc is thus protected from any armed intervention from without, and from within as well.

In this manner we have entered the era of "revival." Incidentally, with considerable support from such illustrious quarters as the Roman Catholic Church in the persons of John XXIII, Paul VI, and John Paul II, in particular. Finally, on June 20, 1981, the leader of the "Opposition" in Communist Poland, the world-famous Lech Wałęsa, declared on state television that the opposition "Solidarity" movement was striving for peaceful cooperation with the (Communist) government, which "must be strong and have the right conditions to govern the country!" [Addendum of June 27, 1981.]

Chapter 9 The Origins of "PAX"

The fundamental concept behind the creation of this subversive organization was the same as that used by the Communists when setting up religious splinter organizations that at one time had broken up the Russian Patriarchal Church from within. All done, naturally, in keeping with the so-called objective conditions. On entering Poland in 1945, the Bolsheviks found that the "objective conditions" that prevailed presented them with considerable difficulties in several respects. Unexpectedly, however, they won an ally for their plans in possibly the most unlikely quarter. And this is how it all began.

"THE RESURRECTING OF THE CONSERVATIVE CAMP"

We have already discussed the situation in Poland that developed under the German occupation. There was just a one-point political program: a blind struggle against the Germans, which included collaboration with the approaching Bolsheviks. Plans for the future were replaced by "faith" in Great Britain and the usual obligatory optimism. To counteract this condition of political inertia, Aleksander Bocheński, the former editor of *Bunt Młodych* [Rebellion of the Young] and of *Polityka* in interwar Poland, advocated resurrecting the ideas of the Polish conservative camp. He was the theoretician of a conciliatory policy toward the invader, and a fanatical theoretician at that. Obviously, such an attitude aroused suspicions of "collaboration" with the Germans. These suspicions were mistaken: Bocheński did promote conciliatory policies, but toward every invader. His influence as a private person was negligible. The whole force of his concept lay simply in the very fact of its existence, at a time when there was no other plan for action in the event of the arrival of the Red Army. Bocheński paraded it mainly in Cracow, during and after the Warsaw Uprising, in the autumn of 1944. He did this especially in a kind of political salon run by Count Adam Ronikier, situated at No. 2, Potocki Street. At that time members of the Polish aristocracy, fleeing from all over the country before the Bolsheviks, and representatives of former conservative thought were all pouring into Cracow. According to Bocheński, "resurrecting" Conservative thought meant in practice the restoration of those conciliatory measures that before the First World War had brought advantageous results in the three partitioned areas, notably under the Austrians.

NOTHING BUT "RUSSIA"

Someone reading this work devoted to the loss of Polish "sovereign thought" might gain the impression that my presentation of the subject is oversimplified and that I onesidedly deny too many Poles the possession of both intelligence and a critical faculty. This impression could be the result of my condensing too much material into too narrow a frame. Obviously, even in conservative circles there were many voices that were critical of Bocheński's concept. Above all: could the nineteenth-century conditions, especially the internal "substance" of the former monarchies of Russia, Germany, and Austro-Hungary, be regarded as analogous to international Bolshevism? In order to evade this supremely important objection, Bocheński became the most fervent advocate of the "Russia" theory. He maintained that Bolshevism or Communism is only the outward instrument, not the actual substance. The content remained the same: Russia! Contact should be established and a compromise modus vivendi found, not with Russia's international but, on the contrary, its national interests. This switch of terminology to "Russia" was the basis of the whole theory, since it would have been rather awkward within that gathering to appeal for conciliation with international Bolshevism. And so this notion, Russia, nowadays regarded as the proper reason for nationalist anti-Soviet propaganda, simultaneously became the only reason for possible conciliation. Nothing should be simplified. Today's subversive agency called PAX really owes its beginnings to a political, not to a subversive, concept.

THE MEETING AT THE "POD RÓŻĄ" HOTEL

While reserving for myself the right to publish my sources at a time I consider appropriate, I shall tell what happened next. The Bolsheviks entered Cracow on January 18, 1945. However, most of the habitués of the "political salon" in Potocki Street preferred to flee to the West. Also—just in case—Bocheński himself, together with Dominik Horodyński, his messenger boy, and several others hid in an apartment belonging to Count X. The reason was that Bocheński was suspected of collaborating with the Germans. Nevertheless, he decided to take this very risky step, which subsequently proved decisive in the whole affair, notwithstanding the fact that, apart from winning the support of some half-dozen titled personages for his concept, he had hitherto not enjoyed any significance or played any kind of political role.

Within a few days of Cracow's being taken by the Communists, Jerzy Borejsza (Goldman) appeared in the city. At the time, he was a high-ranking dignitary with special duties, especially involving the establishment of contacts with "internal" émigrés. Later, as we know, the contacts extended to "external" émigrés, too. Borejsza-Goldman, who is no longer alive, was a man of quick wit and a high level of intelligence. He was greatly valued by the party's upper echelons for the speed with which he could grasp various concepts and for his ability to differentiate between the essential and the inessential. That is why he was entrusted with particularly sensitive missions. All those who knew him during that period point to the exceptional qualities of his character. This is how Wojciech Żukrowski, a Communist writer, characterized him on the tenth anniversary of his death:

> He was a good psychologist and knew that activity got people involved and that attitudes change quicker through work than through discussions. . . . Borejsza was a born activist, organizer, and politician who disregarded hard and fast lines of division. He believed that one should approach one's opponents, seek bridges, even briefly unite with one's opponents to engage in joint action and, in the event of a rupture, steal from them, abduct a few of their most prominent people. How he loved those friendships above the lines of the ideological front: he made forays to capture Stanisław Cat-Mackiewicz and Wańkowicz, both of whom at the time re-

garded a visit to Poland, Red Poland, as a betrayal of London's imponderabilia. . . . And then they both came over to us.[1]

And so Bocheński could really have done no better than to approach Borejsza. Borejsza stayed at the Pod Różą Hotel in Floriańska Street. This is the conversation that took place (I repeat that I reserve the right to publish my sources at some time in the future):

"I am Aleksander Bocheński."

"Oh . . . That's interesting. Apparently they're looking for you."

"I know that, but I would like you to give me one hour of your time."

"Unfortunately I have to fly off in twenty minutes."

"Then telephone the airfield and cancel the flight."

"Will the conversation be as interesting as all that?"

"I can assure you that it will."

A quarter of an hour later, Borejsza did telephone the airport and arrange for his flight to be delayed. Bocheński unveiled before him a complete program for a concord between the extreme right wing, the intransigent "counterrevolutionaries," the Catholic camp, and the new Communist régime, more or less along the lines we know today, that is, along lines that generally conform to those that were termed "poputnichestvo" [fellow-traveling] in the atmosphere of the Leninist NEP we have already depicted but that also conform to the current "realistic politics."

"And whom would you suggest putting at the head of such a group?" asked Borejsza.

"Bolesław Piasecki, if he is still alive."

"Is this supposed to be a joke on your part?"

"No, I couldn't be more serious."

And so Bocheński deployed the well-known arguments about preventing the emergence of a rightist Underground movement. That was the first condition for the success of the whole plan. Obviously, the anti-Soviet partisan movement would not be totally put paid to, but the enormous potential force, represented undoubtedly by the nationalistic young people who adored Piasecki, would be restrained. Piasecki's execution would bring no benefits, while his appointment as chief of a "Catholic-rightist opposition," an opposition that was legal and constructive and that recognized the new authorities as "Polish," would be enormously beneficial.

Borejsza swiftly grasped the importance of these arguments. At that stage, the first requirement of the new authorities was obviously that they should be recognized by the nation not as "occupying powers" but as "Polish authorities," regardless of people's emotional attitude toward them. Bocheński's plan was the most classic example of the concord between nationalism and Communism. That very evening, Borejsza flew away, carrying in his briefcase the complete plan.

THE HANGMAN'S NOOSE OR "LEGAL OPPOSITION"?

Piasecki's story during that period is presented quite differently in the evidence of Józef Światło, a high-ranking Bezpieka official who fled to the West in 1954. According to Światło, Piasecki was arrested by NKVD [Narodnyi Komissariat Vnutrennikh Del—People's Commissariat for Internal Affairs] operational units and was to be tried and hanged not only for his anti-Soviet partisan activities to the east of the Bug River but also for his alleged contacts with the Gestapo. Trying to save his life, Piasecki addressed to General Żymierski a memorandum that supposedly fell into the hands of Ivan Serov, chief of the NKGB. Apparently, Serov became interested in Piasecki's proposals, and so on. This is a great oversimplification that is in keeping with the nation's mood but not with the truth. Matters of this kind were decided at a much higher, political, not police, level.

According to information I have in my possession, the matter was examined by the party authorities responsible for making high-level decisions as a result of the Borejsza-Bocheński colloquy. It is true that Piasecki, caught by the NKVD, was faced with the choice: the hangman's noose or "legal opposition." He chose the latter. As for Bocheński, he emerged from hiding and was given the directorship of the nationalized breweries, "Okocim," and, it was said, a "ministerial salary." (Before the war he had owned a brewery in Ponikwa.) In this case, also, the matter should not be oversimplified to the effect that this was some kind of "payment for services rendered." Bocheński acted not as an agent but as a politician. It was in the interests of both sides that he have freedom of movement as an "independent politician," with his livelihood secured, and be able to concentrate on recruiting ideological supporters.

THE POLITICAL LINE

The whole business began by no means with the breaking up of the Church's unity but with political steps that, for the Communists, obviously constituted a form of tactics "for that particular stage." In the years 1945–47, these still conformed completely to Gomułka's tactics in the years 1956–58, and they had analogous effects. For the time being, PAX was doing exactly what ZNAK [Insignia] is doing now: "Poland is one"; "common interests"; "recognition of the factual state of affairs"; and, above all, the rejection of the thesis that Poland was under "Soviet occupation" and the claim that the "Polish state," albeit with Communists in charge, really did exist. For the time being, the same people wrote both for Cardinal Sapieha's *Tygodnik Powszechny* and for Piasecki's *Dziś i Jutro* [Today and Tomorrow].

It was Underground action that the Communists feared most. In Warsaw, it was expected that such action would be supported and conducted by General Anders's Second Corps. It was to prevent this that Count Horodyński and Count Łubieński left for Rome in 1945–46 and made their way to nearly all the centers where Polish exiles had gathered. Once again, this followed the pattern of journeys by NEP-era emissaries, sent from Minsk and Kiev to the Byelorussian and Ukrainian centers of emigration. And so these two managed to reach émigré decision-making centers and to establish a "common platform" on the most important points at that stage of development. Despite the Soviet invasion of Poland, the Polish constitutional government did not regard itself as being in a state of war with the Soviet Union, shielding itself behind the then well-known slogan of "saving the nation's biological substance." It was a time when the figures quoted for human lives lost in the war were astronomical, with PAX, of course, leading the way both in Poland and among the exiles. (*Dziś i Jutro* once gave the number of those who perished in the Warsaw Uprising as being in excess of 700,000!) Consequently, there has been a widespread view among the émigrés that any idea of an underground struggle in Poland must be not only rejected but even condemned as a "provocation." The accepted line has been "not international Communism, but 'Russia.'" In this way, efforts were made to blur comparisons with NEP, with "poputnichestvo" [fellow-traveling], with "smena vekh" [changing one's colors], or with National Communism, while the genesis of the common platform was traced back to Positivism, with its idea of "organic groundwork," or even to the ideas of Count Aleksander Wielopolski, "the Cracow conservatives," and so on, all of which, naturally, sounded much more pleasant and provided moral support in the form of models taken from the previous century. This explains the high percentage of titled personages and former conservatives in the ranks of PAX.

AGENTS OF SUBVERSION

The chief characteristic of Communist "stages" is that when each one ends, it leads to the next. The first "political stage" turned out well for the Communists, and they concluded that the time had come for the next: the destruction of the Church by the same classic methods that, after 1927, had broken Metropolitan Sergii in Moscow. Obviously, in Poland the Communists' task was much more difficult because the Catholic Church was supported by a central body beyond the reach of Soviet power, something the Orthodox Church did not have, since the Ecumenical Patriarch in Constantinople is not like the Pope in Rome, being merely *primus inter pares*.

Thus, Piasecki's present role began only with the ending of the "political stage" and the initiation of the stage of direct Communist pressure. Political "grey eminences" were removed, since they were no longer required. The concept of "conservative thought" transformed itself into the practice of subversion. The internal content of international Communism was not like the content of the conquering and annexing monarchies of the nineteenth century. Sooner or later, every compromise had to end in subversion, simply because international Communism is not interested in any real, bilateral compromises; it knows only the *tactics* of compromise.

According to Józef Światło, Piasecki was controlled by the Fifth Department of the Security Service, by Colonel Luna Brystygier, to be exact. Once again, this is a gross oversimplification, but of no great consequence. Such oversimplifications divert attention from the essentials. Piasecki came to lead a huge subversive operation that was political, as well as psychological and religious. The instructions flowed from the teachings of Lenin; in practice, they lay in the domain of the party, not of the Security Ministry in Warsaw or its counterpart in Moscow. To represent Piasecki as an agent receiving cash with his instructions from Colonel Luna is to denigrate the enemy and to make the truth look as optimistic as possible, to create a deliberate anachronism that reduces an agency of the world socialist system to the category of some tsarist Okhrana, something at which all the Polish versions of the story are particularly adept. No Okhrana in the world could possibly successfully canvass as many Catholic monsignors as did this godless Communist agency of subversion. And herein lies both the enormous, organic difference and the tragic paradox.

Piasecki was granted extensive concessions: INCO—the Foreign Trading Association—was established as early as 1947, as also were PAX and Veritas, initially with a capital fund of three million zlotys. It was a two-pronged operation: abroad, mainly in France, to win over "progressive" Catholic groups, and at home, to destroy the Church's unity in Poland.

As regards operations abroad, Communist plans for undermining the Catholic Church were very ambitious. Incidentally, they ran parallel to the subversive activities of the Moscow Patriarchate within the Eastern Church. That was the time of the endless trips to France and elsewhere of the well-tried duo Horodyński and Łubieński and others. The Dominican Prof. J. M. Bocheński, an outstanding expert on international Communism, considered the supposedly Catholic writer Jan Dobraczyński, whose books enjoyed great popularity in the West and among émigrés, to be the most dangerous figure in that team.

At home, in Poland, this major agency of subversion was extended and developed into various powerful organizations. Following the Bolshevik model, it assumed the appearance of an entity analogous to that of the "Living (Orthodox) Church" of the twenties and thirties. All kinds of bodies were created, such as the Priests' Commission, Patriot Priests (the Caritas Priests of today), ZBoWiD [Freedom and Democracy Fighters' Union], and so on. Caritas was taken over in 1950, and in that operation the well-known writer Paweł Jasienica, lauded nowadays in ZNAK publications, played the role of provocateur. A powerful "Catholic" press was created. Two examples will demonstrate the extent to which it was "Catholic" in inverted commas.

Monsignor Jasielski from the Priests' Commission proposed a new kind of examination of conscience, which included this point: "How many times have I remained silent about a grievous sin of another, even though I should have reported it to my superiors or the authorities?"[2]

During the second congress of the Priests' Commission, Monsignor Kotarski, hearing of the death of Andrei Vyshinsky, the prosecutor at the great Stalinist trials and thus jointly responsible for the death of millions of people, began his speech on November 23, 1954, with these words: "This morning came the sad news of the death of Minister Vyshinsky. Let us pay homage to his memory.... His name is a symbol of the struggle for peace.... He was a great friend of Poland. All mankind will remember that noble figure and praise for ever the name of a tireless defender of peace. Praise be to his memory!"[3]

This is what this "progressive Catholic movement" looked like, having at last, after numerous reorganizations, changes, and congresses, ending in a final unification, passed under the undivided directorship of Bolesław Piasecki. The concessions and funds at his disposal continued to grow, so that he would shortly come to be called "the richest private person between Vladivostok and

Berlin." No one in the entire Soviet bloc has as many business concessions as Piasecki.

THE MOGUL OF PROVOCATION

Gone are the times when Azef, an agent provocateur of the tsarist police, was regarded as the "king of provocateurs." Those were the days of individual agents and individual tasks assigned by the police. Our time is the time of collectives of provocateurs and mass tasks, assigned not by the police but by the party. It was Piasecki who headed one of these provocation collectives. In 1957, all the PAX organizations, societies, enterprises, and publications achieved the record-breaking figure of nearly half a billion zlotys in their annual turnover.

Gomułka withdrew PAX's overseas agents of subversive operations because their activities had been unmasked by the Vatican and they had thus been totally compromised in the eyes of the Catholics of Western Europe. He replaced them with a team of different people, people from the ZNAK group.

Chapter 10 Pharisaism Versus Subversion

Lenin was not only the creator of classic tactics in combating faith in God. Lenin personally suffered from a phobia: he hated God. In one of his letters to Gorky, he called God "a putrescent corpse, the stench of whose putrefaction has poisoned the atmosphere of the globe." Bolshevism's victory over Russia's Orthodox Church, whereby it was transformed into an agency serving the godless party, is generally ascribed to that Church's traditional structure and docility in the face of all kinds of tyrants. However, a little-known event shows that the Orthodox Church in Russia was actually the only Christian Church on Bolshevik-controlled territory that undertook an open struggle against Communism and acted not only as a "victim of persecution" but as a declared enemy. On January 19, 1918, Patriarch Tikhon placed an anathema on the Bolsheviks: "On the authority of the power lent to us by God, we forbid you Christ's Sacraments and pronounce an anathema upon you, if you still bear Christian names, even if you belong to the Orthodox Church only by virtue of your birth."

This was the source and the beginning of the once notorious antireligious Bolshevik terror, which seemingly did not fit in with Lenin's pliable tactics and which was initiated by a state of open conflict.

In 1945, after the Bolsheviks seized Poland, the Polish Catholic Church did not intend to fight the Communists. On the contrary, from the very beginning the Church maintained complete loyalty toward the new authorities, despite the existence in exile of a legitimate constitutional government.

Nowadays, when one reads how the Polish people were cheated and how the Western powers withdrew their recognition of the legal Polish government in London, even if one views that government's policies with aversion, it is hard to resist a feeling of great depression and sadness in the face of such tragic injustice. This is not the place to investigate the validity of the reasoning behind the interpretation of its legal status, due to which the Catholic Church in Poland, not separated from the State, ceased to recognize the country's constitutional government, while giving de facto and, as shown by subsequent documents and declarations, de jure recognition to the Communist government. Nevertheless, this affected the internal situation in the country more than the withdrawal of recognition by the Western powers.

Despite this situation, so favorable for the Communists, the application of classical tactics did not lead to the Church's capitulation as it did in the case of the Orthodox Church. Furthermore, the Communists achieved important concessions from the episcopate thanks not so much to PAX's subversive activities as to the conciliatory policy of people grouped around the *Tygodnik Powszechny*.

Doubtless, there is only one genuine attitude toward God: a profound faith that whatever one does and thinks, God sees man's thoughts and the true intention of his deeds. Anyone who, while hiding behind God's name for the purpose of thus concealing his private or political objectives, loses his sense of this omnipresent Knowledge, either in his private or in his public life, is a Pharisee. People both from PAX and from ZNAK know that one of the final aims of Communism is to destroy all faith in God on earth. However, the PAX group degenerated very quickly into an overt agency working for the advancement of Communism, so it can hardly be accused of being pharisaical. Not so the ZNAK group.

THE ZNAK GROUP

The *Tygodnik Powszechny* group that constitutes the core of the present-day ZNAK has never fought against Communism, although this was how it was frequently presented among the émigrés. Quite the opposite. From the very beginning, it strove for a modus vivendi: its aim was a compromise with the Communists. Basically, it was ZNAK, not PAX, that fulfilled the essence of the Borejsza-Bocheński agreement. If the people from *Tygodnik Powszechny* failed to attain their objective in Bierut's time, the fault lies not with them but is a result of the fact that the objective of the Communists was different.

At first, Catholics from the *Tygodnik Powszechny* openly sided with PAX. The split occurred only when Piasecki and his comrades descended from the "political stage" to the stage of overt subversion, since the *Tygodnik Powszechny* group was trying to remain at the "political stage" and thus retain the ability to influence the masses of the faithful on the one hand and the episcopate on the other. The nature of the prevalent mood was (and is) that the masses of the faithful were ready at any time to support the Church in its potential struggle against the Communists; the principal concern of this "political" group was to forestall such a struggle and to exert pressure on the episcopate so as to prevent its unwittingly causing an explosion. However, PAX's overt subversion obstructed this road of "political" conciliation. Hence the fundamental difference in opinions, usually given an erroneous interpretation in the West and among émigrés.

Thus, when Bierut judged the first "political stage" to have ended and decided to start on the next, he considered the role of the fellow-travelers and political pedlars of compromise to be finished, and embarked on the liquidation of the *Tygodnik Powszechny* group.

THE AGREEMENT OF APRIL 14, 1950

On April 14, 1950, an agreement was signed "between the Church and the State." This was an important victory for the Communists, and it was received in Rome with surprise and amazement. What followed on the part of the Communists was not, as was generally presented, "counter to the agreement" but quite the opposite: it was its logical consequence. The Communists concluded that the Church was on the brink of capitulating and increased the pressure. There followed a period of ruthless persecution. The bishops were forced to swear an oath in 1952; on February 9, 1953, came the notorious decree on Church appointments, which went so far as to encroach on the *forum internum* of Church jurisdiction; Primate Wyszyński was arrested on September 26, 1953. Two days later, on behalf of the episcopate, Bishops Klepacz and Choromański signed a declaration that has never been published in the émigré press. It was a degrading act that, instead of protesting the primate's arrest and persecution, contained submissively loyal words with regard to the Communist authorities. Where historical analogy is concerned, it corresponded both in spirit and in content to the defeatist declaration of Metropolitan Sergii in 1927.

That was the zenith of the oppression of the Church in Poland, and the Communists thought they had successfully brought about its total disintegration; so far, everything conformed to the pattern established in the case of the Patriarchal Church in Moscow. But now they were mistaken. The error of their calculation was that in Moscow they had in their hands the highest-ranking ecclesiastical personage, since, as already mentioned, the Patriarch in Constantinople is merely a *primus inter pares,* not the head of the Eastern Church. But it is the Pope in Rome who is the head of the Western Church, and the Church in Poland is subject to him. So the Communists' arms proved too short. It is true that they had the powerful PAX organization, ready, once it received the signal, to establish a "State Church" to serve the party, but it was clear that the Catholic nation in its entirety would not break with Rome, and would instead become a Church of the Catacombs. And that would scuttle all the Communists' plans. Rabid attacks on the noble person of the unyielding Pope Pius XII began, but they failed to provide a way out of the impasse. There then followed a "thaw" in the Soviet Union, and Gomułka came to power in Poland shortly after.

THERE WAS NO NEW AGREEMENT BETWEEN GOMUŁKA AND THE CHURCH

People generally believed that, with Cardinal Wyszyński's release from prison, some kind of new agreement had been signed between him and Gomułka in December 1956. Nothing of the sort happened. All that happened was that the agreement of April 14, 1950, was confirmed in toto; to the Church's disadvantage, paragraph "b" of Article 10, referring to prayer in schools, was crossed out. Apart from that, there were some slight stylistic changes pertaining to the notorious decree on Church appointments. The decree itself was retained in force. The essence of the famous "concordat" lay elsewhere, namely in Gomułka's solemn promise to honor the undertakings that the agreement of April 14, 1950, imposed on the authorities. But, in exchange, he demanded support in the elections for the single Communist list.

The episcopate lent its support to the elections. It was the first time in history that the Church of Rome became so deeply engaged in collaboration with a Communist government. For his part, Gomułka for the time being kept his promise, in accordance with Lenin's directives at the Eighth Party Congress in 1919, warning against engaging in a fight against religion while there were "more important problems" to solve. The chicanery and the repressive measures ceased. And so there was a kind of return to the "political stage."

It seemed that those who had advocated conciliation and compromise had triumphed and that the subversive agency PAX, paid for by means of various concessions, had been humiliated. There followed the creation of the "Club of the Progressive Catholic Intelligentsia" under the chairmanship of Jerzy Zawieyski, who declared: "We realize that the PZPR [the Polish United Workers' (Communist) Party] is the only force capable of directing the nation's fate. We place our trust in it and wish to cooperate with it."

COMPETITION

Shortly afterward, the Sejm (Parliament) group "ZNAK" came into being, with Zawieyski (a member of the "Council of State"), Stanisław Stomma, and Stefan Kisielewski at its head. But they met with disappointment: Gomułka was obviously not so stupid as to get rid of his "living Church"; he continued to maintain it to keep both the Church and ZNAK itself in check. That was the moment when ZNAK and PAX began to compete for pride of place in the confidence of the Communist Party. And, of course, this competition suited the Communists very well. ZNAK's policy toward the Communists seemed to be one of persuasion, more or less along the lines of "Why should you support fake Catholics, compromised agents, since we, authentic Catholics as well as realistic politicians, are agreeable to any kind of political collaboration with you?" As we know, Communists cannot be "persuaded"; one can only fit in or not fit in with their tactics at a given stage. And it suited Gomułka's tactics at the time to keep both groups in the game. Piasecki continued to be the richest man between Berlin and Vladivostok, while ZNAK was brought out for use in Western Europe.

AN AGENCY OF PRO-COMMUNIST PHARISAISM

Gomułka effected a peculiar kind of "evolution": he replaced the subversion agency abroad with pharisaism. In place of somewhat ludicrous figures of little ability like Horodyński, there appeared in the West serious, dignified people, very erudite in theology and politically sophisticated. They were not spoken of out loud as "agents," but they were quietly said to be "people close to the person of the Primate." In turn, they sometimes corrected the whispers, and sometimes they did not hear them.

On May 9, 1957, Kisielewski appeared at the Congress for Cultural Freedom in Paris; on May 13, Stomma spoke at the Centre intellectuel des catholiques français; on May 15, Zawieyski was interviewed by *Le Monde*. All these events on French territory enjoyed the active patronage of Maurice Vaussard, a representative of the "progressives" who had hitherto introduced guests from PAX. And the content and meaning of all that was said and written corresponded with the well-known theses of PAX emissaries: Polish Catholics accept the system; Poland wishes to remain in the Socialist camp; the Church should participate in the great changes engendered by Socialism, rather than remain petrified in conservatism and clericalism. In due course, *Życie Warszawy* evaluated all those words politically in the following fashion: "Kisielewski, Stomma, Zawieyski, and other ZNAK members are removing the monstrous prejudices against Socialism abroad and are contributing to the creation of a climate of co-existence."[1]

Just when the émigré community and the American Poles were trying to secure loans and supplies for the "Polish nation," when the Communist government in Warsaw, hungry for hard currency, imposed draconian duties on gifts sent to families in Poland and reduced to a minimum the number of permits for private people to travel abroad, let us look at a list of foreign visits by ZNAK deputies:

> Jerzy Zawieyski is going to the Inter-Parliamentary Union Conference in London and to the International Conference of Catholic Parliamentarians in Lourdes.—Stanisław Stomma is going to Italy, France, and the countries of Latin America.—Miron Kołakowski is leaving with a parliamentary delegation for Finland.—Paweł Kwoczek is going with a delegation to Belgium.—Wanda Pieniężna is traveling to the DDR [Deutsche Demokratische Republik—German Democratic Republic] and to a conference of women's organizations in Vienna.—Konstanty Łubieński is attending the Inter-Parliamentary Union Conference in London and a session of the Union's Council in Nice.—In the summer of 1960, a "Train of Peace and Friendship" leaves for the Soviet Union carrying, among others, a ten-man team of members of the ZNAK group.—Stefan Kisielewski, the most indefatigable traveler of them all, visits France and England in 1957; Romania in 1958; Denmark, France, Italy, Switzerland, and Germany in 1960; in 1961, he "acquaints himself with the achievements" of the Soviet Union; and, in 1962, he is once again in France and West Germany.

Irrespective of these trips abroad, receptions and meetings were organized in Poland for Catholic tours and groups from all over the world. And the Club of the Progressive Catholic Intelligentsia under the aegis of ZNAK played host. Church services were held, lectures given, and discussions organized on the subject, for instance, of "the decadence of the United States," "the decadence of Western Europe," "the improved understanding and effectiveness of co-existence," and, above all—in accordance with the latest demands of Soviet foreign policy—the threat to the world posed by German revanchism.

But let us return to the chronological presentation of events.

THE FIRST ROUND

In 1958, it seemed to Gomułka that the time was ripe for taking advantage of the compromise with the episcopate, and, like Bierut, he embarked on the next stage by beginning to persecute the Church (e.g., the notorious entry into the monastery of Jasna Góra). The subversion agency PAX immediately approved all the directives issued by the Communists. ZNAK did not do so openly but made frantic efforts behind the scenes to persuade . . . the episcopate to adopt "a spirit of concession and compromise." On August 27, 1958, Zawieyski gave *Le Monde* another interview, declaring that "there can be no question of any persecution of the Church in Poland." It seemed, nevertheless, that ZNAK had lost the first round of the contest with PAX. But then, suddenly, everything changed!

STOMMA'S ACHIEVEMENT

Pius XII, a great pope and a great enemy of Communism, died on October 9, 1958. Faced with new tactical opportunities, Moscow ordered a halt to religious persecution. Secretly at first (the relevant directive appeared only two weeks later, on November 7, 1958), ZNAK was granted a licence for the publication of religious books. At the same time, Stomma, armed with a diplomatic passport, traveled to Rome in the entourage of Cardinal Wyszyński.

The Polish Embassy at the Vatican had always been a thorn in the Communists' side. This came out very vividly at the time of the trial of Bishop Kaczmarek. The minimum demand of the Communists was the closure of this Embassy. It is no secret to anyone, except perhaps . . . the Polish émigré press, that the liquidation of the last Polish diplomatic mission to the Vatican was accomplished as a result of the intervention of Cardinal Wyszyński, with the active assistance of Stomma. And the fact that Free Lithuania's mission was simultaneously liquidated as well was a welcome additional present for Moscow.

A new era began for ZNAK, founded on the trust it had won within the Communist Party. Konstanty Łubieński became its vice-chairman, the same man who in Bierut's time had been PAX's most active agent abroad and who had been decorated with the Communist version of the Order of Polonia Restituta. However, it was Stomma and Kisielewski who now moved to the fore. ZNAK was granted new business concessions in the country, including, among others, the profitable "Libella" company, run on the principles of PAX's industrial enterprises, while simultaneously, for the very first time, PAX suffered cuts in its concessions. Articles written by ZNAK members were touted for publication in the émigré press.

THE SECOND ROUND

In this second round of the contest with PAX, there were no longer any doubts as to ZNAK's attitude, since its camouflage was progressively reduced: "We now live in times when the policy of the ruling party is in line with our nation's raison d'état.—The policies of People's Poland have come to stand on strong foundations by choosing to make an alliance consistent with national interests, an alliance consistent with our nation's prospect of development. This is the alliance with the Soviet Union.—Catholicism must overcome the ossification, the routine, the conservatism that attend it.—If it worries you, don't say "Queen . . . " [of Poland—in the litany]—The American world system is slowly disintegrating. . . . Our own strength can come only from a close alliance with the Soviet Union. . . . The most important problem of our national existence is to make our entire nation aware of this and to convince it that such a concept of our raison d'état is right."[2]

Obviously, these are only quotations. The columns of *Tygodnik Powszechny* and the *Znak* monthly contain concepts such as "Realpolitik," "raison d'état," "positivism," "Maritainism," and so on, clothed in rich eloquence, frequently expressed in terms of lofty erudition and philosophical deliberations of pharisaical subtlety, carefully measured out and distributed methodically. But they are all reducible to the fundamental conclusion: "We have stated on many occasions . . . that we regard as right and proper the overall direction of sociopolitical development outlined for Poland after World War Two. The changes that have been implemented in the People's Poland have at last given us a healthy structure."[3]

If we compare these statements with the statements of the Piasecki group in the years 1945–47, we shall see that they were nothing new. We have already read them in PAX publications, though perhaps the form was less hypocritical and less permeated with a spirit of concern for the good of Catholicism and apprehension lest "it be left behind": "Truth is always God's, it is always Christ's, Catholic, ours, even though it bears the emblem of a different world outlook. Open wide the doors and the windows. . . . Don't be afraid to admit that others may be right, to recognize, accept, and enjoy people . . . even if they don't believe in God."[4]

Well, well, these are truly beautiful words. For seventeen years, Communist schools have been trying to instill atheist convictions into children's heads, and, behold, Tadeusz Mazowiecki, a Catholic ZNAK deputy, ascends the Sejm's rostrum and declares: "Seventeen years of development in universal schooling have given Poland enormous social achievements. . . . This enormous development of education is not the result of coincidence but the consequence of the principles of the Socialist system in our country."

SUBVERSION AGENCY NO. 2

The law of the downward slope is the same for everyone. Whoever begins to slide continues to descend. And so we can now observe the ZNAK group descending from the "political stage," via the "pharisaical stage," to the stage of being an overtly subversive agency. This is shown both by its falling in with all the demands of the Communist bloc's foreign policy and by its subversive work among Catholic groups in the West, as well as in Polish émigré centers.

On October 8, 1961, *Tygodnik Powszechny* came out with a huge article entitled "Proposals for Émigrés." These proposals harmonized completely with the instructions of the former "Mikhailov Committee" in East Berlin, now called "the Committee for Contacts With Fellow-Countrymen Abroad," whose aim was subversive work among émigrés from the Soviet Union: "Support 'your country's' interests abroad." The only difference was the higher quality and the improved, and thus more effective, form of these new proposals.

In its issue of March 1962, the Paris *Kultura* published Stefan Kisielewski's "Letter to the Editor," containing in essence exactly the same suggestions as those made forty years previously during the provocative activity of the well-known GPU "Trust": "Present-day Communism is really Americanism for the poor. . . . Polish Communists are nothing other than representatives of the eastern orientation of the Polish (state)," they are conducting a "constructive policy with Russia . . . opening up great possibilities," because "Communism is becoming pragmatic and liberal." We can witness here a "universalist evolution of Communism. . . . All the wise people in the Party are striving to transform the system, to detotalitarianize it, to democratize and liberalize it . . . the organic work of renewal" is beginning. And the fundamental conclusion from all this was that the only thing needed was a halt to all anti-Soviet and anti-Communist activities!

Finally, in an article published in the June issue of *Kultura* (1962), Stefan Kisielewski, the very same representative of revolutionized pharisaism, brings the exiles a consoling piece of news: "For me, Prime Minister Khrushchev symbolizes the practical approach. The man is fortunately not a philosopher. . . . He simply has eyes and wants to put them to proper use. What a cheering thought that he is an empiricist!"

Nevertheless, although all this was somewhat skeptically received by émigrés, it did contain a note of direct appeal to the imagination of the Polrealists: "In our corner of the wretched peninsula we call Europe, Polish people still have no choice other than the choice between Russia and Germany."

It would be naive to think that, given the actual discipline to which a "Sejm Deputy" is subject in Poland, Stefan Kisielewski could permit himself to promote a thesis that was basically in conflict with the theses of the "Socialist camp," were such suggestions not in the tactical interests of the Communist Party, the master who had delegated him to go and speak abroad.

Chapter 11 The Second Great Provocation

THE MEANING OF WORDS

It is not true that one's choice of words is of no major significance. Sometimes it makes a tremendous difference. When it was said in 1927 that Metropolitan Sergii of Moscow had "made a deal with the Bolsheviks," it sounded awful; when it is now claimed that an "agreement between Church and State" has been worked out, it sounds dignified and respectable. In both cases, however, the gist of the matter is identical. A politician who said, "I have decided to become a fellow-traveler of international Communism" would no longer be regarded as a respectable politician; if, however, he stated, "I have decided to devote myself to organic groundwork in my country," he would be regarded as a realistic politician. The same applies to the replacement of words such as "collaboration" by "positivism," or "Sovietization" by "structural change," and so on. In all these cases, the basic condition that justifies compromise is the fact that the People's Poland is referred to not as a province of the Communist bloc but as the legitimate Polish state. And so even during the first steps on the downward slope, in 1945, émigrés refrained from using terms such as "Polish Communists," "Polish Bolsheviks," "collaborators," "Soviet Quislings," and so on and resorted instead to the nebulous term "régime." Used without an adjective, it suggested that one was referring to the "régime" governing in . . . the Polish state.

GOMUŁKAISM

These were the props on the stage on which Władysław Gomułka, an old Bolshevik agent, was to perform.

Gomułka was arrested by the Polish police in 1932 in Łódź and sentenced to seven years in prison. After only one year, on the basis of a Polish-Soviet agreement concerning the exchange of prisoners, he was turned over to the Soviet authorities. In Moscow, Gomułka attended special courses on diversionary tactics, and, three years later, via Denmark and Germany, he returned to Poland to expand the range of seditious activities. Arrested for a second time in 1936, he remained in jail until the outbreak of the 1939 war. On the basis of a tacit agreement between the Nazi and Soviet invaders, the Nazis allowed him to leave for the Soviet-occupied area of Poland. He stayed in Galicia and, following a party instruction of the time, refrained from any kind of anti-Nazi action but continued his propaganda work against "bourgeois Poland."

In 1943, he was ordered by Moscow to go to Warsaw and rebuild the Polish Communist Party under the name of the Polish Workers' Party (PPR). The later course of events is well known: friction between Gomułka and Bierut arose during the German occupation and concerned differences in their views on tactics. This animosity later became so acute that it led to the temporary imprisonment of Gomułka in the People's Poland. This was of course nothing new in internal party relations. Yet there were never any ideological differences between them. Gomułka, more intelligent than Bierut, favored a more flexible policy, which he thought would be more effective. At the same time, Bierut, schooled in the discipline of the INO [Inostrannyi Otdel NKVD—Foreign Section of the NKVD], preferred more rigid, fossilized tactics.

Gomułka's entire emotional life was devoted to his struggle to subordinate Poland to the Soviet Union, his battle against the independent Polish state. This explains his unquestionably enormous knowledge of the enemy's territory and psychology. He could rightly be called the "Polish Lenin." The Russian philosopher Nikolai Berdyayev, who died in 1948, was of the opinion that the basic motivation for Lenin's activities was his hatred of the political system of Russia and his desire to destroy it. Lenin subordinated all other goals to this one major end. Similarly, Gomułka also sacrificed everything to one goal: effective tactics for the achievement of his major aim.

A Brilliant Hoax

Gomułka worked in complete accordance with the instructions of Lenin. In a discussion with Rosa Luxemburg and Pyatakov in 1916, Lenin used the famous words about the "diverse roads to Socialism" and about the "monotonous greyness" of all those who would like to change everything in compliance with a single model. On March 19, 1919, at the Eighth Party Congress, Lenin stated: "One of the Polish Communists to whom I said: You will do it differently, replied: No, we will do the same as you, but we will do it better than you!"[1]

Lenin was extremely satisfied with this answer. What Gomułka did could not be essentially different from the things Bierut had done. In certain respects, Bierut's first stage was much more "liberal" than Gomułka's "Polish October." Let us recall that, during the first Bierut stage, *Głos Ludu* [The People's Voice] wrote: "We reject as fantastic, even as provocative, all the enemy's insinuations that the party is aiming to collectivize agriculture. . . . We support the idea of individual peasant farms unflinchingly. Our party has never proposed collectivization and does not have a plan for collectivization in its program. It is a fact, however, that the reactionaries have succeeded in hoodwinking some peasants."[2]

The "agreement with the Church" made at that time was so far-reaching that Bierut (an old agent of the INO NKVD) used to sit in the front row during solemn Church services on state occasions; he took an oath using the words "So help me God"; some of the cabinet members and the police participated in the Corpus Christi processions, and so on. Bierut was still adhering strictly to the instruction about the "different stages," so his subsequent tactics were rigid and characterized by the aforesaid "monotonous greyness." Gomułka avoided all Bierut's errors and decided to do "the same, but better." The essence of the Gomułka tactics was that, while he relied on the old NEP model, he adjusted it to the prevailing mood of the time. He not only had his finger on the pulse of the nation; he acted as if he had his ear close to the living body of Poland, and, in deciding on what steps to take to reach his immediate goal, he was guided by an infallible diagnosis. In this way, he brought about what amounted to a brilliant hoax, resulting in a degree of solidarity between the masses at large and the party that had probably not been achieved by any Communist leader before him. This enabled him to save Communism in Poland without bloodshed in 1956, the year of crisis, and to earn the just gratitude of international Communism. During the conference of eighty-one Communist parties in Moscow in 1960, the delegate of the Italian party, Luigi Longo, stated: "The bold analysis of the political causes of the Hungarian counterrevolution and the events in Poland made by the international Communist movement, and especially by the brave comrades who are presently in charge of the brotherly Polish Party—this analysis has proved correct."

The work of Gomułka can indeed be called great, since he has undertaken a tremendous task, the transformation of Poland from the traditional so-called bastion of Christianity directed against the East into an offensive redoubt of international Communism directed against the West. His Polish People's Republic has become a shop window of "good Communism" and, at the same time, a hoax that is capable of misleading Western opinion about the "evolution" of Communism more successfully than the old provocation of the GPU "Trust" was ever able to do.

Gomułka Was Appointed by Khrushchev

There is no Polish state in the guise of the Polish People's Republic. The Polish People's Republic is not a continuation of the history of Poland but a continuation of the history of the 1917 Bolshevik Revolution. The Polish People's Republic is not a continuation of the Polish state but a continuation and an integral part of the Communist bloc. Gomułka assumed power, as Marchlewski was meant to assume it earlier, and as Bierut did, not contrary to the intentions of the Communist Center in Moscow but by its appointment.

On February 16, 1956, the Twentieth Party Congress, which included the famous anti-Stalin speech of Khrushchev, began in Moscow. On March 12, Bierut unexpectedly died. His death coincided with the de-Stalinization projects of Khrushchev. On March 20, the Central Committee of the Polish party held a meeting in Warsaw that was attended by Khrushchev. Edward Ochab was appointed First Secretary of the Party. Ochab was a "Khrushchev man" body and soul. There followed the well-known events that shook the monolithic Communist Party. In June 1956, anti-Communist riots occurred in Poznań. Gomułka, who had already been freed from prison, thanks to Khrushchev's intervention, as an "anti-Bierut" and "anti-Stalin" man, proposed that the orders initially given by the Prime Minister, Józef Cyrankiewicz, to deal with the "Poznań affair" should be repealed and that the riots should be regarded not as anti-Communist but as "anti-Stalinist," which was completely in line with the views of Khrushchev. On July 18, 1956, at the Seventh Plenum of the Central Committee in Warsaw, Ochab delivered a fiery speech glorifying

Khrushchev, but both Ochab and the rest of his comrades belonged to the old Bierut group. Because of the ferment in the country, it became necessary to put a "new man" forward. This "new" man, with a distinctive "anti-Bierut" hallmark, was Władysław Gomułka. It would have been rather difficult to find at that moment a better man. He was then proposed as a candidate for the position of First Secretary of the Party. By whom? Undoubtedly as a result of an agreement between Ochab and Khrushchev. But, let us stress, for the time being he was proposed only as a *candidate*. The appointment depended on Khrushchev.

Ochab called the Eighth Plenum for October 19, 1956. It was convened to decide not only about the election of the new Party Secretary but also about the entire future tactical line, if not the fate of the Polish People's Republic. There was, therefore, nothing surprising in the fact that, in view of such important decisions, the Presidium of the Central Authority, represented by Khrushchev, Kaganovich, Mikoyan, and Molotov, arrived in Warsaw. The situation in Poland was full of tension. The survival of Communism in Poland was at stake. We know what happened at the Eighth Plenum from the report in *Nowe Drogi* [New Paths].[3]

Ochab met Khrushchev at the airport. *After talking to him*, he declared at the Plenum that the Politburo intended to nominate Gomułka as First Secretary. At the same time, he proposed to adjourn the meeting until 6 o'clock.

> COMRADE JAWORSKA: "Why is it necessary to adjourn the meeting until the evening?"
>
> COMRADE OCHAB: "Because of the need to talk to the delegation of the Presidium of the Communist Party of the Soviet Union."
>
> COMRADE JAWORSKA: "I move that the election [of the First Secretary of the Party] should take place before the adjournment."

The motion of Jaworska was supported only by Comrade Tatarkówna. It was defeated by sixty-one votes against the votes of the two women. All those present realized that the outcome of the "election" depended on Khrushchev's decision. Only one of them dared to ask a question.

> COMRADE GRANAS: "Could the Plenum be told the subject of the discussions between the Politburo and the delegation?"
>
> COMRADE OCHAB: "The problem of Polish-Soviet relations."

As far as a "sovereign party of a sovereign state" is concerned, both question and answer were quite characteristic in their brevity.

But Gomułka was not a member of the Politburo. Ochab, therefore, tabled an additional motion that Comrade Gomułka should also "go to the meeting": "Who is for the motion? . . . Good. Who is against it? No objections."

The staging of this scene is worthy of the early days of Leninist Bolshevism. As we can see, from beginning to end it was stage-managed by the Khrushchevist Ochab.

The meeting with the Soviet delegation, however, went on long after 6 o'clock. There was nothing strange about that. It was necessary to agree on tactics at this decisive moment. We do not know what happened. We know only the later tactics of Gomułka. He must have presented his plan to Khrushchev and gained his complete approval. Otherwise, the course of the Plenum meeting the following day, October 20, would certainly have been quite different. This is how it went.

In a secret vote to elect members of the Politburo, Gomułka received seventy-four votes, as many as Loga-Sowiński but fewer than Ochab, who received seventy-five votes. In the elections to the Secretariat of the Central Committee, Gomułka again got only seventy-four votes, as many as Jarosiński but fewer than Ochab and Gierek, who received seventy-five votes each. In both cases, then, Gomułka was not the first choice of the Plenum. Then Ochab got up and declared: "I propose that we hold open elections [for the First Secretary]. Who is against this? I don't hear any dissent. . . . The Political Bureau proposes that Comrade Władysław Gomułka—Wiesław—be elected. Those for, raise your hands. Who is against? No objection."

Gomułka was "elected," and Khrushchev and his companions, their minds set at ease, left for Moscow. These are the facts. Everything else, the strange myth about a supposed Gomułka-Khrushchev clash, and so on, which was spread all over the world, was, from start to finish, a Communist provocation to the world and the Polish nation, staged in accordance with the feeling prevalent at the time. The only truth among the many rumors concerns the deployment of the military in the country. This fact cannot be questioned. But these troops were not directed against Gomułka; rather, they were meant to ensure his safety. They were directed not against the "Polish road to Socialism" but against the nation, which wanted to get rid of all kinds of "Socialism." Actually, thanks to Gomułka's tactics, it was not necessary to employ these troops.

The "National Hero"

The version of events that, although not official, soon became obligatory, briefly ran as follows: "Gomułka acted with his hands tied. He wanted to save

Poland from Soviet tanks at any cost. He had, therefore, no other choice but officially to declare Polish-Soviet friendship. In return, in the bargaining with Khrushchev, he won his agreement to the idea of a 'Polish road to Socialism' and promised not to countenance any counterrevolution. Therefore, any kind of anti-Soviet or anti-Communist action would have destroyed Gomułka's patriotic work and provoked events like those in Hungary. Society, therefore, felt obliged to support Gomułka and not to listen to provocations. The 'Polish October,' the 'Polish road to Socialism,' was simply the first evolutionary stage and would be followed later by further liberalization and by more independence from 'Russia.'" Complete calm followed in Poland, and the version outlined above became obligatory not only in Poland and among émigré circles but in the entire free world. In some Polrealistic circles, Gomułka nearly became a national hero, all the more so when Moscow not only decided not to send in any tanks but even recalled Rokossowski.

We can see, therefore, that the "Polish October" (1956) became virtually a model for the subsequent manipulations of this nature in the years 1980–81. [Addendum of June 27, 1981.]

Po prostu [Plain-Speaking]

After assuming power, Gomułka came to the conclusion that, because of the anti-Communist feelings that had developed in the country, the most pressing need of the moment was to allow people to give vent to these feelings, and so he decided to establish a kind of lightning conductor that would divert them into a direction desired by the party. In practice, this meant "taking the wind out of the sails" of anti-Communist elements and transferring this energy to Communist elements. This could be done by directing people's criticism not against the Communist system as such but against the people who were in charge of the system before October 1956, that is, against the "Stalinists," the "party conservatives," the "Natolin" group, in a word, against all those people whom Gomułka wanted to remove—not against the principle but against the method of application of the principle, not against the doctrine but against the bureaucrats of the doctrine. As a result, the Communist youth paper *Po prostu* was allowed to indulge in seemingly unlimited criticism.

The assertion that *Po prostu* was a spontaneous development is obviously nonsense. In a Communist system, nobody is allowed to publish a paper independent of the party, since even the technical conditions do not exist to make such an independent publication possible. No other paper of this kind came out, although it is undoubtedly certain that dozens of them would have appeared immediately if there had been real freedom of the press. On the surface, *Po prostu* went beyond the framework of admissible criticism, but the enthusiasm it created at home and abroad brought no detriment to the Communists; on the contrary, it benefited them. *Po prostu* was outdoing the antiparty elements in its criticism, and by passionately demanding "improvements of the system" it drew attention away from the demands to "abolish the system" altogether. It is not an exaggeration to claim that Gomułka owes 90 percent of his popularity abroad to *Po prostu,* including the fact that the émigré community has almost completely decomposed and even, perhaps, the present American loans (received through the State Department, which is delighted by the confirmation of its thesis about the "evolution of Communism"). Once the preplanned closure of *Po prostu* had occurred and the students' demonstrations had been dispersed, one can say that the next stage was reached.

Further "Evolution"

This did not bring about any slackening in the relations between the Polish People's Republic and the Soviet Union; on the contrary, it created a closer union. A new factor entered in the form of the personal confidence and friendship between Khrushchev and Gomułka ("our dearest friend and comrade").

We may regard the "Joint Polish-Soviet Declaration" of July 22, 1959, as the culminating point of this development. For the first time, a term was used that, due to tactical considerations, had been avoided even in the official declarations of the Stalin-Bierut period, namely that Poland was moving toward full Communism. The actual words of the text solemnly stated: "The Polish nation and the nations of the Soviet Union have a great goal in common—the building of a Communist society."[4]

The next statement of *Pravda,* published on July 25, 1959, once more dispelled all illusions: "The nations of the Soviet Union and Poland spurred on by . . . are building, with confidence and inspiration, the radiant future of mankind—Communism."

During a reception at the Polish embassy in Moscow on the occasion of an industrial exhibition, six weeks later, on September 4, 1959, Khrushchev declared: "Though Comrade Gomułka is not present here, he is with us in his thoughts. We wish him good health, and the rest he will do by himself. . . . We are of the opinion that relations between the Soviet Union and Poland, and with the leaders of the Polish People's Republic, are better today than they have ever been before. These relations are more durable and deeper than at any time in the past. . . . We are proceeding along the same road shown to us by Marx, Engels, and Lenin, and we shall arrive at the longed-for goal—the building of a Communist society."⁵

The optimistic prognostications of the West have so far failed. American aid ("for the Polish nation") is being used to strengthen the economic potential of the Communist bloc. The greater part of the American grain is used to expand the production of meat, which is later exported, sometimes at dumping prices, to get hard currency. This hard currency is needed for sending Polish "instructors," that is, Communist agents, to Nigeria, Liberia, Senegal, Congo, Ghana, and so on. Students are enticed from these countries to Warsaw, and in this way the Communist infiltration of the world is accelerated. The Polish People's Republic supports the Lumumba group in the Congo, Fidel Castro in Cuba, and all Communists in all parts of the globe. The "Rapacki Plan" is actually the "Khrushchev Plan," as all the actions of the diplomats of the Polish People's Republic on the international scene are really the actions of the Communist bloc. The diplomats and the spies along with the tours of the Moscow ballet, the "Mazowsze" group from Warsaw or the "Śląsk" group, and so forth, are all involved in these efforts at infiltration.

The Techniques of Disinformation

The main difference between the original NEP and this third NEP à la Gomułka is that the old one was designed, in the main, to win over the country's nationalists at a time when the Western world on the whole was still maintaining some kind of self-restraint and skepticism. The latest version of NEP, however, is designed much more for the foreign market and is even supported by the Western world. In this way, the nationalists in the countries enslaved by Communism find themselves, metaphorically speaking, under fire from three sides. The whole construction has three elements: Communist tactics, pious national hopes, and the pious hopes of the West. This combination is supposed to replace the actual reality, but it is obviously far removed from this reality. In line with this new type of "political realism," there has also developed a new information system, which has replaced the system previously in force in the free world.

Let us ignore the apocryphal writings that are published in the West and presented as "underground literature" smuggled out of the Soviet bloc and supposedly proving the internal "evolution" of attitudes there. Let us rather deal with the usual methods of information. It has been generally accepted until now that the work of any politician or statesman should be assessed on the basis of two sources: (a) his words, and (b) his actions. Now a new source has been added: (c) his thoughts. And so, for instance, the words and actions of Gomułka are in complete harmony, and there can be no doubt about their meaning. It appears, however, that the political (dis-)informants are now able to penetrate Gomułka's thoughts and his secret intentions, which apparently contradict his words and actions. This clairvoyance is especially characteristic of the correspondents of Western newspapers who are accredited in Warsaw (that is, tolerated, or welcomed, or inspired there). That being so, many speeches of Gomułka and many of his political moves acquire a different, "real" meaning, because "Gomułka had to say this" or "Gomułka was forced by Khrushchev to do that." What he himself thinks about it is clearer to the journalists than to Gomułka himself. One does not have to add that, in most cases, what they "know" is what their Western headquarters and their Eastern sources of inspiration would like to hear from them.

The network of people disinforming Western opinion is very extensive. It includes the press of different and frequently divergent political orientations. Disinformation obviously acquires more importance as the authority of a paper increases. To mention just a few examples, let us begin with the well-known Warsaw correspondent of the Paris *Le Monde*, Philippe Ben, whose interpretations have been circulated all over Europe. The Hamburg paper *Die Welt* has such "objective" information from Warsaw that even the Communist Warsaw papers refer frequently to its "objectivity." And, of course, the Bavarian paper *Münchner Merkur*, close to the Christian Social Union, has nothing in common with the political views of the "Polish desk" of the American Radio Free Europe or with the Viennese paper *Die Presse*. But for a long time they had the same Warsaw correspondent, Dr. Ernst Halperin. On the surface, the individual pieces of information relayed by Halperin from Warsaw could not arouse any reservations. However, were one to summarize their "general line," it would sound more or less like this: "There are two good Poles, each in a very difficult situation, Gomułka and Cardinal Wyszyński. Together, and each in his own way, they are trying to save Poland from the evil Khrushchev." This general drift has influenced the above-mentioned German Catholic paper, the Polish service of Radio Free Europe, Austrian public opinion, American academic research, and government departments in Washington. These are, naturally, only minor, certainly not the most important, examples. They nevertheless characterize the situation in which one never knows the real source of the slanted information. In this example, is it Halperin himself, the State Department, or the Communist disinformation service?

In subsequent years this model will be used again, the only difference being that the former "duumvirate Gomułka—Wyszyński" has been transformed into a "triumvirate: the Communist Party—the Opposition (the leader of "Solidarność," Lech Wałęsa)—the Catholic Church (Pope John Paul II)." [Addendum of June 27, 1981.]

Chapter 12 Along the Road of Classic "Poputnichestvo" [Fellow-Traveling]

"THE POLISH OCTOBER"

Although Gomułka has now exposed his cards with regard to his tactics, not one of the politicians of the Polrealist camp who had previously given him moral credit has openly admitted his mistake, has admitted that he was duped. On the contrary, the Polrealistic version has it that "Gomułka is abandoning his position of October 1956." In this way, the previous assessment remains accurate, and the interpretation of the "Polish October" is still correct and positive. We called attention earlier to the fact that the acceptance of certain words frequently has a decisive influence on the substance of reasoning. In this case the acceptance of the term "Polish October," as indicative of a kind of neo-positivism, brings with it far-reaching consequences for a political stance. It means the acceptance of a new type of national interest.

What is concealed under the phrase "The Polish October"? We do not say "The Polish Kościuszko" or "The Polish 3rd of May," but simply Kościuszko and the 3rd of May. It would, however, be correct to use such terms as "the Polish Bonaparte," "the Polish Thermidor," and so on, to underline the analogy—the fact that this is a "Polish version" of a historic person or event from a different period and country. The name of the month October is used throughout the whole world to describe the victory of Bolshevism in Russia in 1917. It has no other meaning. Calling something which happened in Poland the "Polish October" can therefore mean only that we are talking about an analogy, a Polish version (of Bolshevism). One may regard it as objectively or subjectively better only because it is a Polish version, but it is impossible to deceive oneself about the implications of the word itself.

WHAT IS PROVOCATION?

The encyclopedia definition states: "An insidious inducement to action, which may bring about detrimental results to the provoked person and to third parties." Were we to limit ourselves to this definition only, we would discern elements characteristic of a typical provocation in the activities of the Communist "Association for the Development of Contacts with Fellow-Countrymen Abroad," whose task is to convince émigrés that they should cooperate in all matters which are in the common "interests of the country and the nation" while abroad. (1) These activities are "insidious," since the slogan "interests of the country and the nation" is a screen for the interests of international Communism. (2) They have "detrimental results to the provoked person," since if we understand the word "person" to involve the whole nation, it is directly encouraged to contribute to the consolidation of its own slavery. (3) They are also detrimental "to third parties," since collaboration with international Communism constitutes a potential danger for other nations.

The term "provocation" in its common usage, however, has broader implications. Even if we go back to such an anachronistic model of individual provocation as the Azef affair, we find within it elements of "double-dealing" which are so difficult to distinguish in any kind of provocation. Were the assassinations of Plehve and Grand Duke Sergei, organized by Azef, in the interests of the Socialist Revolutionary Party terrorists? Definitely. That is why, on the one hand, General Gerasimov, a departmental chief of the Okhrana, shouted at Azef in a moment of bad humour: "From this moment on, no more double-crossing!" On the other hand, however, after Azef was unmasked by Burtsev, the Central Committee of the Socialist Revolutionaries "simply let him slip away," as Lopatin expressed it. And it was rumoured that the Central Committee had known even earlier about his contacts with the police . . . A provocation, therefore, is always to some degree a double game. Communist provocations invariably contain more or less concealed elements of "poputnichestvo," that is, of an apparent compromise. This compromise allows for diverse interpretations, and consequently one does not know for sure where the apparent interests of the target of the provocation end and where the interests of the provocateur begin. The provocation operation is therefore arranged in such a way that the quantitative weight of the benefits to the planners are greater than the quantitative weight of the compromises on minor matters made to the target.

The "Gomułka" type of provocation as applied to Polish émigré circles is in complete accordance with the instructions of the already mentioned diversionary association. This latter does not demand that the émigrés return home or abandon their ideological positions: it demands only that they support the supposed interests of the "homeland" in the most important matters; that is, the interests of international Communism, which are concealed beneath this slogan.

POLISH EMIGRANTS ARE NOT "ANTI-COMMUNIST"

This is the line of Polrealism, which argues as follows: "We are not a 'White' émigré community, we are an anti-Soviet, or, rather, an anti-Russian community." To what extent this thesis has permeated the consciousness of Polish political leaders is evident from the fact that it is actually accepted by all the official Polish political groups. As a consequence, although such a general instruction has never been circulated, the organized Polish émigré community has kept itself aloof from alliances with any kind of ideological anti-Communist front, and only formally does it show solidarity with the representatives of those Eastern European countries which were the victims of direct Soviet aggression after World War Two.

This is a fundamental stance, and one should keep it in mind so as not to deceive oneself and others. The official position of Polrealism is not ideological; it is claimed that it is "realistic." Polrealism is not an a priori enemy of Communism; rather it is an ally of "everything which is Polish." One can call such an attitude sincerely patriotic, and even super-patriotic, if one takes into account the fact that it does not hesitate to collaborate with Communism to achieve its aim. One cannot deny, however, that as long as Poland is ruled by the Communists this gives the National Communists an excellent opportunity to make political moves on the patriotic chess-board which ensure both maximum success at home and a maximum degree of infiltration into the ranks of the émigré community.

THE "COMMON FRONT" WITH THE COMMUNISTS

This is both open and hidden. The various signs of penetration by Communist agents are associated with the hidden front. Since there is also overt cooperation, it can never be stated for sure whether a given political stance has been adopted at the instigation of an agent or out of sincere convictions which have developed under the influence of the prevailing atmosphere. Let us give an example which could be called a classic in this regard: a talented Catholic writer, Jan Bielatowicz, a man above all suspicion as far as Communist influences are concerned, can write: "Anti-Communism . . . cannot serve as a political program. . . . The émigré community has as its goal the welfare of the Polish nation . . . The Oder-Neisse border is a national question and therefore the nation fights for it as best it can without considering whether this suits the Communists or not."[1]

This is the statement of a (true) Catholic, that is, of a man subscribing to a certain world-view and thereby committed to a particular ideological stance. And despite this, he says that "anti-Communism" cannot be regarded as a program and he sanctions actions which "suit the Communists," if this is in the interests of the nation. Thus he puts what he sees as the national interest above the interests of humanity and above the interests of his Church.

At a meeting of the Italian section of the Polish Combatants Association (SPK) in Rome on November 18, 1961, the last ambassador of free Poland at the Vatican, Kazimierz Papée, stated: "There are common problems, fundamental questions, which are obligatory for all Poles and which demand a common effort. We know this is the case since we have worked for many years on these questions. . . . But I will tell you, to cheer you up for a moment, about an event from the fairly recent past. One of our diplomats presented to his partners in one of the Western countries our arguments for the speedy recognition of the Oder-Neisse border. He received the following response: 'This is interesting, since I heard the same arguments only yesterday from the ambassador of People's Poland.'"

As can be seen, Ambassador Papée did not even countenance the thought that what he calls "cheering news" might in reality be the sorry result of a Communist provocation which has led to the situation whereby, during a period of global tension (over Berlin) between the free world and the bloc enslaved by the Soviets, one of the last diplomats of independent Poland shares the opinions of the diplomats of the Communist régime and even boasts of this.

In a brief exposition it is impossible even to list all the available examples of this "common front" with the Communists. In addition to the Oder-Neisse problem, there is the myth current in the West that the Polish People's Republic is somehow better than the other members of the Communist bloc and therefore deserves more assistance and material aid. The Polrealist thesis, namely, that this involves assistance not to the "régime" but to the "Polish nation," is particularly inconsequential and openly demagogical. In the same way, dozens of other nations enslaved by Communism could also try to get assistance. This would mean that the free world would keep on sending large amounts of material goods to Prague and Budapest as well as to Kiev, Moscow and Peking. It would have to grant them loans and aid. It is difficult to see why only the Polish and the Yugoslav nations should be recognized as so much better than all the others. Obviously this is not so, and no sensible person believes in this aid for the "nation." It is clear that what is meant is overt assistance for the "régimes" because of their apparent "evolutionism," "revisionism" or "Titoism." Meanwhile reality shows the falsehood of such conjectures. The bloc of international Communism has been utilizing Gomułka's Poland as a Trojan horse particularly well suited to infiltrate the West and it even received loans from the West for this purpose. No doubt it has had a quiet laugh about this naiveté. Lenin's thesis about the "deaf, dumb and blind" has found, in this case, an unusually pertinent confirmation. One has to state, however, that the disinformation activities of the Polrealist program play no small role in this regard.

We find a kind of synthesis of this program in an article by the former cabinet member Zygmunt Berezowski, lately chairman of the Political Committee of the National-Democratic Party and chairman of the Commission for Foreign Affairs of the Provisional Council of National Unity in exile:

> Poland . . . is contributing to the evolution taking place in Europe independently of official governmental policies . . . and which is slowly shaping its future. The settlement and integration of the Western areas, which have made the Oder-Neisse line not an internal frontier within the Soviet empire, but a border of the nation . . . the continuous resistance to Communism which has made it impossible to transform the society into a "Soviet people," the entire position adopted by Poland—these all constitute a valuable contribution to the politics of a free and secure Europe. They are a new form of defense against the flood which threatens it.
>
> Therefore it is not diversionism or economic reprisals forcing the country into the general Communist mould which should become the objective of Western policy, but a careful and keen perception of the different roles and significance of the various countries behind the Iron Curtain.[2]

One could say that this declaration is as patriotic in its intent as it is false in its content. Not a single point reflects the objective truth: Poland is not contributing to any evolution . . . the Oder-Neisse has not ceased to be an internal boundary within the Soviet bloc . . . Poland's position is not a contribution to the politics of a free Europe . . . it is not a defense against the Communist flood . . . economic reprisals and diversionism do not amount to forcing everything into the Communist mould . . . it should not be an objective of Western policy to differentiate between the various nations under Communism. In other words, everything is exactly the opposite of what was stated in the article quoted above.

The so-called Rapacki Plan, as far as disengagement in Central Europe is concerned, was indirectly supported by the Paris *Kultura,* otherwise a magnificently edited journal on the highest intellectual level. Also in favor of the Rapacki Plan was the former American congressman Kowalski, a Democrat from Connecticut. A particularly intensive campaign in favor of the Rapacki Plan was staged, with the considerable support of the First Secretary in the Washington embassy of the Polish People's Republic, Kmiecik, amongst Americans of Polish descent. The Rapacki Plan, which stresses "German disarmament," was also supported by an absolute majority of Polrealist circles abroad.

It should be stated here that the tactics of utilizing the nationalist feelings of émigré circles for the purpose of achieving Communist diversionary goals have always been carried out in accordance with Leninist principles. They are in no way the invention of Gomułka. One year before he assumed power, in October 1955, on the initiative of the Party, a meeting took place in Warsaw at which "Polonia—the Society for Liaison with Poles Abroad" was established. Presiding over this meeting was Professor S. Kulczyński. In his address he underlined the fact that "in émigré circles there is a strong desire to develop and strengthen contacts with the Homeland." Members of this Society included such important people as the former Prime Minister of the London government, Hugon Hanke, the writers Arkady Fiedler and Edmund Osmańczyk, the poet Antoni Słonimski, the well-known PAX agent Dominik Horodyński, a member of the State Council, Professor Oskar Lange, and many others whose names, it was felt, would increase the prestige of the organization. The Warsaw radio station "Kraj" [Homeland], established to broadcast diversionary propaganda to émigrés, stated on November 1, 1955: "It would be unjust to assert that the masses of Poles living abroad are unpatriotic, that they do not feel affection for their country, that they do not suffer from homesickness."

And in a broadcast of July 29, 1958: "It seems to us that with every passing day the unity of the homeland and Poles abroad is increasing, despite the borders dividing us, that with every passing day there is less distrust and reserve. . . . We note with delight that the Cold War is coming to an end in their relations; together, both at home and abroad, we are working to solve the most pressing Polish problems."

There is no doubt that Gomułka singularly contributed to the "ending of the Cold War" and that he made all these actions more vigorous and effective. The performances of various companies whose main aim is propaganda have been promoted throughout the West. Such groups as "Mazowsze" and "Śląsk" are frequently received with tears of emotion, despite their blatant political message, identical to that of the song and dance troupes from Moscow and other Communist countries. Art exhibitions from Warsaw, films, theatres and academics are all now supported and promoted.

As a special example of this political attitude we may point to a resolution accepted at the annual meeting of the émigré Journalists' Association on January 17, 1959: "The congress of the Journalists' Association sends greetings to their colleagues at home who work in difficult conditions, being restricted in their opportunities to express personal views and being subject to Communist Party control and official censorship."

Even a superficial analysis of this resolution is bound to reveal its unusual degree of falsehood. It is phrased as if the journalists sending the greetings were of the opinion that the journalists in Poland were working on Polish papers which were merely "under Communist control and censorship." But this congress of the best informed people, that is, journalists, knows perfectly well that there is no censorship of the press in Communist countries, since all the newspapers are simply owned by the Party-Government; that there likewise exists no "control" in the common meaning of the word, since this is simply replaced by Party instructions; that the journalists work on these papers of their own free will and what they write is just Communist propaganda which contributes indirectly to the deepening of Poland's slavery. Let us return to the comparative method: during the German occupation a Polish writer, Emil Skiwski, published a monthly, *Przełom* [The Breakthrough], which proposed the conclusion of an agreement with Germany to fight together against the Bolsheviks. Already then he was declared a traitor to the nation, although he never called the arrival of German troops "liberation" or the country under German occupation "free Poland." After the war he was annihilated as a writer, destroyed and crushed as a person, once and for all, and nobody even knows whether he is still alive. On the other hand, for instance, Gustaw Morcinek, a writer who completely debased himself, a deputy of the Communist parliament who proposed changing the name of Katowice to "Stalinogród," received highly favorable reviews in the émigré literary press. This is only one of literally innumerable examples. The average journalist working today for the Communist press in Poland outdoes Skiwski many times over in "collaboration" with the invader. But, as we see, he is considered worthy of "greetings" from his "émigré colleagues."

This comparison would be too drastic if it were examined separately from the reality, and the reality now is not as it was then. The reality shows us that Polrealism has ceased to consider the present political situation in Poland, both de facto and de jure, as an occupation, whether Communist or Soviet.

"ONE LITERATURE"

A peculiar position in the fellow-traveling phenomenon of Polrealism is occupied by the field of literature. This is an area especially important for the Communists. The most suitable area for Communist penetration is not so much politics or economics as human psychology or emotions. Therefore the Communists are very anxious to create the impression that literature and science should preserve as "Polish" a façade as possible. We know that wherever the Communists seize power, they first attempt to communize literature and science. This is a well-known fact. Under the influence of Polrealism, however, émigré circles have accepted the principle that "Communist" refers only to the content of printed materials which at one stage were called Communist propaganda, that is, materials which serve the purpose of direct agitation. All other materials are regarded as Polish literature, although there are no private publishing houses in People's Poland and books are produced only by agencies of the Party-Government. The drawing of analogies with Polish literature under Russian rule is a device which distorts reality. Under Russian rule a national Polish literature was still in existence; it was printed by Polish publishers and only censored by the authorities. Today Polish literature is published by the same authorities which regulate, inspire and control it. There is no space here to list all the quotations which would leave no shadow of doubt about the matter. Here is Gomułka's statement at the Third Congress of the United Polish Workers' Party in March 1959:

> The main basis of our cultural policy is . . . the grounding of all creative activities on the world view and methodology of Marxism-Leninism. . . . We support . . . the sort of literature which is realistic in form and socialist in its ideological expression. The leading role of the Party consists in the fact that socialist ideals and a scientific

world view should inspire the content of literary creativity. . . . We refuse today and will continue to refuse to publish works which are a political weapon for the propaganda of anti-Socialist forces. . . . We want an art which, in its artistic form, will illustrate the process of forming new, socialist social relations and changes in human psychology. . . . The major task of the Party on the cultural front at the present time is to fight for the final elimination of the influence of anti-Socialist creative tendencies, since that is the major obstacle in the development of Polish socialist culture.

This should suffice. The same is being repeated today. [Addendum of June 27, 1981.] Obviously, within the wide range of the stated program the occasional valuable book will be printed, a book not related to the program and with the characteristics of a work of normal Polish literature. This is, to a certain extent, part of the strategy of Communist infiltration. This literature is a Communist literature, however, not just in the case of particular books, but as a whole. Similarly, there is no Russian literature in the Soviet Union, only Soviet literature which has been accepted and evaluated as such in the West for decades. Leon Kruczkowski, a writer and member of the Central Committee of the Party, speaking at the same Third Congress, was right when he said, on behalf of literature in Poland, that: "The existing socialist literature, as a whole, as a specific tendency in creative dynamics, is becoming more and more alien to bourgeois creativity."

Yet, in spite of these obvious facts, in the field of literature there has been a complete reconciliation of views between Polrealism and Communism concerning the "unity of Polish literature" at home and abroad. At the same time, through literature, the way has been opened up for the most effective Communist penetration of the West. After Gomułka's "October," many émigré writers started to write in such a way as would make it possible for them to be published at home, and this is what duly happened. In a program broadcast on February 20, 1958, the Communist radio station "Kraj," speaking about émigré literature, used the following very flattering words: "The art which has been created by émigré artists is only to a minor extent an art . . . engaged against the ideological situation and system existing in Poland. These novels and poems are published by us; they are widely read; they are by no means hostile! What then will finally determine the position of the émigré artist, of the émigré writer? His art is not an art different from that created in Poland. With the exception of the books of Józef Mackiewicz, no stance fundamentally hostile to ours has been expressed in any other works."

Michał Rusinek, delegated by Warsaw to attend the Thirtieth Congress of PEN-Clubs in Frankfurt, characterized the relationship between émigré writers and writers in Communist Poland in this way: "In the course of these meetings we have renewed old friendships and created new ones. Among the conversations which interested us the most were those with émigré writers, with Kazimierz Wierzyński, Aleksander Janta-Połczyński, Paweł Mayewski.... After all, it is only in the last few years that Congress participants have seen Poles 'from both sides' sitting at the same table, treating each other with respect. This is confirmed by the Congress minutes, which up to now have not noted a single case of an attack mounted by a writer from Poland against a Polish émigré writer, or the other way around."[3]

The atmosphere created by Polrealist literary circles in exile can be clearly seen in a report by Stefania Niekraszowa from London, published in *Ostatnie Wiadomości* [The Latest News]: "Through the efforts of the Association of Writers and Journalists and the Students' Association ... outstanding guests from home read their literary works and essays nearly every Thursday in the General Sikorski Institute in London.... The rooms of the General Sikorski Institute cannot accommodate the masses of people; the corridors and stairways are full of people longing for intellectual contacts with home."[4]

Unanimous rage, both on the part of the Communists in Warsaw and the Polrealists abroad, is the response to any attempt to call literature in the Polish People's Republic by its real name. For instance, the "Kraj" radio station stated on July 10, 1958: "The London *Wiadomości* carried out a survey on the subject of émigré writers and literature in Poland. Nearly all those asked spoke of the organic unity of Polish literature and opposed the division into an émigré and a home literature. Nearly all, since obviously Józef Mackiewicz stated that we have not a Polish, but a Communist, literature, but, coming from a former collaborator with Nazi propaganda, this is quite understandable."

Three weeks later (July 29, 1958): "We are not concerned with the case of Józef Mackiewicz personally. The statement of Józef Mackiewicz is of interest to us as a problem, as a wider question than the sum of the political views of this otherwise brilliant writer. We have here the case of a possible point of view, of a certain principle in evaluating events, which ... may be regarded as absurd, harmful and anti-intellectual."

Reacting to a similar statement in a survey conducted by the émigré newspaper *Dziennik Polski,* its literary editor, who was also the Chairman of the Association of Polish Writers in Exile, said: "Among the replies published today, the readers will also find the answer of Józef Mackiewicz. Mr Mackiewicz seems to regard all literary activities in our homeland as Communist literature. This notion is so obviously erroneous and—I do not hesitate to use here a harsh word—so *ludicrous* that in my opinion it is not necessary to start a polemic against it."[5]

TO "OVERTHROW" OR TO "REFORM"?

In the political attitudes of Polrealism those émigré centers which have generated Polish groupings working for the Western powers frequently play a substantial role. We refer here to bodies apparently working for the cause of Polish politics, but in reality only servicing the foreign policy of another country, especially America. We find there, for instance, the powerful apparatus of the Free Europe Committee and its radio stations. The changes it undergoes depend on the changes in American foreign policy. Fundamentally, therefore, these Polish bodies cannot be regarded as representing an independent Polish viewpoint and should be seen as reflecting the American stance or the stance of the other Western powers. They do actually have some kind of influence in Poland, through the provision of information and expertise, especially with regard to the "evaluation" of events and of the situation there.

As for the activities of the Western radio stations broadcasting in the languages of the Communist bloc, including Polish, they certainly do more good than harm. One could even risk saying that they are of enormous benefit in that they broadcast news items which are notoriously covered up or distorted by the Communist media. It is even rather difficult to imagine what would happen if people under Communism were deprived of that limited amount of objective news which they now receive from the West. Even the broadcasting of mildly oppositionist views during periods of hopeless coexistence may mean a ray of hope for the people on the other side. Therefore these broadcasts are consistently jammed by a Communist system which does not allow any kind of opposition.

(In the Communist bloc 100 jamming stations were in existence in 1948; one year later, 150. There were 1,000 in 1950. Between 1961 and 1962 there were 2,500 jamming stations, erected at a cost of about $250 million and with an annual budget of about $100,000.)

The situation is quite different as far as political tendencies are concerned. The policies of the Western powers, and especially of America, as we know, put their money on "Titoism," "Gomułkaism," "revisionism," "evolutionism," etc. To support this optimistic line, a constant flow of information, or rather disinformation, is necessary, since otherwise the policy of coexistence could not be maintained. In this respect the Polish bodies previously mentioned constitute an important source in support of the prevalent wishful thinking. This support comes about not only because these groups work hand-in-glove with their bread-and-power-givers, but also because they have accepted the Polrealist general line which, to a large degree, and as far as Communist Poland is concerned almost completely, corresponds to the premises of peaceful coexistence.

A Communist emissary abroad once argued: "One cannot simultaneously try to overthrow and reform the same thing." A very astute comment. Either, or. Either one is an enemy of the Communist régime, or a loyal oppositionist. It seems that Polrealism has quite definitively chosen the second: not to overthrow Communism in Poland, but to reform it by "evolutionary methods."

The overall picture is of a compromise which corresponds in all major respects to the fellow-traveling of these nationalists who, forty years ago, were deluded by the tactics of the first example of National Communism in its Leninist NEP version. The "basis" upon which Lenin was able to construct his "superstructure" of National Communism was also, in essence, very similar. Let us recall the conclusion he drew from this historical experience, that nationalism, if faced with a choice between an alliance with a neighboring nationalism against Bolshevism, and an alliance with Bolshevism against a neighboring nationalism, would, as a rule, select the latter. In reference to contemporary Polrealism, the old antagonism of the Byelorussian and Ukrainian nationalists against Poland has been replaced by Polish antagonism against Germany. The Communist Provocation, therefore, tries to feed this antagonism and to keep it in an active emotional state, as similar as possible to the complex which developed during the bloodthirsty Nazi occupation.

Chapter 13 The German Complex

THE FETISH OF A SUCCESSFUL PROVOCATION

Turning now to the "German complex," I shall not treat it with the "caution" and "tact" with which so-called painful and delicate questions are commonly treated. This is the line adopted by some Poles who recognize, on the one hand, the necessity of getting out of the anti-German impasse but who at the same time insure themselves by selecting a special stylistic form so as not to vex public opinion and not to become the target of more or less brutal invective and abuse. Perhaps, from their point of view, they are justified in trying in a real and practical way to win readers over to their political standpoint. I personally never try to win anyone over, nor do I wish to impose my views on anybody. I would like only to try to unveil ever so slightly certain truths that are not talked about, to show the other side of the coin, and, by so doing, to stimulate thought. Recourse to stylistic flourishes would be contrary to my own conviction and could undermine the sincerity of my writing. I do not feel bound to spare international Communism, nor am I bound by any kind of obligations to its interests. I am convinced, however, that the German complex *in its present form* is the result of Communist provocation. It is not a Polish problem or a Polish-German problem; it is an integral factor in the global Communist conspiracy.

The situation seems clear to us. Communism has not changed from the days of Lenin and Trotsky as regards its goal of taking over the entire world. It confirms this at every step in both word and deed. In qualitative terms, Europe is still the most important part of the free world. In Europe, Germany occupies a key territorial position, just as it did in 1920. The capture of Germany is the number one goal of Communist planning. In 1920, the achievement of this goal was prevented by the existence of the Polish bulwark. If this bulwark still existed today and if it constituted, in the present balance of power, as strong a bastion as then, the thrust of international Communist aggression would undoubtedly be directed not against Germany but against Poland. But this bulwark has been breached. The front of the Communist flood has moved west. The last bulwark in Europe today is West Germany, supported by the forces of the free world. Therefore, the attack is consistently concentrated on this bulwark, with the aim of breaking through or undermining it. The range of operations mounted to achieve this goal is wide. On the one hand, there are attempts at a new "Rapallo"; on the other, there are even tactical alliances with otherwise anti-Soviet elements, provided they are anti-German. What is at stake is the undermining of the existing line of defense of the free world.

Polrealism has allowed itself to be indirectly ensnared in this global Communist conspiracy. This takes the form of an emotional patriotic engagement that creates a state of obsession and practically excludes any discussion *ad rem*. The political pretext is the alleged German threat to the Western border of the Polish People's Republic on the Oder and the Neisse.

THE ODER AND THE NEISSE: THE MAIN GOAL

Either one starts from the position that Poland has lost its independence to the Communist bloc, or one does not start from this position. In the first case, it means that if one believes that Poland has lost its national sovereignty, one cannot recognize as the borders of a sovereign state those new borders that have been brought about by this loss. If Poland has lost its independence, then it cannot have "recovered" any territories. It is impossible to recover a part while losing everything; this would be a formula inconsistent with logic. The so-called Oder-Neisse line is simply an internal line of demarcation between the Polish People's Republic and the German Democratic Republic, that is, between two parts of a single, uniform Communist bloc that have been given these names at whim. One may demand such a border for the future, but one cannot recognize it as a currently existing border. It is quite absurd to make this line, arbitrarily drawn by Stalin, an integral part not only of one's entire policy but even of the entire moral stance of the nation.

There are quite a few wise and enlightened Poles who have perceived the fatal results of the paralysis caused by elevating the Oder-Neisse line to the pedestal of a national fetish previously unknown in Polish history, a paralysis affecting not only practical policies but Polish political thought in its entirety. Sometimes one hears—obviously only in private conversations—that this was a "stroke of genius on the part of Stalin," by which a permanent rift between Germany and Poland was created. Presumably, he also had in mind a major objective, which has been achieved today, that is, the recognition of the Polish People's Republic by Poles as the "Polish state." Only by recognizing the Polish "state" can one arrive at a recognition of the Oder-Neisse line as a state boundary; likewise, the recognition of the Oder-Neisse line as a state boundary encourages Polrealism to recognize the Communist occupation as the Polish state.

A Border Strip That Is More Important Than Independence

An event hitherto unknown in Polish history has occurred. At a time when the state, the whole nation, has found itself under what is undoubtedly foreign domination, no matter how we interpret it, liberation from this foreign domination is not the supreme national concern; rather, it is the question of one section of the frontier assuming primary importance. "If we had the choice of changing the system at the price of losing the areas on the Oder and Neisse, we should retain the Recovered Territories, even if this meant the prolongation of Communist rule," writes the Paris journal *Kultura*.[1] The doyen of émigré journalists and writers, Zygmunt Nowakowski, in a nice short story entitled "Anusia's Health,"[2] describes a patriotic Polish child who, in an imaginary situation, asks the President of the United States not to liberate Poland but to recognize the Oder-Neisse border. A great number of public statements and memoranda in émigré circles indicate clearly that the "question of recognizing the Oder-Neisse line" is of more importance than the question of Polish liberation and independence. The resolution of the Provisional Council of National Unity in London passed on April 14, 1962, ranks the "main Polish desiderata in the light of the international situation" as follows: "The Council of National Unity demands: First, the formal recognition by the West of the border on the Oder and Neisse as the final border, without postponing its decision in this matter. Second, the maintenance of the prohibition against arming Germany with any kind of atomic weapons. Third, the right of self-determination for Poland and other nations of East-Central Europe."[3]

The Congress of Americans of Polish Descent, the most powerful Polish organization in America, presented to President Kennedy and Secretary of State Rusk a memorandum: "The first part of the memorandum points to the necessity of maintaining the economic, technical, and cultural assistance given to the Polish nation. The second points to the danger of German revanchism for European peace and security."[4]

This happened at just the time when the dark clouds of Khrushchev's diplomatic offensive on Berlin were hovering over Europe. It is, therefore, not in the least surprising that the memorandum of the Congress, though it also contained some anti-Soviet references, was accepted and cited with great enthusiasm by the Communist press in Warsaw. Similar examples could be cited ad infinitum.

The Significance of Double Standards

The choice of the Oder-Neisse as the focus of political attention is quite striking. Let us remember that we are dealing not with other borders of the Polish People's Republic or with its borders in general but with only one section of the border and with precisely that section that is less in danger than any other. Any sensible person is aware of the fact that, given the nature of power within the Communist camp, there can be no guarantee against the arbitrary change of any border within the bloc and that these boundaries may become flexible at any moment that is deemed proper and appropriate by the Moscow center. But no one ever speaks about this permanent danger to the other borders of the Polish People's Republic. Only a few people, for instance, know or remember that on February 15, 1951, an "agreement was signed" on the basis of which an "exchange of territories" with the Ukrainian Soviet Socialist Republic took place. In this agreement, the Polish People's Republic gave up 480 square kilometers on the Upper Bug River with the cities of Bełz, Uchnów, and Waręż, thus losing a section of the railway line from Rawa Ruska to Kowel and the coalfields in this area. In return, it received the area of Ustrzyki Dolne. The population of these areas, against its will and without being asked, was simply expelled and transferred. This kind of manipulation may be carried out by the Communists at any moment, in any territory. Some years ago, there was talk about an intended "adjustment of the border" in the area of the Białowieża Forest between the Polish People's Republic and the Byelorussian Soviet Socialist Republic, to the advantage of the latter. There was not the slightest protest about this plan.

The significance of these double standards becomes especially marked if we recall that the center of gravity has been transferred to an area that did not belong to the Polish state before the war. At the same time, the question of the borders and territories that did belong to independent Poland and that were violated by the Soviet Union has simply been removed from the political agenda. It is true that the official émigré authorities have never renounced the Eastern Territories, but if one simply compares the approach to these two problems, the lack of consistency shown by the émigrés and the consistency of the Communist provocation are revealed. This is how things are: occasionally, during patriotic celebrations, demands for a return to the eastern borders of 1939 are expressed by the émigré community. The form and tone of this demand, however, as compared with the stress placed on the Oder-Neisse question, leave no doubt that this is a rather Platonic declaration that is not taken too seriously by the participants in the celebrations. In the memoranda presented to the Western powers, the "recovery" of the Eastern Lands is no longer even mentioned. Let us continue the comparison: despite the fact that the émigrés have not recognized the "agreements" between the Polish People's Republic and the Soviet Union concerning the renunciation of the Eastern Territories, the most serious Polrealist publications have quite openly relinquished these lands. The Paris *Kultura,* for example, publicly justifies the cession of these areas by Poland once and for all. This does not provoke the slightest outrage; it does not result in any protest resolutions or the boycotting of *Kultura* by Polish public opinion. On the contrary, the magazine still enjoys the greatest esteem, and the most famous Polish writers are published there. Some years ago, when somebody wrote an open letter attacking the attitude of *Kultura* to this question as lèse-majesté, the letter was treated as a joke. This is all happening at a time when the motto of the day is the solemn slogan that "there is not a single Pole" who is not in favor of the Oder and Neisse border and the "Recovered Territories." Moreover, this same *Kultura* that jokes about the ridiculous die-hards who demand the return of the Eastern Lands of the Republic also writes: "Given the present situation, if a Pole, even in the name of the most sublime concept of anti-Communism, agreed to the detachment of the Western Lands from Poland, then such a person, from the Polish perspective, would be acting as an agent to the detriment of his own nation."

Without going into the merits of the case or trying to judge whether it is right or wrong to renounce the Eastern Lands or to revise the 1921 Riga Treaty borders, one cannot deny that, as an important and contentious matter, it is rightly discussed and that it is also reasonable that there are differences of opinion concerning the border that was in existence thirty years ago. And yet we find, in the same conditions and within the same society, that it is not permitted even to mention the possibility of a discussion concerning a frontier that ceased to exist six hundred years ago! And every Pole who dared to dispute it in any way would be called a traitor.

The question then arises, who really decides about this application of double standards that allows no appeal, this application of standards that are so shockingly contradictory? And in the name of what law is this done, a law that can be found not in any of the legislation of the Polish Republic but only in the laws of the Communist People's Poland? But let us not amuse ourselves by asking questions without answers. It is the influence coming from the other side that is decisive.

Why the Silence About Königsberg?

A part of Eastern Prussia also belongs to the so-called Recovered Territories that have been incorporated into the Polish People's Republic. One look at the map would have sufficed to show that if the Polish-German border of 1939 was to be adjusted in Poland's favor, then the most rational solution would have been to round off the frontier by incorporating Eastern Prussia, especially since Eastern Prussia up to the year 1657 (not six hundred years ago, like the Western Territories) was a feudal area that owed its allegiance to the Polish Crown. If we were to be logical, Eastern Prussia should be the most important factor as far as the "Recovered Territories" are concerned and should, therefore, present the greatest interest to the Polrealists. Yet, as we well know, only the southern part of Eastern Prussia was incorporated into the Polish People's Republic, while the more important northern part, including the capital, Königsberg, a port of tremendous significance, and a stretch of coast, and so on, were incorporated into the Soviet Union as the "Kaliningrad region" (in a way that breaks up the unity of these areas in a ridiculous fashion). And now we are faced with a strange paradox: Polrealism makes no claims to Königsberg, that part of the "Western Territories" that would seem to be the most essential. At any rate, it does not present any memoranda to the Western powers on this matter, and we might also mention that a unanimous silence prevails everywhere concerning the "Kaliningrad region."

We can see, therefore, that in a case like this, which would be incompatible with the interests of the Soviet Union, the slogan that states "There is no Pole, who . . . " and so forth is no longer valid. On the contrary, there are very few Poles who would demand the "recovery" of Königsberg. As a result, we have the following formula: one must accept willy-nilly the status quo of those territories that Communism has captured by force and that it now holds, whereas the claims of a disarmed Germany present a "threat to Poland and to Europe."

IS "GERMAN REVANCHISM" A REAL DANGER?

Communist propaganda does everything possible to create the impression that German revanchism is a threat. This propaganda has nothing in common with Polish interests, whether we deny the sovereign existence of Poland in the form of the Polish People's Republic or whether—as the Polrealists wish—we recognize the Polish People's Republic as the "Polish state" with its own external state boundaries. Even if we accepted this latter position, we would still have to come to the conclusion, after an objective assessment of the situation, that the Polish People's Republic is not threatened by Germany at the moment and that it is impossible to imagine such a threat emerging.

A look back at history tells us that there has probably not been a single moment in history when nobody had a claim to a crown, a succession, a territory, or the property of another state. There have always been "revanchists" around. The existence of "revanchist" tendencies does not in itself constitute a threat. Such a threat does not arise even if formal support is given to the revanchists by a neighboring state with a government that does not recognize the existing status quo. Thus, for instance, in 1938, under the pressure of a Polish ultimatum, diplomatic contacts between Poland and the Lithuanian Republic were established. Before long, they began to engender friendly relations. This was generally regarded as a great success of the Polish government, even though the treaty between the two states contained Lithuania's solemn declaration that it did not renounce its claims to Wilno. In this way the Lithuanian government was in reality supporting the "revanchism" of the whole Lithuanian nation. The argument that a small Lithuania was too weak to threaten a more powerful Poland was certainly correct. But the contemporary German Federal Republic is incomparably weaker than the Communist bloc and incomparably weaker than Lithuania was vis-à-vis Poland at that time.

A real threat occurs only when a state is determined to use force to bring about a "revision" ("revanche") and has this force at its disposal. The German

Federal Republic has neither the will nor the means to revise its frontiers. The policies of the German Federal Republic with regard to its eastern neighbors are de facto under the supervision of the United States, and the small German army is under NATO control. There is no possibility of a military, or even a political, move by Germany without the agreement of the Western powers. The Germans at the present time are not even able to plan for the defense of West Berlin, so how, in this situation, could they plan an act of aggression against the Oder-Neisse border? Given the present balance of power, the assertion that the German army, with its three hundred thousand men, even if it were completely controlled by the "revanchists," could be a threat to the twenty-million-strong army of the Communist bloc is absurd. In the existing situation, when the world is facing the threat of a Communist invasion, to assert that "German revanchism threatens Europe" is grotesquely sinister. In the existing circumstances, when the whole of Poland is in Communist captivity and when nobody has even drawn up any plans to liberate it, the appeals of those Poles who call on the free world to defend them against "German revanchism" seem grotesquely incongruous.

As we know, the Communists, in their actions both at home and abroad, do not hesitate to use grotesque slogans. It is enough to recall that, in December 1939, they claimed that they were "threatened by Finland" (the population of which is barely as large as the population of Moscow) and that Finland had attacked the Soviet Union, not the other way around. No one who knows anything about Communist methods can be surprised that at the very time when their plans include the takeover of Germany, they are claiming that it is not they who are threatening Germany but Germany that is threatening the Soviet Union and the various "People's Republics." One has to wonder, however, about those Poles who, knowing all about Soviet methods, still give them credit and assistance, instead of exposing them before the whole world.

It is said that Germany may in the future attack Poland, since it has done so before. This is quite possible. In the future, anything may happen or not happen, repeat itself or not repeat itself. In the future, any political treaty or any formal recognition of a border may likewise be kept, or it may be torn into pieces. The Soviet Union, for instance, has kept merely 5 percent and violated 95 percent of all the treaties signed during its existence. It is difficult to talk about a realistic policy when one directs one's own attention and the attention of others against someone who, at an undetermined time in future, may become or may not become an aggressor, instead of directing it against someone who is an aggressor today and who most certainly will remain so tomorrow. That the Communists are especially interested in diverting attention from this is naturally understandable.

THE OFFICIAL THESIS OF POLREALISM

In an abbreviated form, it is roughly as follows: "The matter of our western frontier is also important from a psychological point of view. The fact that the Soviet Union is the only one of the great powers that recognizes the present Oder-Neisse border binds the Poles against their will to the Soviet camp. A recognition of this border by the Western powers and the German Federal Republic will loosen this Polish tie with the Communist bloc. In their stubbornness the Germans are pushing us into the arms of the Soviets and are preventing a loosening of our bonds." Since we do not know what Polrealism imagines such a "loosening" would look like in practice, let us assume that it would mean an increase of pro-Western feelings in Poland and, one can also imagine, an automatic increase in anti-Soviet feelings.

This seemingly logical formulation contains, however, a serious element of illogicality in that it assumes that an essentially anti-Soviet goal can be achieved by cooperating with the Communists. It is widely known that the Polish Communists, as well as the whole Soviet bloc, all Communists, pro-Communists, fellow-travelers, and, finally, the "coexistence-mongers" of the whole world unanimously support the Oder-Neisse line and are striving for the recognition of this border by the Western powers and the German Federal Republic. On the other hand, we also know that it cannot be in the interests of the Communists either to loosen the ties of Poland with the Communist bloc or to increase pro-Western feelings in Poland (and, thereby, to increase anti-Soviet feelings). To remove this obvious and essential contradiction, one would have to assume that (a) it is not true that the Communists are trying to obtain recognition of this border, or (b) this is what they are striving for, but they are not sincere, or (c) if they are sincerely striving for this, they are so stupid that they are not aware that they are acting to their own detriment.

Not one of these assumptions can be supported. Points (a) and (b) are refuted by the frequent statements of Polrealist politicians that "in the common cause of the Western borders of Poland, we are at one with the Communists." To try to substantiate point (c) would clearly lower the level of the discussion. There can, therefore, be only one conclusion: namely that the Communists are not afraid that the recognition of the Oder-Neisse line by the Western powers and in particular by the German Federal Republic will be to their disadvantage and that they are not afraid that there will be any loosening of ties between the Polish People's Republic and the Communist bloc. They are clearly right not to be afraid. What is important for the Communists at the present time is not recognition or lack of recognition in itself but, as we mentioned before, diverting the attention of public opinion from the Communist threat and directing this attention to the apparent "threat of German revanchism."

The influence of Polish émigré activities on international (today, interbloc) decisions is obviously minimal. The cooperation of the Polrealists with Communist tactics and propaganda in the most important area of current politics, on the other hand, contributes emotionally to closer ties between Poland and the Communist bloc. This far outweighs any contribution to the loosening of these ties that might ever arise from the recognition by the Western powers of the Oder-Neisse border.

AN ATTEMPT TO OUTBID OR A PROVOCATION?

A particular error in the political calculations of Polrealism is the so-called concern for public opinion at home. For this purpose, Polrealism regards it as advisable to outdo the "régime" in its anti-German stance. This kind of bidding against the Communists as regards the radicalism of their slogans is nothing new. As a rule, it has been fatal. Its victims have been the competing Socialist parties, such as the Mensheviks and the Socialist Revolutionaries during the first years of the revolution; today, among others, the left-wing Catholic circles suffer. Each attempt to outbid the Communists is completely pointless; they cannot be outbid in anything for the simple reason that this process occurs not on the same level but on two completely different qualitative planes. Communism operates in a sphere that has nothing to do with our notions. Therefore, to engage in this kind of bidding, Polrealism (like, by the way, the majority of the contemporary "realisms" about the Soviet Union) has to bring about an artificial evening out of these levels. As we have seen, this is done by substituting the term "Russia" for the term "Communism," which conjures up a picture of Polish society at home more or less as it was during the partitions. This is supposed to give press statements, resolutions, declarations, and other so-called expressions of "public opinion"—at least to some degree—the appearance of genuinely representing Polish public opinion at home. There is, however, no public opinion, in our meaning of the term, in Poland at all; what is expressed publicly is not an opinion but a decreed utterance. Or political manipulation, already mentioned several times. [Addendum of June 27, 1981.]

What do people in Poland want? Certainly the same as what people in Czechoslovakia, Romania, Hungary, East Germany, Lithuania, the Ukraine, Turkestan, and the whole of Russia want, the same as all people under Communist rule want: the overthrow of the Communists! To such an extent is this a normal human desire that all the various aspirations—of Lithuanian nationalists for the recognition of their right to Wilno, of Byelorussians for Smolensk, of Ukrainians for the recognition of a border from Białystok to the Kuban, of Russians for a "one and undivided country," of Poles for the recognition of the Oder-Neisse line, of Germans for the revision of the Oder-Neisse line—all these are secondary problems for people living under Communism. The recognition of the primacy of the *real* desires of the human masses would, however, demand the acknowledgment of the existence of a superior enemy that oppresses everybody in the same manner: the power of international Communism.

As far as Polrealism is concerned, this would mean—as we mentioned earlier—moving Germany from the position of "enemy number one" to the position of a potential ally in the fight against a common enemy. This would amount to renouncing the entire previous political line and to destroying the emotional basis of the Polrealist concept. Thus the desperate clinging to such formulas as "Russian hegemony," "domestic public opinion," and so on.

To what extent this concern for "domestic public opinion" and the desire not to be "compromised" in its eyes are meaningless and fruitless is shown by previous events. The Communists are, for instance, well aware that General Anders has spoken many times in favor of the Oder-Neisse frontier and that Cardinal Wyszyński has done everything in his power to ensure its recognition by the Vatican. This does not, however, prevent the Communists, at an opportune moment, from pressing the button, and to a man the Polish press will state that General Anders used to be in the service of General Guderian or Gehlen and that Cardinal Wyszyński is on friendly terms with German revanchists. Recently, at the end of 1961, the Communists distributed among émigré Poles an awkwardly camouflaged pamphlet and, on the basis of this pamphlet, using the media in Poland, accused people known in émigré circles as notorious proponents of the Oder-Neisse frontier of acting in collusion with the Germans and even of being German agents and receiving funds from the German embassy in London. And, despite the fact that such accusations and ludicrous assertions have obviously been part of Communist tactics for well over forty years, the "accused" thought it advisable to enter into polemics, to defend themselves, to try to explain, and to call the authors of the articles in the media at home "slanderers." In this way, they created the fiction (disinformation) that really it was only libel and personal attacks that were involved and that it was possible to enter into polemics with the press in the Polish People's Republic, while in reality this was all the result of an impersonal action of a system in which no polemics are possible.

In this way, the advocates of Polrealism fall into the trap that has been set for them. The common assumption that Communists attack only people with whom they don't feel comfortable is a major error. Frequently, the very opposite happens. They attack precisely those whose position of compromise in general, or on a certain subject, is well known to them, and, by increasing the pressure, they hope not to create resistance but to make them compromise even further. Such tactics of intimidation have occasionally brought great success. For instance, we witnessed an increase in the attacks on the episcopate at the very time when it was making greater compromises than ever before. This actually produced an extremely conciliatory declaration on the part of the bishops in 1953. Now the situation is similar: the violent attack on the Polrealist politicians has drawn a wave of anti-German statements out of them, because they wanted to justify themselves in the eyes of "public opinion at home" and to display the "purity" of their intentions, along with a vehement disavowal of "any contacts with the Germans," which means in fact an adherence to the political line necessary for the purposes of the Communists. This has happened at the precise moment when they are very much interested in seeing that no departure from this existing line takes place.

Chapter 14 Culture in the Stranglehold of Compulsory Infantilism

The moral aspect of the anti-German complex has a much wider significance than the political aspect described above. Its consequences may indirectly have a negative influence on the whole development of national culture. For it creates a situation in which there is a substantial lowering of standards, not only in politics but also on the intellectual level, as a result of the renunciation of objectivity and its replacement by demagogy. This situation pushes the whole nation into a kind of compulsory infantilism. I want to be understood correctly: what is at stake here is not only relations with Germany. I refer to a lowering to a level at which the whole nation, including its intellectual luminaries, starts to use, with regard to other nations, the criteria "goody" or "ugh." Naturally, everyone has the right to spend his time making paper cut-outs or building sand castles. This would not be dangerous in itself, were it not compulsory for every Pole and were it not the case that anybody who protests against this game of "good" versus "evil" ends up an outcast.

Communism is the total antithesis of freedom. It attempts to replace the human mind by the mechanism of the party. The first step in this direction is depriving people of objective information. Someone might say that this is nothing new. That is correct. Lies, demagogy, distortions, and bias have always existed and exist everywhere. The difference, however, is in the fact that, while in liberal systems true information is normally provided and it is only later tendentiously transformed into disinformation, it is the Communist habit to provide both false information and false conclusions. This is, therefore, a different technique that cannot be measured by our criteria. And so, for instance, if a correspondent of *Izvestiya* draws attention to the "masses of poor people oppressed by militarism" in West German cities today, we know that this information is published in conformity with a specific Communist technique. In what category, however, should we put the information provided by a free Polish writer—who, by the way, has lived in Germany for ten years—in a free monthly edited by Polish intellectuals in the free world, who writes that "the Germans are trying to avoid remembering the Nazi past," while it is known that German literature, journalism, films, theaters, lectures, and public discussions are overloaded with topics from the Nazi past? It seems to us that this is a case of infantilism. There is a difference between a Communist political textbook (*Politicheskii slovar'*) that tells us that the "Socialist Revolutionaries" were "a counterrevolutionary middle-class bourgeois party" and a leading Polish émigré historian who writes that "at no time in its history has Germany really belonged to Western culture." The former is the kind of disinformation that is in accord with the normal Communist ways of thinking; the latter, since it is not in accord with normal scholarly ways of thinking, borders on a childish tantrum.

The genesis of the anti-German complex, which in some cases has reached the level of frenzy, lies—as we know—in the attack by Hitler's Germany on Poland, the innumerable crimes committed during the occupation, and Hitler's plans to liquidate the upper strata of the Polish population, thereby transforming the Polish nation into a kind of "tribe" comparable to those in Africa. Hitler's crimes were committed, however, not only against Poles but against many other nations, and especially, to an incomparably higher degree, against the Jewish nation. This is all well known. Nobody in the world denies this; first and foremost, the Germans themselves do not deny it.

Those who state that the beginning of all the recent misfortunes that have befallen Poland was Hitler's attack in September 1939 are also right. The fact that Poland fell into Communist bondage, where it remains today, is also a result of this attack. Anybody in his senses would therefore think that, theoretically, the greatest indemnity today's Germany could pay for all the wrongs committed by Hitler's Germany would be to give Poland the moral, material, and military aid necessary to release it from the slavery into which it has fallen through Nazi aggression. But here we confront a peculiar paradox: even the theoretical assumption of such a possibility, of such an apparently logical general "indemnity" paid by Germany to Poland, evokes outbursts of anger from Polrealists, who regard this as contrary to the interests of Poland. This concerns not any specific reservations, of which there could certainly be many, but the general principle, which condemns out of hand every theory involving a possible anti-Communist action along with the Germans. And it is precisely here that Communist interests reveal themselves most fully.

It would be naive to imagine that the anti-German complex would not have arisen in Polish society without the assistance of Communist provocation. Most probably, however, so many years after the end of the war, it would not be as widespread as it is at present without artificial and systematic stimulation. Once we transfer the problem to the ideological level, we detect an obvious lack of consistency. We are opponents of collective guilt; we are opponents of mass deportations; we are opponents of totalitarian systems; we are the greatest opponents of murder and violence; but, under certain conditions, we behave as if we supported all of these things—namely when, for certain reasons, it does not suit us to condemn or even to protest against such actions openly. Reversing the situation, this is a kind of behavior closely related to that of which we accuse the Germans, that is, that they did not know, or did not want to know, what was happening in the concentration camps. If, however, with regard to ourselves, we easily explain this turning of a blind eye by reference to the imperfections of human nature, why should we demand perfection from the Germans? Some will say: what a strange comparison! After all, the Germans committed crimes against us; we have not harmed the Germans! This is correct. Therefore, it should be even easier for us to condemn those acts that were committed against them by the Communists. Yet, with the exception of my own statements and a letter by Professor J. M. Bocheński in *Kultura* (May 1962), I have not read a single published Polish statement that condemns the Communist crimes against the Germans in the years 1945–46. I have read, however, the statement of a Pole, a Catholic prelate so well known that streets are named after him, who praised the Bolshevik crimes against the Germans.

It is characteristic that many people, extremely ill disposed toward the Germans, are not even aware of the extent to which they unconsciously turn the Germans into "supermen" through the various ways and means by which they express their aversion. I recall one of the first postwar German films, *The Murderers Are Among Us*. There was a scene in it showing how a "bad" German sent Jews to their death while a "good" German was angry, suffered, fought with himself, and finally pulled out his gun. "And in the end he did not use this gun!" wrote a Polish critic about this film in a tone of malicious triumph. This remark involuntarily brought to my mind a recollection from my own youthful past:

We had "among us" a pleasant companion, a certain Lieutenant M. A long time had passed since the war of 1920, but Lieutenant M., despite his years of service, did not get any promotion. "Why?" it used to be asked. "Well, there's a nasty little blot in his copy book." During meals in restaurants a remark would be heard: "He hanged about a dozen innocent Hebrews in Iwieniec—or was it in Wołożyn?—ha, ha, ha!" Nobody seemed to remember in which town this had happened, or if it was only in one town, but the story always ended with the same "ha, ha, ha!" Lieutenant M. did not like this banter, even when everybody was drinking; it reminded him of a ruined career, and he would frown. I rather sympathized with him, since, I repeat, he was a really nice person. But the following question did not suggest itself to anyone at that time: how many innocent Jews would have been hanged by Lieutenant M. (and other lieutenants) had such a thing not been treated as an offense but supported and rewarded by medals and promotion, instead of acting as an obstacle to advancement? And is it so easy to call evil all those companions who, while drinking vodka, would dismiss the whole matter with a nudge in the side and a "ha, ha, ha!"?

If literature and literary criticism, out of some higher political considerations, avoid all confrontation with the reality of life, they should, at least, be prepared to deal with problems that are probable in real life. The following question comes to mind: how would I personally have looked in the light of the critical comments made by the Polrealist writer about this film? I took part in the same war as Lieutenant M., and let us assume that I was among other cavalry men while someone, on higher orders, was being hanged on a pine tree. What should I have done? Should I have spurred my horse, ridden out in front of everyone, and protested? Or should I have taken out my saber and attacked the commander? The main effect would have been for the whole company to open their mouths in amazement and wonder, including, probably, the person being hanged. Further, if I had not been shot down immediately, this would have been only because of a sincere conviction that I had gone mad.

Terrible things happened during the German occupation. So much has been written about this that everyone knows the atrocities by heart. What do we know, however, about the acts of revenge in eastern Germany? Silence. If everything that happened there was all right, why are we ashamed? If it was not all right, why don't we condemn it? In the book *Das Ende an der Elbe* [Defeat in the East], Jürgen Thorwald writes that one farmer in a German village was killed and his head was cut off as a joke since he had tried to defend his wife, who was gang-raped by 16 soldiers; this was a quite common occurrence. Nobody knew, however, why, on the same occasion, a fourteen-year-old boy was nailed to a barn wall head down. An American chaplain, Francis Sampson, recalls that in Neubrandenburg, German girls who had been raped were hanged by their feet from branches, their legs pulled apart and their groins ripped open. In Prague, German women were stripped of their clothes and forced to shift rubble; they also had to keep their lips wide open so that every passer-by could spit into their mouths; mothers were tied up in barbed wire and thrown into the river, while children were drowned in reservoirs and people amused themselves by pushing them away from the edges with sticks. The Reverend Karl Seifert recalls that on May 20, 1945, he saw a wooden raft on the River Elbe with a German family with several children fastened to it, their hands and feet pierced by long nails. A former Soviet major, Grigoriy Klimov (*Berlinskii Kreml* [The Berlin Kremlin]), describes how he saw in ditches at the side of the road German women who had had beer bottles pushed between their legs with the butt ends of rifles.

Enough of these quotations. Their number is not what matters. They are cited as illustrative of one category of information that Polish public opinion in general does not have or does not wish to have. And now let us ask the following question: is the mother whose son was nailed to the barn or whose daughter was torn apart between the branches of a tree, after all she has suffered, able to regard this as a "just punishment by God" because her fellow countrymen had committed crimes in other countries? In my opinion, she is not. Neither a German mother nor any other mother in the world is capable of regarding such actions as just. From the political point of view, it is obviously easy to reduce everything to the question "who started it?" But let us appeal to the imagination of those who write about life: is it possible for a human being, faced with the body of his closest relative who has been killed in a bestial way, to draw up a balanced political account and to weep over unknown people murdered in an unknown country? If we could find such a person, he would probably be made of steel and belong to a race of "Übermenschen". I personally do not really believe in a race of "Übermenschen".

If we think the whole matter through, we find that the distortions in both socialist realist and Polrealist war memoirs involuntarily achieve results contrary to those intended by the authors. Thus, it was accepted that all Germans during the occupation had to be and really were "bad." Let us now try to analyze, in accordance with this pattern, the literary characterization of an individual German as a human being during the occupation of Poland. Any German is bad if, at a time when stealing in the occupied country was a "done" thing, he stole along with the native inhabitants: he is presented as a "thief." Any German is bad if, at a time when everybody was dealing in the black market and trafficking, he bribed officials or accepted bribes himself: he is a "briber." But the worst German of all is the one who did not steal and did not give or take bribes but who carried out the orders of the authorities during the occupation: he is a "criminal." If we now were to try to extricate a living human being from this collective literary type, the question would automatically arise: what should an individual German have done to deserve the name of a "good" German? Socialist realist literature has an excellent prescription: obviously, he should have joined the Communist Party. In Polrealist literature, he would have to have been a German who, amid the general prosperity of those who operated the black market, lived a life of an ascetic, using only his own ration cards; someone who allowed black marketeers to flourish and even assisted them without accepting any personal reward; who decided not to carry out the orders of his superiors, thereby risking his head for the welfare of Poles. Let us admit that such a literary figure would be too unrealistic, too infantile and simplistic, too implausible to be true to life, especially in conditions of war. Only a living angel could live up to such demands, and this would obviously be in direct conflict with the intentions of the authors of this literature.

There were many bad and cruel Germans, just as there are many bad and cruel people in the world. But it cannot be the case (nor is it) that millions of living people are stamped with the same common negative characteristic like lead soldiers made from the same mold. Any attempt to prove the fallacy of such a view brings discussion down to an infantile level.

I resort again to the comparative method. Indulging in this kind of infantilism, one could burden the whole Russian nation with the responsibility for

Bolshevism, all Germans with the responsibility for Hitlerism, the Italians with the responsibility for Fascism, and the Jews for the crucifixion of Christ. A free man, if he wants to remain free, should say: Nonsense! I shall not be made a fool! Such a revolt against the demands of a national collective should not be regarded as evidence of sympathy for any of those nations but as a protest in defense of common sense, free thought, and objectivity to which every man has the right, even if he does not consider this his duty.

A general accusation leveled against all Germans (during the war it was obligatory in half the world, and it is now being kept going by Communist provocation among the Poles) is that they did not themselves overthrow Hitler, that, on the contrary, they allowed themselves to be led by him and obediently carried out his orders. This same charge could have been made against the Russians in regard to their being ruled by Lenin and serving in the NKVD. During the war, such a charge was not made, since half of the world supported the Bolsheviks. This is clearly evidence of the conditional nature of such charges.

But the extension of collective guilt to whole nations is not only a propaganda game played in particular political circumstances; it is also a rather tricky ploy. Why could one not make a similar charge against, for instance, the Polish nation, namely that it has tolerated Communism for so many years? As for the general potential of the Secret Service (UB), Border Control Units (WOP), Internal Security Corps (KBW), and similar secret police organizations, they are not numerically smaller than the SS units in Hitler's Germany. After all, the Germans at least made several attempts to assassinate Hitler; not a single hand has been raised against Bierut and Gomułka in Poland. Moreover, at the present moment, every Pole in the world, at home as well as in exile, regards the incitement to assassination or the shooting of representatives of the régime, in short, any attempt to overthrow the totalitarian system by force, as a provocation or crime for which the whole nation would have to pay. It follows that what we regard as a crime in the Germans (their submission to Hitler), we regard as a virtue in ourselves. And vice versa: what for us is a crime was the duty of every German.

The answer to such a comparison, an answer obligatory for all Polrealists until 1956, went as follows: this is something quite different. There is no analogy at all! Hitlerism was a German creation and originated within the German nation, while contemporary Bolshevism has been imposed on Poland from outside and is maintained only by the force of "Russian" bayonets. From this it would follow that a nation is not responsible for "alien" systems imposed upon it by force but that it is responsible for its "own," "homegrown" state system. And, when this thesis is extended further, this latter system bears the stamp of the mentality of the nation and reflects its morality. Should we accept this formula, we are faced with a number of rather difficult problems. For instance, which system was more typical of the mentality of the French nation, the bloody dictatorship of the 1789 revolution, the imperialism of Napoleon, or the Restoration of Louis XVIII? All these changes occurred within twenty-six years. In view of the brevity of these periods, would the length of the following periods be decisive? But, in such a case, one would have to say that the German nation was regarded as a nation of "poets and thinkers" for a much longer time than as a nation of the Gestapo and SS. It would be necessary to solve many more similar enigmas all over the world. By deriving consequences from the differentiation between "homegrown" and "alien" systems, we would have to come to the conclusion that the Germans bear the same degree of guilt for not assassinating Hitler as they would today (in reverse) if they were to shoot at Herr Ulbricht and his comrades. This would be a very convenient interpretation for all "alien" Communist systems all over the globe.

Obviously, such a topic cannot be exhaustively treated by using a few arguments or abstruse formulae. The genesis of power and of the state system imposed on nations is hidden in the darkness of the philosophy of history and belongs to an area abounding in explanations of human psychology and in historical examples. Should we add the injunction of St. Paul that "there is no power but of God," we would find ourselves in a net of immensely contradictory interpretations.

Regardless of the comments made above, the formula that differentiates between "homegrown" and "alien" power systems seems to have one more defect. Since it uses exclusively the term "nation," it omits the existence of a much more concrete factor in life, the individual person. Obviously, mutual relations between the individual and the authorities, whether these be "homegrown" or "alien," are a given. By shifting the center of gravity from the collective, political level to the individual, human level, we are faced with a new complex of tricky criteria. And so, for instance: why should an SS man, who pursues people of another nationality for the benefit of his own authorities, stand morally lower than a Polish cop pursuing his compatriots in the interests of a foreign régime imposed by force? Why, for instance, should those German writers who wrote hymns in praise of their "own" Nazism be regarded as criminals, while Polish authors (and what authors!—Gałczyński, Broniewski . . .) who write hymns in praise of "alien" Bolshevism are excused as unfortunate victims? Because they have to, because of their wives and children? Because they want to live? And did the others not want to live? Didn't they also have wives and children?

One other incidental question arises. Would many European nations at a time of greatly awakened nationalisms (one now writes "patriotisms") fail to produce poets praising their "own" leader (even if he were the worst of the worst), straddling Europe from the Atlantic to the Volga, a man whose power reached from the sands of Egypt to the Arctic Ocean?! You can't be serious! Not for nothing is Hitler, albeit with reluctance, compared to Napoleon. As a result, any answer to the question "What is 'worse'—to praise 'homegrown' Nazism or 'alien' Bolshevism?"—appears at least dubious.

After 1956, this whole subject suddenly became metamorphosed: the position adopted was the complete reverse of what it had been until then. We suddenly learned that Communism per se is not so bad . . . it is bad only when it is "alien," imposed, "Russian." On the other hand, "Polish" Communism, by virtue of the fact that it is indigenous, Gomułka-ite, "homegrown," becomes not only better but perhaps even "good." It is bad only if we move away from the "Polish October" toward the "Russian October." Most people accepted this reversal of the previous argumentation without even realizing the fundamental contradiction that this implied. Only the most intelligent of the Polrealists sensed this tricky contradiction bordering on a collective lie. In answer to unpleasant charges of this sort, we heard indignant outbursts like the following: "How dare you compare Communism with Hitlerism!" Was it then the duty of the Germans to overthrow Hitlerism since it was "their own" if it is the duty of Poles to defend Communism the moment it becomes "their own"? But this is where the triumphal activity of the Great Provocation begins, to the description of which this whole book is devoted. Therefore, in this particular instance, we shall refrain from further comments.

Nobody could say that the smoke of Auschwitz has been allowed to fade into the mist of oblivion. Thousands of reports give off the same terrible, cadaverous smell as Auschwitz did in reality. No one has forgotten, and rightly so. All this has been looked after. What has, however, been forgotten is the most important thing: the human being. It has been forgotten that the objective meaning of the word "crime" is not restricted only to crimes against Poles and Jews but involves crimes against any human being.

And here one has to remark that foreign postwar literature has surpassed ours in its objective presentation of one of the greatest crises of humanity, World War Two. Because of its present tendency to "search for the human being," it is simply more interesting. It is obvious that, in literature, the person is always more interesting than politics and the nation.

Some dismiss the stance of today's Germany by denying obvious facts either through ignorance or ill will or simply by accepting the Communist method of interpretation. Some complain of the lack of expiation on the part of the Germans; others, on the contrary, aware of the degree of expiation, express contempt for their excessive penitence, pointing out their lack of dignity. Thus, no matter what, as long as the outcome is negative. Among the common arguments are such interjections as "Ah, it's only because they lost the war! This is why they are 'good' now, but if. . . ." Let us mention parenthetically that we did not win the war either . . . but what has this got to do with the whole matter? Human ideas have frequently emerged in response to external circumstances; in any case, their content is more important than the conditions that have contributed to their genesis. All that is important is the future that they open up, not the past, which has been buried in a foul mass grave. Is it possible to regard a beautiful book as worthless only because it would not have been written had one, and not the other, general won the decisive battle ten years earlier?

In contrast to the prescriptions of socialist realism, the sincerity of each writer can be measured not only by what he writes but also by what he passes over in silence. Still, everyone should have the right to write what he wants and what is most dear to his heart, what he considers important. Let Semitophiles and anti-Semites write, as well as pro-Communists and anti-Communists, pro-Germans and anti-Germans. The negative side of a human group is not the fact that one of its members writes in a certain way and another writes differently. The negative aspect lies in the fact of no one daring to write differently, of no one daring to express his disapproval or rejection of something, to express his individual, different opinion, even though he lives in the free world and neither the Gestapo nor the NKVD threatens him with Auschwitz or Kolyma.

Certainly, there is still a small percentage of people in Germany today who do not condemn the whole Nazi past and who even defend it. These rare exceptions are immediately noted: "Look what these people are writing about!" Whereas one should say: Thank God! Thanks are certainly due to God, but first of all for the sake of the Germans. A nation that shows too much unanimity of opinion, too much self-discipline, too much sameness of thought, where there is nobody who will say something different from all the others, cannot be regarded as sincere. Such a society looks as if it has been artificially reduced to one common denominator. This is the ideal of a totalitarian, Communist system, and not a free system. In a fine article defending Władysław Studnicki against mass condemnation after he had offered to appear as a defense witness at the trial of General von Manstein, W. A. Zbyszewski wrote once that public opinion in a mature nation should be like an open fan. This is certainly true. Let us add only that the greater the spread of this open fan, the more evidence it provides of the dynamics, the richness of thought, and the culture of the nation. A fan closed by the grip of a strong fist is reminiscent of a cudgel.

The most eloquent proof of the terrible slavery of the spirit in the Communist system is the fact that, among the millions of people living in that system who, for thirty years, had compared Stalin to a living deity, nobody is now prepared to stand up and say a word to defend him.

In the one-sidedness of this German complex, which is close to a state of infantilism, the heart of the matter, the question of Germany, has a lesser importance. As a "complex," however, it is a characteristic example of the depreciation of culture. If the attitude toward one single state or toward one single nation restrains all vital elasticity and becomes a stumbling block on the road to independent thinking, how can one speak about potential Polish "involvement" in or "contribution" to the progress of the world?

An English philanthropist, the Rev. Henry Lansdell, traveled throughout Siberia in 1869 and modified somewhat the opinions of his time about the horrors of the forced-labor system in tsarist Russia. In a book published subsequently in London, he somewhat naively entered into a polemic with a "certain Russian, Dostoevsky." He contended that, in his *Notes From the House of the Dead,* Dostoevsky had exaggerated, presenting things too drearily, and got entangled in inaccuracies. Lansdell did not know what Dostoevsky would come to mean for the world. He treated him at that time as a "certain Russian," but, in presenting the Russia of that time to European public opinion, he defended it against a Russian writer. Reading these pages today, one can imagine the indignation and reviling with which a Polish writer would be treated by his native collective were he to depart so far from the official image of Poland that a foreign author had to defend it before the rest of Europe!

But the name of Russia of that time was made famous to the whole world not by a government writer or a loyal journalist but by this "certain" Dostoevsky. One could add: yes, but this was due to his genius, to his talent, and not everybody possesses these qualities. This is correct. One suspects, however, that if a Polish writer offended the Polrealist complex to the same extent, he would remain a "certain" person even if he were the greatest genius and talent on earth; in other words, he would be buried alive in the house of the dead.

Once, Henryk Sienkiewicz stated: "Woe to the nations that love freedom more than their country." This was a statement that sounded nice in the nineteenth century, when there was still a lot of individual freedom and when slavery was identified solely with the slavery of a nation. People at that time could not even imagine what forms the total enslavement of the human spirit would take in the future. Today, happy the country and happy the people when it is (still) possible to criticize anything in public. I recall that, during the gloomiest period of occupation, a Nazi propaganda pamphlet found its way into my hands; it was entitled, as far as I remember, *The English About Themselves*. This was a selection of statements by English politicians and journalists who devastatingly criticized British actions with regard to other nations in various situations and at various times. This was an attempt by the Nazi propaganda machine to elicit in the reader a repugnance toward England. In my case, this pamphlet only increased the esteem and admiration I felt for England!

One may strongly dislike and even feel aversion to the policies of the United States. Yet, do not the statements quoted below say more about authentic freedom than all the official broadcasts of American propaganda? For instance, the American Admiral Burke publicly stated in April 1962: "We are becoming a danger to the world. Nobody knows what we will do, since we ourselves do not know what we will do." Or consider a statement by former Attorney General, Robert Kennedy, a brother of the President of the United States, at a conference in Indonesia. When asked, "How do you assess the role of your country in the war with Mexico?," he answered: "I think that in this war justice was not on our side."

Today, the world is threatened by a catastrophe. The greatest of all possible catastrophes would not be a war for freedom but a capitulation to total slavery. Transposing the words of Henryk Sienkiewicz to our times, one has to say: "Woe to the nations that love their country more than freedom!"

Chapter 15 The Real German Threat

"ANTI-FASCISM"

Someone once joked that America could easily defeat the Soviets by using a ready-made formula: take the example of Hitler and do everything in exactly the opposite way. Sometimes one also has the impression that the reality of West Germany today could be best depicted according to this formula: take everything the socialist realist and Polrealist press writes about Germany and turn it the other way around.

At the present time, Germany is undoubtedly the most anti-Nazi country in the world, not only in form but also in spirit. Such phenomena as the anti-Negro excesses in the United States, the racism of South Africa, the French OAS [Organisation de l'Armée Secrète—Secret Army Organization], and so on are out of the question in Germany. Still, according to official statistics, there are about thirteen thousand trained Communist agents in West Germany with an annual budget of 120 million marks; there are more than thirty crypto-Communist organizations that operate openly under various fronts; some one hundred thousand copies of secret Communist pamphlets and papers are distributed. Furthermore, Communist infiltration is carried out through a multitude of diverse and changing methods, the description of which would take up too much space. Perhaps more dangerous than this direct infiltration, however, is the indirect infiltration of many shades and various strengths.

Any excess brings about negative results. In West Germany there is an excess of . . . anti-Nazism. This observation may evoke derisory cries and the usual invective. But even the most coordinated howl of protest could not change the fact that so-called anti-Fascism in every country has been under the control of international Communism, which uses it for its own, clearly unilateral, objectives. We are concerned here with this unilateralism, not with anti-Nazism per se. It is not possible to set any limits on the condemnation of such a grim totalitarianism as Nazism. But, without using the comparative method, which alone is able to provide an objective view of events, it is easy to go to the other extreme. The artistic, literary, and intellectual circles and the youth of West Germany are perhaps not more pro-Communist than the corresponding groups in France, Italy, and other European countries in terms of absolute numbers. They are more so, however, if we take into consideration that Germany borders on the Iron Curtain and that half of it is under Communist rule. The ratio of German films with anti-Nazi tendencies to those with anti-Communist tendencies is perhaps 1,000:1. In all likelihood there has not been a single play with anti-Communist tendencies, while an adaptation of *The Diary of Anne Frank* has had a huge number of performances in German theaters. In literature, compared with a hundred good anti-Nazi novels, there is not a single good novel about life in East Germany, although this should be of interest to everybody. All kinds of "young avant-garde movements" and various literary groups are not only inexorably anti-Nazi but also, to a large degree, "progressive," along the lines of the contemporary coexistence-mongers. Sometimes one has the impression that German literary circles consider the topic of anti-Communism, regardless of the literary value of the work, as kitsch, similar, for instance, in painting to the theme of a castle and a lake with swans found in lithographs that adorn third-rate inns. Many key posts, especially in the German publishing world and in the press and radio, date from the time of the granting of licenses by the allies after 1945, when any sign of anti-Communism was prohibited.

Such a situation is obviously not without influence on the formation of public opinion—especially since, under the slogan "Nie wieder Krieg!" ["Never again must there be war!"], an aversion to any kind of active battle against

Communism dominates in the main. The Communist provocation is well aware of this state of affairs and, through its own channels, not only exploits it for its own objectives in Germany but also tries to frighten Germany by mobilizing world public opinion, thus forcing it continuously onto the defensive. While the numerous murders committed every day by the French OAS, for instance, are regarded only as statistics, one German teenager who paints a swastika on a fence can alarm the opinion of half of the world, thanks to the Communist provocation.

The stance of Polrealism is similarly inconsistent. In other words, it sees danger in a single swastika, although there is no one behind it, while it does not realize the danger of the millions of hammers and sickles, behind which is the power of international Communism—the same power that is currently enslaving Poland.

"RAPALLO"

More significant, however, is the fact that the political assumptions of Polrealism correspond in essence to the political assumptions of the so-called German "revanchists" (or at least of their most extreme group)—not only because they too regard the Oder-Neisse question as the most important. Both start from the assumption that the Polish People's Republic is a continuation of Polish history, that the Polish People's Republic is a continuation of the Polish state, that Poland is still located between Germany and Russia; both of them attempt to infer from this the independence of Gomułka's initiatives, and both attempt to emphasize the instability of the agreement between Gomułka and Khrushchev on the Oder-Neisse question (even pointing out supposed frictions in this matter); both the German revanchists and the Polrealists regard themselves as each other's main enemy, and both are inclined to treat "Russia" as a lesser evil. In the Soviet Union, they both discern Russian imperial interests that, in certain conditions, through a compromise, could be put to use for their own national objectives. It will suffice to give a few quotes from the *Pressedienst der Heimatvertriebenen* (*hvp*) [Press Service of Those Driven from Their Homeland], published by the Göttinger Arbeitskreis, to reveal this general tendency.

The usual tenor is that the Soviet Union is not really interested in the Oder and Neisse . . . and, between the lines, that Khrushchev is not as irreconcilable as Gomułka. One could talk with Moscow, but the Poles, both the Communists and the émigrés, are the obstacle. A certain "mood of apprehension" in Warsaw is constantly noted; this results from some Moscow move, as if there existed an autonomous political stance in Warsaw not dependent on the directives of the Communist headquarters. Also characteristic are the frequent references to the Polish émigré press. The commentaries are, by the way, quite naive: "Gomułka is putting pressure on Khrushchev to present the Oder-Neisse problem to an international forum.—Gomułka did not mention Khrushchev's name even once in his speech! . . . But he spoke about partisan activities during the last war. . . . This is a clear hint for those who know how to read and how to listen. . . . Those are no idle rumors that say that Poland will take up arms should the Soviets agree to concessions with regard to the Oder-Neisse frontier. In Warsaw changes in the Soviet attitude are followed with suspicion. Should China one day become an atomic power, the Soviets might be interested in recreating good relations with Germany. . . . After all, Russia annexed Eastern Prussia in the Seven Years' War, but returned it later to Germany."[1]

These quotations are sufficient to enable us to realize how unfitting to this picture would be a remark that the Soviet Union is not the Russia of the Seven Years' War and is not Russia at all but something quite different. Having made such an observation, one would not be able to reach the following final conclusion: "The whole thrust of Polish politics [in Warsaw] with regard to Germany is aimed at preventing Russian-German negotiations from being carried out in accordance with the principle of equality."

Once again, we notice here the reversal of reality: it is not the Soviet provocation that makes a Polish-German reconciliation impossible, but, on the contrary, it is the Polish provocation that makes a German-Soviet reconciliation impossible. We observe here, as in Polrealism, the appeal of a so-called Realpolitik, which is based on overlooking the real facts and acting as if there were no international Communism, which aims not only at the maintenance of the Oder-Neisse line, not only at the capture of the whole of Berlin, not only at the capture of the whole of Germany, but at the domination of the entire world. As a result of this intentional oversight, we are only one step removed from a favorable attitude toward the renewal of a "Rapallo" policy with Moscow, an attitude still camouflaged but already quite evident: "The contacts of Dr. Kroll, who comes from Upper Silesia, with Khrushchev have caused some alarm among Poles.—Gomułka tried to warn Moscow against a possible 'Rapallo' course of action.—Rapallo brought great benefits to the Soviet Union. . . . Cooperation in military affairs also developed . . . since there was a fear of further annexation of German territories by the Poles . . . the Soviets were afraid of Poland making trouble again. . . . It was therefore a clearly defensive peace policy that led the German government to 'Rapallo.' . . . It is a historical truth that

'Rapallo' happened only because both the Soviet Union and Germany were equally afraid of Poland."[2]

These are quotations taken at random from a single source. One also hears, however, that the Free Democratic Party, a current partner in the government coalition, is showing a serious tendency to renew the pro-Rapallo policy toward "Russia" as an expression of its "realistic" eastern policy. And so we can make some kind of equation between Polrealism and "German realism," neither of which takes into account historical or present-day experience.

Also significant is the generally accepted term of German political vocabulary "Wiedervereinigung" (reunification) with reference to the major aim of the "unification of Germany." In this case, the word "unification" is quite misleading. One can unify Europe, one can unify two divided parts of the same country, but one cannot "unify" an area taken away, seized, and occupied. One can only liberate it or not liberate it, but the verb "unify" does not fit such a case. This term was certainly imposed by the Western powers so as not to sound too provocative to the Soviets. Still, it has been generally accepted in Germany, a country that shows a desire to come to an agreement with the Soviets in an amicable way. This is an official desire, and certainly a noble one. It will not, however, change by one iota the fact that neither the German Democratic Republic, nor the Oder-Neisse line, nor any other area occupied will be returned freely by the Soviet Union to Germany or to a free Poland. This is not because these lands are "Polish" or "German" but because they are Communist and constitute an important gateway for an attack leading to the capture of Western Europe.

Also erroneous is the Polrealistic notion that in certain left-wing German circles there is an apparent understanding of the "Polish point of view." Actually, this is a result of the developing anti-anti-Communist atmosphere and of the search for ways of coexistence with "the East" through a "Rapallo" with the People's Poland, the existing Poland, Communist Poland.

Today, a serious "German threat" can arise only from Germany's making the same mistakes as any other nation that conducts its policies with eyes closed to reality. This is the policy that was once characterized by the motto "any means is right," as far as the particular interests of the nation are concerned. Today such a policy belongs to the realm of illusion. We have learned this from reality and experience since the time of the Bolshevik Revolution in Russia. Since then, not every "realistic" policy has been realistic. Since that time, the world has become more complicated and also more universal. Hegel said once (quite rightly): "The particular is for the most part of too trifling value as compared with the general."

Chapter 16 "Realisms" Versus Reality

"RUSSREALISM"

It is not true that Communism threatens "Western civilization" and "Western culture." It threatens every civilization and culture: Roman, Byzantine, Chinese, Indian, Arab. As the enemy not of nations but of man tout court, it is also the enemy of man's God and of all the achievements of humanity. Unfortunately, the attitude of man toward Communism and the attitude of a politician toward the Soviet bloc frequently differ.

The overthrow of Communism in general and the liberation of the peoples of Eastern Europe in particular seem to be rather difficult to achieve—as we have seen earlier—without German participation, but without the participation of the Russians they are simply impossible. Russia, therefore, cannot be our enemy in the fight against international Communism, but it should be our prime ally. At the present time, Russian anti-Communism is the "purest" anti-Communism, that is, without secondary interests, concentrating completely on the overthrow of the Communist system. It is uncompromising precisely because of its purity. Russian anti-Communism and coexistence in any form are mutually exclusive. Therefore, the most logical approach is the *nepredreshenchestvo* stance adopted by Russian émigrés, that is, "not prejudging," not taking any decisions in advance with regard to the future national, state, and territorial aspirations of the enslaved nations in view of the more important task of liberation from the common yoke. This stance would be in accord with the priority of the term "man" over the term "nation" if we were to treat the proposed ideals literally. In politics, however, as we know, they are not treated literally.

The nationalists of the other enslaved nations take the opposite stance: *predreshenchestvo,* deciding in advance, that is, their national aspirations and those territorial boundaries to which they have claim are to be recognized beforehand. Nationalists are most certainly opponents of Communist internationalism. On the other hand, since, because of their principles and the nature of their ideology, they are opponents of every kind of internationalism and cosmopolitanism, they are automatically opponents of an international solution of the Communist problem. Therefore—as we have pointed out many times —they tend to negate the international character of the Communist threat by replacing it with the threat of national Russian imperialism. Their program clearly puts the "nation" first and "man" second. Furthermore, they let it be unequivocally understood that, should their claims and national aspirations not be satisfied in advance, they are ready to withhold participation in the common effort to overthrow Communism or in possible liberation actions initiated by the West and that they are even ready to switch over to the Communist side. One could draw the conclusion from all this that the Byelorussians would prefer to remain in Communist slavery unless Smolensk is promised to them in advance; the Lithuanians, unless they are allowed to keep Wilno; the Ukrainians—Lwów; the Poles, unless the Oder-Neisse line is internationally recognized; the Cossacks, unless a "free" Cossack state is promised them, and so forth. But this attitude obviously clashes with the interests of the enslaved people. There are probably few human beings who would refuse to leave prison unless they received a guarantee of certain living conditions and of a particular job and so on and who would prefer to remain in their prison cell if such a guarantee was not granted in advance.

Therefore, the principle of "not prejudging," as proposed by the Russians, seems to be more rational than the principle of "prejudging." The contrast between these two principles becomes, however, substantially blurred after a closer look. Just as it would be erroneous to assert that all Communists, since they renounce their national interests in favor of internationalism, are ideological victims of Russian imperialism (because the Russian Communists are the only exception, having as their goal not international interests but exclusively Russian national interests), so, too, it would be erroneous to assert that the Russians are the only exception, having no nationalistic objectives. On the contrary, Russian nationalism is just as apparent as that of other nations. Its major slogan is the so-called *neraschleneniye Rossii,* that is, the integrity, or nondismemberment, of Russia. This "advance condition" contains the same elements of "prejudging," that is, the recognition of their territorial and border aspirations beforehand, since, after all, this is what the retention of the entirety of the former Russia amounts to. The similarity of this position to that of other nationalisms is emphasized when some Russian groups "let it be understood" that, should Russia be divided up, they will not side with the anti-Communist forces . . . they will perhaps even support the Soviet side. There are also many declarations proclaiming "the solidarity of all Russians in this respect, whether they are at home or in exile." And here we notice a similarity to the declarations of the Polrealists ("all Poles at home and in exile," and so on); that is, we may speak of "Russrealism."

Just as, for the Polrealists, the major opponent is not international Communism but Germany, just as, for the German realists, the major opponent is not Communism but Poland, just as, for all national realists, the major opponent is not Communism but Russia (or Poland), so for the Russrealists the major opponent is not Communism but those who "attack the entity of the former Russian empire." We can see that, in all these cases, Communism is not regarded as enemy number one; in all these cases, egoistic, nationalistic interests are superior to the common interest of both liberation from and a defense against the common enemy. This is a rather saddening picture. Naturally, these attitudes create a wide-open field for the activities of the Communist provocation, which endeavors to benefit from this state of affairs and to maintain it. Let us not deceive ourselves into thinking that Poles are unique in their stance. Just as some Polrealists travel to Warsaw and are well received there, so some Russrealists travel to Moscow and also find an understanding for the "common cause."

THE "REALISM"—OF MANNA FROM HEAVEN

As if in line with a special rule, all these captive "realisms" are united only in criticizing the policies of the Western powers, which, with regard to the Communist bloc, pursue their own apparently "realistic" interests. Against this general background, can we be absolved or comforted by the fact that this criticism is really correct?

As we have seen, Poland, acting in its own national interests after the First World War, contributed substantially to the rescue of Bolshevism. In the Second World War, for national reasons, it openly took the side of the Bolsheviks; after the war, for these same reasons, it has considered it expedient to support "its own road to Socialism." It does not matter here whether these reasons were right or wrong. Let us even assume that in each instance they were really weighty. We want only to state the bare fact itself.

With regard to the present situation, we have to say that the "Polish People's Republic" is neither "Polish," nor a "republic," nor of the "people." It is a member of the Soviet bloc and a branch of international Communism. Those Pol-realists who do not notice this, or do not want to notice it, deprive themselves of the basis for any criticism of the Western powers that also do not notice, or do not want to notice, that a similar fate may await them in the future if they continue in their anachronistic policies exclusively based on following a "sensible" interpretation of their own interests.

A consideration of global problems would extend the scope of this book. At this point, we wish only to call attention to one aspect of this endless criticism of the West, which can be explained by reasons other than the easiness of shifting the blame onto somebody else. More frequently, this is a very suitable pretext for the conduct of a "realistic policy," that is, for not opposing Communist slavery and for switching to a stance of "organic" collaboration or of "positivism"—because "the others" do not want to liberate us. If we think this matter through, it means that a country that in turn is going to be occupied by Communism should not resist it but should reach a compromise in the name of realistic politics and wait for others to decide whether to liberate it or, more likely, not to liberate it—as if history knew any instances in politics where the love of one's neighbor was greater than the love of oneself. Let us agree that it is difficult to imagine the provocation of international Communism developing a program more useful for itself.

This is a topic that usually rouses the "realists" to fury and that, therefore, is not permitted in public discussions, especially in the Polish émigré press. The prohibition a priori of a certain topic also deprives people of the right to ask questions that constantly present themselves: Why should the Americans have more desire to liberate us than we have ourselves? Why should the Americans die for us, if we do not want to die for ourselves? This kind of question is generally regarded as "lunatic" or even "criminal," since it is assumed that no spontaneous resistance can withstand the world powers of today or have any success. Reality, however, tells us something different. Those who sit with their hands folded are neither given recognition nor taken seriously. Had a small group of Jews not started to struggle against the British Empire in 1946, today there would be no Israel; had the Cypriots not done the same, today there would be no independent Cyprus; had the Algerian Arabs not started a seven-year war against the French Empire, they would not have lived to see an independent Algeria in 1962. These examples could be extended to include such countries as Morocco, Egypt, Syria, and Indonesia. One Negro of genius, Tschombe of Katanga, threw down the gauntlet against the whole world, and, although it is still uncertain whether it was not actually he who shot down a great evil-doer from the position of Secretary-General of the United Nations, nothing happened to him despite the massacres carried out by United Nations troops. And all this happened although not one of these spontaneous movements and countermovements had an atomic bomb or even tanks. We shall not assess how justified or unjustified these individual cases were. We shall limit ourselves to stating a simple fact: despite the general condemnation of war, only those who act gain recognition of their rights and respect in the world. The legend that it is possible to buy the Soviets by politeness is only a legend, similar to that of the possibility of prevailing upon them. During World War Two, Finland was involved in two wars against the Soviets, one on the side of Hitler, and still, among all the countries between the Arctic Ocean and the Black Sea, it later got the best deal.

As is well known, the Soviet Union affirms and very much supports all those actions that are directed against the Western powers, but it describes any such actions as "criminal incitements to war" when they are directed against its own interests. The Western powers neither affirm nor, as a rule, support any such actions against the Soviet Union. And, although they show an aversion to "counterrevolution," they take the factual situation into account; since they are accustomed to counting people like dollars, they have respect for all large numbers, wherever these are found.

The attitude of our "realists" toward the Western powers, and toward America in particular, is logically somewhat topsy-turvy. Instead of treating America as our ally—good or bad, wise or stupid—we regard ourselves, at best, as America's allies (with many conditions attached), while it is our liberation that is at stake. As though it is not *we* who should fight and seek America's assistance in the struggle, but the other way around: America should do the fighting, and we (possibly) should assist her. As if America was living under the Communist yoke at present and not we.

Undoubtedly, it would be in the interests of the Western powers to support the aspirations to freedom of the people of Eastern Europe and to become their faithful allies in this cause. Does this mean, however, that, if our ally leaves or betrays us, we should not only give up our aspirations and the fight but even switch over to the enemy's side so as to punish our disloyal ally in this way? If we behave like the child who "cuts off his nose to spite his face," should we still call this "a realistic policy"?

Since we have already broached many sore subjects that are generally not discussed, let us go a little further into these prohibited topics and say something about the Hungarian uprising. We know that the people rose there in the name of freedom and that they did not receive any assistance from the free world. As far as the free world is concerned, this was the kind of stupidity that makes you sick. The West officially explained its decision as coming from a desire to avoid a third world war. We will not make any comment on this "realistic" position and this moral pharisaism. We are concerned with a certain detail generally shrouded in a veil of silence. Perhaps the West would not have taken this position, or would have been forced to take a different one, had the Hungarian uprising been total. A total uprising was not in the interests of the West, but it was in the interests of Hungary. We know, however, from secret sources that the Hungarian army did not revolt. True, we have seen pictures and documentary films, but the Hungarian army as such was not present in them. We saw individual soldiers, officers, perhaps individual units, but the Hungarian army as a whole did not take up arms. Perhaps it was waiting for the West to help, for the West to make a move. But the West used the army's inertia as an excuse not to act. Could it have done so if the insurrection had spread to Poland, to Czechoslovakia, to East Germany, and even further? But such speculations would lead us away from the issue.

Some unpopular things sometimes have to be said if we want to determine the real state of affairs. One of the tasks of this book is an attempt to do just this—reveal the truth. Perhaps some individual factual errors have been committed while doing this. I do not think, however, that it is an error sincerely to wish to identify this real state of affairs.

Chapter 17 Pathos Versus Pestilence

In view of the overlapping of international interests, there is today no longer a place for state sovereignty of the old type. If a nation wants to remain sovereign, it should understand that such a possibility exists only through being an integral part of the free world. The motto should not, therefore, be "one's own road to Socialism" but rather the "common road to freedom," not one's own path "for the benefit of the nation" but the common path "for the benefit of humanity."

In view of the position of the "international socialist system" and with regard to the territories occupied by it, today every humanitarian ought to become a revisionist.

The leading Polrealist journalist, Aleksander Bregman, one of the few first-rate writers in that camp, analyzing the stance of Polish journalism, described it as one of duty, encompassing different points of view but nevertheless serving the interests of Poland. However, a policy that serves exclusively the interests of the state and of the nation is an anachronism today. Today's politics should serve the interests of humanity in order to safeguard it from global catastrophe. We have to be conscious of the fact that a great process of transition from the advocacy of national interests to the advocacy of human interests is taking place.

We have to renounce the principle of the primacy of national interests over the interests of the idea of freedom. Actions detrimental to humanity cannot be justified today by any considerations relating to a nation. There are no reasons—be they geographical, territorial, divine, or human—that should force one to abandon freedom. Let us not be afraid of this pathetic cliché. Whether this holds pathos or not, a man needs freedom as much as he needs the air he breathes and the water he drinks. The only object of our interests, the object of our politics, and the object of our death or life struggle, in view of the current Communist threat, is freedom within the limits humanity can achieve on earth. This is what is at stake.

If it were possible to convince the Communists of anything, to point out to them unequivocally that they are acting in an evil cause, one could continue the policy of negotiations and coexistence. But any discussion with the Communists is futile, since for them black is white and white black, which makes any kind of satisfactory conclusion impossible. The Communists engage in negotiations only with a view to breaking the resolutions made at these negotiations when it suits them. According to Lenin, coexistence is only a *peredyshka*, a pause to catch breath. Thus, there is no option but to switch from a position of negotiation to a position of strength. If it seems utopian to hope for other nations to agree to this, any other plan would seem to be much more utopian.

The errors committed by the Western powers vis-à-vis international Communism have been enormous. Their greatest error, however, is the one being committed at present, namely that they put their money on National Communism, as there is an allegedly spontaneous tendency on the part of the so-called satellite states to become independent from the center of international Communism. Such plans for the destruction of the Communist monolith would make sense only if they were to lead to a final liberation of those states from the Communist community. The tactical error in this case is that "national Communist separatism" is viewed in the same way as is a religious heresy. Or the dissident movements that are so highly praised. [Addendum of June 27, 1981.] The difference here, however, is that any religion, any faith and, therefore, any religious heresy must in the end have the support of the faithful masses, since it cannot maintain itself without such support. In the case of Communist splinter groups, in contrast, we are dealing with the games of a small clique of party leaders, cliques that do not have the support of the masses anywhere. All Communist régimes, wherever they exist, actually rule against the will of the population. Communist rule is imposed upon the population by force, fraud, and deceit. Once this force is undermined, the Communist system is bound to fall apart. The leaders of the various Communist parties are well aware of this fact—at least more aware than the West seems to assume—and do not forget it even when they are engaged in disputes among themselves and in intraparty struggles. They would be swept away in every country where the authentic will of the people got the upper hand. It is not possible to "win someone over" by promising him as a reward his own destruction.

Where did this hope for the "evolution of Communism" come from? Let us be quite open: it is the product of a situation that is not talked about and thus something that one can pretend to be ignorant of. Nevertheless, every sensible person knows that Communism cannot be overthrown by any means other than war. Since nobody wants war and nobody wants Communism, either, one should admit that policies thus far have led the world into a dead end. No self-respecting politician will admit, however, that he has led his constituents into a blind alley. It has therefore become necessary to conceive a device, an ersatz device, that would suggest a way out of the cul-de-sac and then to come to believe in this new way out. Hence, the old concept of the "evolution of Communism" was taken out of the attic, and people cling to it since it is the only alternative to war. The fact, however, that it may be the only alternative does not prove that it really exists. In reality, not only does it not exist, but, like every kind of self-deception, it weakens the resistance of those who are threatened and strengthens only those doing the threatening.

At this moment, the free world is still the stronger side, and this may be a source of authentic optimism, not the illusory optimism brought about by the everyday disinformation. The Communists themselves still give us a great chance of winning, since they frequently prove to be more stupid than their opponents and than one would expect of them. The stupidity displayed by banging a shoe against a lectern, the stupidity that we saw in the Pasternak affair, the stupidity that puts off those who do not want to be put off—this still offers us a substantial degree of protection, but for how long? Today the triumph of the Communist provocation is already incontestable in many areas of the ideological, political, and emotional fronts. And one may be justified in fearing that this triumph will be complete the moment the Communists become cleverer than they presently are. To forestall such an eventuality, we should, first and foremost, stop examining the mistakes of others and rather attempt to understand the errors of our own making.

The free world is also different from the enslaved world in that there cannot be too much discussion in it, too much exchanging of ideas on important matters. The merit of free thought is to be measured not only by its objective worth but also by its subjective sincerity.

There are some who question the correctness of the thesis that Communism constitutes a threat to the free world and who assert that this is only a slogan, a pretense that serves as a screen for other goals. It is impossible to deny that in many individual cases this may be true. But these particular cases should not prevent us from discerning the heart of the matter, namely that the international socialist system, as far as its actions and effects are concerned, could be best described—using human language, which is so deficient in exact definitions—as a psychological pestilence. This is not a new definition. After 1918, it was in common use in Russia; the "Bolshevik pestilence" was not just a term of abuse, however. Winston Churchill wrote, ten years later: "The Germans . . . transported Lenin in a sealed truck like a plague bacillus from Switzerland into Russia."[1]

There exists a widespread body of opinion that describes anti-Communism as an obsession of people who are not able to think in "sensible" and "realistic" categories; they are, as it were, affected by an incurable disease, and it is therefore a waste of time to treat them. We can only dismiss them with a shrug of the shoulders. This view of an alleged anti-Communist obsession has been created by political "realists" and intellectual conformists not only for their own use but also for the use of a large part of the petite bourgeoisie in different parts of the world, that is, of people whose daily interests and desire to conform are devoid of any fantasy. To those who ignore the warnings of anti-Communists and shrug their shoulders, I would recommend that they do a little thinking about an example such as that of Berlin and ask themselves:

Would it have been possible fifty years ago to find in Europe a single sane person who would not have regarded as the product of an unbalanced mind the prediction that, not in some distant Shanghai or on an island of horrors but in the center of Europe, in the middle of one of the greatest cities of the world, there would one day exist a border above all other borders, a wall dividing the meaning of human words, a wall bristling with machine guns? Would it not have been inconceivable that shots would be fired from this wall even at children on the street and that such actions would not be punished, that passers-by would be kidnapped as they walked along, that people would build tunnels like prisoners trying to escape from jail, and that all this would be happening under the eyes of the entire civilized world, which would regard this situation not as a state of war but as peaceful coexistence and that "cultural exchanges" would be carried out with the other side? Yet, today, the loss of perspective has gone so far that nobody is even surprised that the government of the same country whose capital has been divided by this wall, a wall previously unknown in history, is seriously considering the granting of billions of marks in loans to those who shoot from behind this wall! This is a situation that could never have been understood before World War One; it is not only without precedent, it is clearly fantastic. No, no man from our fathers' generation would have believed in the possibility of such a fantasy becoming reality.

Human nature has a great capacity for resignation and for adaptation to existing conditions, but no realism should deprive people of imagination, since then it ceases to be realism. A comparison of the habits of the world in 1912 and those in 1962 gives us some kind of basis for imagining, although not in concrete forms, to what kind of situation people will be forced to adjust "sensibly" in the year 2012! That is, if the center of the psychological pestilence has not been eradicated by then.

The death of half the human race in an atomic war is not the greatest catastrophe. The real catastrophe would be for all mankind to be living under the rule of the Communist system.

Perhaps the longed-for time will come when all this will be forgotten, when this book will have vanished into oblivion and Communism will have been eradicated from the face of the earth; when we will all return to old disputes that existed before Communism. This is how a great sickness passes; pestilence fades away into nothingness and not even a trace of it is left. And then people no longer remember and do not want to remember. But it also happens that the sickness does not disappear by itself and that a great effort must first be made to beat it into submission. It also sometimes happens that the sickness proves to be triumphant. I am writing in a time of great sickness.

Part Four **Let Us Hope . . .** [1982]

Attempts to define what is happening in the Polish People's Republic are rendered very difficult by the flood of disinformation, ignorance, and misrepresentation of the truth, the latter either unwitting or deliberate. We must include here not only the disinformation launched by the Communist headquarters in Warsaw and Moscow for political *tactical* reasons but also various kinds of nationalist wishful thinking by those nations under the control of Communism, which for their part confuse the governments of the free nations so far as their relations with the Soviet bloc are concerned.

Cardinal mistakes include:

I. The identification of the Soviet Union with old Russia, its traditions, aspirations, "spirit," and so on, in short, with "Russian imperialism." In actual fact, the opposite is the case: not only are the nature and aims of old Russia alien to the Soviet Union, but so also are the crucial characteristics of classical imperialism. The principle of every imperialist power is its exploitation of the conquered countries for the benefit of its own country (the metropolis) and its own people, while neither Russia nor Russians within the Soviet Union are reaping any benefits from the aims and activities of international Communism; they are rather its prime victims, not infrequently living in worse conditions than people in allegedly "colonial" countries, namely those that have been conquered by the Communist headquarters in Moscow.

This turning of reality topsy-turvy, so to speak, is, nevertheless, part of the nationalist program of the captive nations, which clearly seek not to overthrow the Communist system but to gain within that very same Communist system more rights and liberties of a strictly nationalist nature. An example of this is the frequently encountered slogan that Polish (Ukrainian, Byelorussian, and so on) Socialism (Communism) is not so bad, as long as it is not Russian.

II. International Communism, with its headquarters in Moscow, is not "imperialism" within the ordinary meaning of the word but an effort to dominate the globe, the whole world, all nations, in order to force on that world the totalitarian Communist system. Communism's aim neither was nor is Russification but is solely and exclusively the imposition of the Communist system on the world. We know the means employed to this end: infiltration, indoctrination, propaganda, both general and particular, all lead to this goal. This is the greatest danger to threaten the world since it began.

To define this threat as "imperialism," especially as the imperialism of only one nation, is not only to mislead world opinion but, above all, to underestimate the threat itself. Hence—indirectly—it is in Moscow's interests to exploit this definition in different ways for tactical purposes, and this is what it does.

III. International Communism in its present form is a kind of psychological PESTILENCE, and no national or economic factors have anything to do with this. Freedom, true freedom, can come only with the overthrow of Communism, with the destruction of the system, regardless of the language it uses. This destruction is not a prescription for solving any kind of problems concerning boundaries, nationalities, the economy, or other such matters in countries under Communist control. It is solely a prescription for the *restoration of freedom*. People will remain what they always were: "good" or "bad," but they will be free from the Communist threat.

IV. Does the world desire, is it striving for, the restoration of the freedom of pre-Communist times? That is the question we are all faced with. Sometimes it seems that the world does indeed desire this but is not striving for it. And this applies not only to the world that is still free, the so-called Western world, but—paradoxically—the Communist-controlled world, as well. There are different reasons for this. First of all, there is the psychosis of the fear of war (of so-called confrontation). The Western world has placed all its hopes on "the evolution of Communism," while the Communist-controlled world, that is to say, its political elite, backs the idea of an improvement in living conditions, but without bloodshed.

V. What the "opposition" in the People's Poland and other Communist-controlled countries is after is, doubtless, not the overthrow but the improvement of Communism. But these two outcomes are mutually exclusive. Stefan Kisielewski, my political adversary, who is regarded as a "dyed-in-the-wool oppositionist" and who now propagates the "Finlandization" of Poland as a political formula, once rightly noted that "one cannot simultaneously 'overthrow' and 'improve' the same thing."

There is no doubt that the Solidarity movement in the People's Poland never strove to overthrow Communism but to improve it, to improve both economic and social conditions. "More bread and freedom!" It was consistent in this. It accepted the dominant role of the Communist Party, as long as it did not depart from its Polish-Catholic version. And, anyway, it is impossible to strive for something ("overthrowing the system") if you call the very idea (counterrevolution, the use of force, and so on) "slander," "provocation," or the like. In its efforts to attain a "National Accord," the Solidarity movement was given full support by the Church, starting with Primate Wyszyński and ending with Pope John Paul II. And it was here that the lack of consistency became apparent, as well as a certain deceptiveness of words, slogans, gestures and comments, and the refusal to look reality squarely in the face—because with whom was this National Accord to be attained?

VI. I will again quote here a seemingly slight example. In one of his letters to Gorky, Lenin wrote: "God is a putrescent corpse, the stench of whose putrefaction is poisoning the whole world." He never withdrew that opinion, and everyone knows that to the end of his life he never changed it. The whole world also knows that Leninism or Marxism-Leninism is the highest aim and ideal of international Communism and that Lenin is its greatest prophet to this day. So the question arises whether the present Pope, who avoids uttering the word "Communism," knows about this letter of Lenin, about the real aim of every kind of Communism, which is the destruction of all faith in God. And so we have the paradoxical situation where, in the course of a demonstration of Solidarity workers in Gdańsk, in the Lenin shipyard, the Pope's portrait was hung on the wall next to the portrait of Lenin. Such an act should have been considered a grave insult to the Vicar of Christ, instead of which it was universally hailed as an act of homage to the Pope, evidence of the Catholic spirit of the workers and a manifestation of "oppositionist" aspirations to freedom. This is just one small example in a string of inconsistencies, confusion of ideas, etc., which we will not enumerate here.

Can something permanent be built on inconsistency and muddled thinking? I do not think so. And we must place in this category the belief that we can create a Communism that guarantees people their personal, political, or economic freedom, or any other freedom for that matter. Yet this belief continues, despite the obvious evidence, which has existed since 1917, that unless Communism is overthrown, it is of little use to dream of any kind of "freedom."

A CLASSIC PRECURSOR

Sixty years ago, we had a classic example of what is now happening in Poland, in the so-called Kronstadt Events (Kronstadt Revolt) near Petrograd, in March 1921.

People do not like analyzing these events. As early as August 1920, riots erupted in the Tambov Province (the Antonov Rebellion), followed by riots along the Volga and in the Ukraine, the Caucasus, western Siberia, and so on. Inflation and the economic crisis got worse. In January 1921, the Bolshevik government reduced food rations. In February, workers began to strike and demonstrate in Moscow. On February 23, there were strikes and street demonstrations in Petrograd (which had not yet been renamed Leningrad). Initially, the government mobilized flying units of Red Cadets, eventually declaring a state of emergency and at the same time calling on the workers to return to work. On February 27, leaflets appeared in the streets of Petrograd, printed by a Workers' Committee, with the following appeal to the workers: "Comrades! Preserve the revolutionary order. Demand the release of arrested Socialists and those workers who are not members of the Party! Demand the abolition of the state of emergency!"

On the following day, six thousand workers from the Putilov Works went out into the streets. The Bolshevik government managed to crush the demonstrations: it brought in soldiers and large detachments of militia. At the same time, the workers' food rations were increased. News of the events in Petrograd reached Kronstadt. The crews of the battleships *Petropavlovsk* and *Sevastopol* called meetings, which submitted all kinds of demands—but—without breaking with the system. These demands included, among others, "Power to the Soviets, independent of the Party!" And, at the same time, "Down with counter-revolution, both from the right and from the left!" The classic "Socialist" tone was maintained.

The protesters denied any connection with the anti-Communist counter-revolution and treated any suspicions of such a connection as "slander" and "provocation." They asked that "no blood be shed" and appealed for calm and solidarity. The Bolshevik government massed its troops. The revolutionary committee of workers and sailors replied with this manifesto: "Let it be known throughout the world that we are defenders of the power of the Soviets [councils] and that we are guarding the achievements of the Social Revolution. We shall either win or die!"

These slogans failed to draw the whole country into an uprising. They discouraged many people from participating in the movement. The Bolsheviks destroyed the worker-sailor "opposition," and its leaders fled to Finland. And the Western powers? . . . On March 16, 1921, Great Britain signed a trade agreement with the Bolshevik government, and on the same day Turkey signed a treaty of "friendship" with it, while, on March 18, Poland signed a peace treaty with Moscow. Earlier still, on March 8, at the Tenth Party Congress, Lenin proclaimed his famous manifesto introducing NEP. Then, as later, this tactical turnabout was considered to be "irreversible." Peasants joyfully returned to work "on their own land."

This "Communism with a human face" lasted for several years. Then there followed collectivization, expropriation, mass deportations of the "kulaks" to labor camps, and terrible poverty all over the country, as happens everywhere under Communist rule.

LENIN'S STRANGE DISAPPEARANCE

It is clearly a striking fact that present-day anti-Communist declarations, especially classic Western propaganda, contain very few, if any, pejorative references to Lenin and his Bolshevism, while there are plenty of references to Stalin, Stalinism, neo-Stalinism, and so on, as though all the evils began with Stalin and not with his predecessor, Lenin. Why is that? The reality was quite the opposite.

It was Lenin who was the first to introduce concentration camps, of which the most notorious was situated on the Solovki Islands. It was Lenin who ordered tsarist officers to be drowned in leaking boats in the White Sea. It was he who ordered the murder of the Tsar's entire family, including the children and faithful servants.

The time of Lenin's NEP, regarded as a prototype of "Communism with a human face," was also the time of the bloody rule of the Cheka and the GPU by a Pole, Dzerzhinsky. It was the time of the greatest religious persecutions:

thousands of adherents of the Orthodox, Catholic, and other denominations, priests and pastors, bishops and archbishops were murdered; churches were turned into warehouses or even into stables. There took place the show trial of the Catholic Bishop Cieplak and of the Vicar-General Butkiewicz, who were sentenced to death. Cieplak was subsequently released to go to Poland, while Monsignor Butkiewicz was shot in the cellars of the Cheka. At that time, the Moscow *Pravda* of March 31, 1923, published an article calling for a death sentence to be pronounced on the Pope as the fountainhead of all counterrevolution in the world. In that period, all the areas in the Bolsheviks' domain were engulfed by antireligious terror.

And today there is a sudden silence on the subject. The whole interpretation of events has been reversed in the West, more or less according to this formula: "good" Lenin overthrew the evil Tsar, but "bad" Stalin spoiled Lenin's work. The American Radio Free Europe broadcast in February 1982, with a certain note of triumph, a speech by the Spanish Communist leader Santiago Carillo, in which he denounced the introduction of the state of emergency in Poland and said that present-day Communism in Moscow "deviated from the ideals of the October Bolshevik Revolution." This sounds like a mockery. But then the Polish periodical *Poland in Europe* [Polska w Europie], published in Rome and undoubtedly enjoying the support of Vatican circles, in its issue no. 1 of 1982, quotes, alongside the statements of various episcopates, declarations in Poland's defense by Enrico Berlinguer, Secretary of the Italian Communist Party; Tetsuzo Fuwa, Chairman of the Presidium of the Communist Party of Japan; Kenji Miyamoto, Chairman of the Communist Party of Japan . . . stressing, in a benevolent tone, that: "The Communist Parties of Japan, Italy and Spain have shown their solidarity where Poland is concerned." So, is this an anti-Communist paper or a pro-Communist publication that enjoys "solidarity" with those parties? The information is communicated to the other, Communist-ruled, side, to hearten and encourage our fellow countrymen. And, incidentally, this is also in line with the stance of the whole of the so-called West.

This stance can be explained in two ways. First, in the West the term "revolution," any revolution, is customarily treated as a positive concept. The term "counterrevolution," any counterrevolution, is treated as a negative concept, even as an insult, particularly in the United States, which regards its secession from Great Britain in the eighteenth century and the establishment of an independent country in America as a "revolution." The same applies in Europe, where it has been accepted that the Great French Revolution was the beginning of a new, progressive era. And so, in the current policies of the so-called free

Western world with regard to Moscow, the policy is not to overthrow Communism (that would be counterrevolution!) but to place one's hopes on *evolution,* on "real Socialism," on a search for allies on the left, and especially for "opposition" among the Communists themselves, that is, in Euro-Communism, in Red China, and so on. But one cannot seek Communist allies under an anti-Communist banner or besmirch the prophet-figure that Lenin represents for all Communists. One can, however, denounce Stalin and "neo-Stalinists" who have "distorted Lenin's teachings."

Hence, the terms "counterrevolutionaries," "Red Fascists," and so on are used in broadcasting as words of abuse in relation to Moscow; likewise, " General's [= Jaruzelski's] junta," "neo-Stalinists' junta," "party conservatives," "gang of Red reactionaries," and other such epithets are used in connection with the Polish state of emergency introduced by Jaruzelski. But it would be unthinkable to brand them, for instance, "a Bolshevik gang"!

And yet this would be a more exact description. General Jaruzelski is neither a traitor, as he is called in some émigré circles, nor an eighteenth-century Targowica conspirator, which anyway sounds ridiculous when transferred to modern times. Jaruzelski is simply a Communist. He would be a traitor if he betrayed the Communism he serves. And this is precisely what many dissidents and oppositionists are incapable of understanding. Despite all the lies and tactical twists of Communism, a certain moral strength of the Communists is indicated by their sincerity. Similarly, among the writers in the People's Poland, Jerzy Putrament is sincere in his stance. I knew him before the war; he has always been a Communist, and he remains one. What he writes is against everything I stand for, but I know it is sincere, while the pleiad of contemporary writers, with their convolutions, understatements, self-censorship, adaptation to "national conciliation," and so on, is full of inward mendacity; they are writing not out of innate sincerity but out of concern "not to go too far" in speaking the truth, not to "stick out one's head" too much, concern to conform outwardly. That is their weakness. They include both people with an anti-Communist past and former Communists who have gone over to the "dissidents."

Neither the West nor the opposition movements within the Soviet bloc—largely manipulated by the party—are fighting or wish to fight Communism as such.

"PREVENT BLOODSHED!"

This is the most prevalent slogan all over the world, particularly emphasized by the supreme moral authority represented by the head of the Catholic Church —prevent bloodshed in the struggle against Communists.

I live in Germany, and I came across a tiny newspaper notice quoting some German statistics: last year, that is, in 1981, 11,800 people were killed and 470,000 injured in road accidents in the Federal German Republic, and, of the latter, a considerable percentage subsequently died in hospital or suffered permanent injury. This is not the place to quote and analyze comparative statistics. This is the situation in one not very large European country. But what about the world as a whole? Such figures, provisionally rounded off, would come to millions. And added over ten years, for instance, would amount to. . . . It would, of course, be unreasonable to expect the Pope or any other moral authorities to condemn the development of motoring in the world or to demand its abolition. But one can imagine the uproar that would begin if as many people lost their lives in the fight against Communism as in traffic accidents. And yet the domination of the world by Communism seems an infinitely more important matter than the development of motoring. People may justly laugh at this comparison, but it does show that the concern is not for the loss of blood as such, but for the cause in which it is spilled.

And the same applies to the condemnation of war. Any war, it is said, should be condemned. But not every war is. In 1979, Philip Van der Est, a well-known British journalist, produced a lengthy work that included the statistics on murders committed by the Communists. According to this work, starting with the year 1917, that is, with the "Great October," Communists have murdered 143 million people. That is many times more than Hitler managed to murder. (Let us note, incidentally, that, in tsarist Russia, barely 997 people were executed in the period between 1821 and 1906.) But it would be difficult to imagine the Pope and moral public opinion nowadays describing the war against Hitler as a crime. Of course, it is unimaginable. Everyone will agree that it was a just war and that without that war Hitler's Nazism would have continued on its path of destruction. In that case, then, why should war against Communism be a crime? It seems to me that any war against a criminal régime is a just and proper war.

Anyhow, it is impossible to eliminate wars from human existence. During the past three hundred years, we have had only sixty war-free years. And, since

1945, that is, since the end of the most recent World War, there have been forty wars in various parts of the earth.

A super-bogey has been invented: nuclear war, capable of destroying our planet. After every new invention, beginning with a new type of bow, through artillery, machine guns, and poison gas, there have been prophecies that the age of war would end because war had become too destructive. None of these predictions proved to be true. Hiroshima continues to be regarded as a deterrent, but no mention is made of the fact that during the Second World War the bombing of Dresden by the Allies with ordinary bombs dropped from the air created four times as many victims as Hiroshima. Nothing is said, because . . . it would not do to say such things.

In fact, this "it would do/not do to say" constitutes a great hindrance to our intellectual development in general and to our political development in particular.

ONCE AGAIN: THE TRUTH TURNED UPSIDE DOWN . . .

The Soviet Union is presented as being a great military power (armed to the teeth). But the reality is quite the opposite: the Soviet Union must surely be the weakest power in history. There have been all kinds of powers, but never one where 90 percent of its population desired its downfall.

Anyone who lived through the last Soviet-German war and saw with his own eyes what went on at the beginning. . . . No, it would not do to talk about it out loud. Because Hitler's invasion of the USSR in June 1941 was universally welcomed by the entire population, including especially the Russian population, as a "liberation." But anyone who declared himself for Hitler is "bad" in the eyes of public opinion, so to quote this example is also "bad." I shall not cite examples that are generally known and recorded in numerous published works: entire Soviet armies surrendering and going over to the invader, whom the population welcomed with bread and salt. The number of POWs during the first few months reached the incredible total of several million. And yet Hitler lost the war.

We know Hitler and his system of countless crimes. However, his boundless stupidity and the stupidity of his system and his political ideas are less well known. Before he crossed the Soviet borders, he could have been sure of victory. And he did everything to relinquish this victory. Hitler did not fight Communism. He is a prime example of this "nonstruggle." He fought nations and "races." He considered not Communism but the Jewish race and the Slavonic nations to be the enemy. For him, Bolshevism was a creation of the Jewish race, and he treated the people of Eastern Europe as subhumans. Being himself a revolutionary and, above all, a National Socialist, he hated any counterrevolution—or, for that matter, any "right-wing movement"—with all his soul. He stated many times that German soldiers were fighting the Soviets in the East not to create a counterrevolutionary situation in Russia. He compared the Russians to "mud people." And so the "liberation" they expected turned into a bloody suppression of human dignity. He turned the "liberation" into his own defeat. But, in spite of that, there were still millions of people (1,800,000 Russians, Ukrainians, Byelorussians, Baltic peoples, inhabitants of the Caucasus and the Don, Central Asians, and so on) who stayed on Hitler's side, the anti-Soviet side, fighting to the end, such was their hatred of the Communist system.

And there really is much of this "Hitlerism" nowadays in the attitude of the so-called West (not excluding Poland), in its view of the Soviet bloc. People wish to see not Communism there but "Russia" and the "Russians." Yet the destruction of that bloc depends not on military force but on the strength of political propaganda. There is a ready-made formula: take the example of Hitler's policy and do everything opposite to what he did . . . namely, change the role of invader into that of an authentic liberator.

But, even from the purely military point of view, the Soviet Union is many times weaker than the West. The Stockholm International Peace Research Institute recently published some results of its studies in the periodical *L'Est*. These constitute a detailed analysis of all the strategic zones, types of weapons, and so on that had been compared with those of the West. It proves that on land and sea and in the air, the Warsaw Pact is militarily one-fifth as strong as the Atlantic Pact, and not vice versa, as people usually prefer to present it. And that is taking everything into consideration, including atomic weapons.

Thus, the Soviet Union and its whole bloc is a power that fears open war ("confrontation") most of all, since, given that the free world makes a correct assessment and then applies a correct policy, the Soviet bloc will disintegrate into splinters in the first clash of war. And the whole offensive, the psychological network of Communism that now entangles and threatens the globe, will disintegrate as well.

A SIMPLE CALCULATION

International Communism reckons simply: why risk war (doom), when it is possible to dominate the world without a war, using one's bare hands, so to speak? Hence, the entire offensive plan of the Communists is closely intertwined with their plans for defense. We know all about infiltration, indoctrination, disinformation, about Communists seizing control of influential groups in the free world, of all kinds of leftists, "progressives," pacifists, and so on. As early as the twenties, the provocation known as the "Trust" was intended on the one hand to sow the conviction in the West that there were great, internal, "evolutionary" changes taking place in the Soviet Union and on the other hand to warn against a war that would annihilate these changes and reinforce the uncompromising nature of Communism. Since then, hopes in the free world of Moscow's evolution have not ceased, given the excellent support of various "dissidents" who are manipulated by the Soviets. Communist Peace Congresses became famous after World War Two. They recruited all and sundry, especially among intellectual "progressive" Christians. Nowadays, they are no longer required, since following the Second Vatican Council successive Popes have made PEACE the supreme virtue and raised it to the level almost of a holy canon: anything but war! Anything but bloodshed! Not only in an external war but—God forbid—in an internal counterrevolution! This is why a "nonantagonistic opposition" in the Communist countries was launched on a grand scale and in a new edition. This kind of opposition strives for an evolutionary improvement of Communism but rules out its overthrow by force. It began in the Soviet Union itself, back in Khrushchev's time. The first pieces of "samizdat," which even included the addresses of their authors and editors, which made them semi-overt publications, became renowned throughout the world. Their significance was all the greater because they simultaneously confirmed the West in its belief that the Communist bloc was undergoing the EVOLUTION that everyone had dreamed of, the "evolution" that was the alternative to war and even excluded its possibility. In this way, such "oppositionists" as Sakharov and Solzhenitsyn gained fame and were followed by a whole galaxy of others. All the famous Sakharov hearings organized in the West were distinguished by the fact that, despite their alleged anti-Communism, they heard only the "innocent victims of the Communist system" but not, as a rule, the enemies of Communism. ("It's the latter's own fault if they are subjected to repressive measures.") Solzhenitsyn, who was allowed abroad with his whole family and archives, reached the summit of his fame in the West. His activity consisted precisely in propagating from the very peak of "anti-Communism" three theses of the utmost importance to Moscow: (1) that the West was rotten and incapable of fighting (it was Lenin who said that the West was "ready to sell even the rope for its own neck just to make money"), so it was useless to count on the West; (2) that Communism was a great military power that, as he said, did not even need the atomic bomb because it could destroy the West with its bare fists! (And the West was frightened out of its wits.); and, most important, (3) that the only way to fight Communism was through a spiritual transformation, love of truth, prayer to God, but never, as he wrote in his *Gulag Archipelago*, "with dagger, sword, or gun"! Moscow needed these three theses. To use Lenin's expression, Moscow could "spit on" all Solzhenitsyn's other words (and some of them were excellent). Obviously, all this would have no significance if it were propagated by a Soviet agent. Its significance lay precisely in the fact that it was proclaimed by someone regarded as an "apostle of anti-Communism."

This same line and pattern were followed by other nonantagonistic "opposition" movements in the Soviet bloc and elsewhere, in the first place by the so-called Euro-Communism.

The very name itself is indicative of a major disinformation ploy, because Marx and Engels and Lenin himself were all born in Europe, and present-day Communism is neither Asian, nor African, nor American but something that has been grafted there from Europe. Communism has always been "Euro-Communism." Lenin taught the methods of spreading it and of applying the tactics of "anything, so long as it's effective."

Naturally, there was no "invasion of Czechoslovakia" in 1968, nor any application of the so-called Brezhnev Doctrine. It was not in accordance with the new doctrine of Brezhnev but in accordance with the old one of Lenin—likewise in Hungary, in Gomułka's Poland, in Romania, earlier still in Yugoslavia, and, finally, in Jaruzelski's present-day People's Poland, with its "state of emergency."

A word of reservation is in order here. Such partly manipulated nonantagonistic opposition movements are not the work of the KGB or other security services, as is generally held. Police forces in the Communist system have minimal freedom of initiative. This is understandable in totalitarian systems: the party rules everything. If some contacts do occur between the party and certain "oppositionist" activists, these take place only on the basis of a secret agreement between the party headquarters and the leaders of those movements for the purpose of some previously determined compromise. Again, this does not mean that everyone can see where this is leading or is supposed to lead. On the contrary, 90 percent of those who take part in such opposition movements undoubtedly do so in good faith and in the profound belief that this is what should and must be done.

This is the case with today's "Solidarity" in the People's Poland, which recognizes the primacy of the Communist Party and denies any aspirations for the overthrow of this party or for any political role for itself.

WILL "QUANTITY BECOME QUALITY"? . . .

Marx taught us that it will. Please God, he will be proven right.

So far, it has suited Moscow to have "opposition" movements in the Soviet bloc that deny any counterrevolutionary tendencies, since their activities are aimed at improving, not weakening, Communism. But we are all human. The Communists who strive for world domination are only human, too. And errors and miscalculations are human. If they become widespread, if they slip out of the control of their Communist controllers, the internal upheavals in the Soviet bloc might suddenly change from quantity to quality. Given favorable circumstances outside, they might even lead to the overthrow of Communism. Imponderables play an important role in the lives of people and nations, in the concatenation of various historic circumstances. An "opposition" in some measure manipulated by the party, growing in numbers, might suddenly change into a huge collective cry: "Doloy sovetskuyu vlast'!," "Down with Soviet rule!" Down with fraternizing with the Communists, down with this game of mutual understanding and national solidarity in the name of "state interests"! This cry, rising like a storm, will fly across frontiers and embrace everyone, not for the sake of "national reconciliation," or "social reconciliation" but to eliminate the pestilence of Communism from society—a cry that will restore common sense to the captive and oppressed and to those who are still free.

Let us hope that it is still possible for this to happen.

Józef Mackiewicz: His Life, Work, and Views

This chronology provides biographical information on Józef Mackiewicz and elucidating quotations from his writings and the writings of others. Extracts by Mackiewicz are followed by the year of publication in parentheses, with a full source citation in the Notes section. Extracts by others have just a source citation in the Notes.

1902

Józef Mackiewicz was born in St. Petersburg on 1 April (19 March Old Style) 1902, and his birth certificate described him as being "descended from the Wilno (Vilnius) Province landed gentry." His father, Antoni, was a co-owner and director of the "Fochts and Co." wine importing partnership. His mother, Maria, née Pietraszkiewicz, came from Cracow [Kraków].

> Poland has often been called Russia's Ireland, and there was, indeed, a great deal in common in the relationship of these two countries with the dominant nation—the religious controversy, the historical conflict, the ruthlessness of domination. On the other hand, it had never been Great Britain's policy to develop Ireland's industry, whereas Poland became one of

the more industrialized regions of the Russian Empire and had, on the whole, a higher standard of living than Russia itself. Besides, its Roman Catholicism drew it culturally into the Western orbit as much as the Orthodox Church linked Russia with the South-East of Europe. All this enhanced Poland's sense of cultural superiority over Russia and made it view Russia with a contempt embittered by the knowledge of its helplessness. Nevertheless, the Polish nobility continued sending their sons to Russian élite schools and Guards regiments and accepted the highest posts in the Russian administration and at the Russian Court, where they were much admired for their polished manners and their westernized elegance. Warsaw was regarded as a kind of Slav Paris, where Russian ladies with means to do so liked to order their dresses. To every Russian, Poland was, after all, "Europe"—or very nearly. For, to Russians, "Europe" was less a geographical fact than a cultural concept in which they never dreamt of including themselves. If they ever said about a compatriot that he was "a European," they invariably meant it as a term of praise, connoting probity, good manners, education, and a reasonable attitude to life.[1]

1907

The Mackiewiczes moved to Wilno. Józef spent his childhood surrounded by a large family, which subsequent events divided into Poles, Lithuanians, and Bolsheviks, separating them for good by state borders and to an even greater extent by ideologies. The husband of one of Mackiewicz's cousins became a foreign minister in the nationalist Lithuania, and the husband of another cousin became the head of the GPU in Minsk.

> In the very old days, that is, before 1914, we almost never used the word "cousin": we would say "a sister once removed." The common folk, then called "the ordinary people," would just say "a sister," and that was it. The husband of a sister once removed was, therefore, a brother-in-law.
>
> It happened that this daughter of my aunt was, for us, the nearest, that she was loved and liked more than any other. Fair-haired, with blue eyes and an oval face, she grew into a beautiful girl. Katarzyna.... Of course, it must have been my aunt's calamitous husband, and her own father, who drew her into the Bolshevik sphere. Before the Great War, he was a doctor practicing in Wilno, a sometime army doctor; but he was not much in demand because the treating of people occupied him less than the treatment of a political and social system. For he was an atheist and socialist; I do not know whether he was a Bolshevik before the October Revolution, but he certainly was after it.
>
> He played some part at the time of Lit-Biel [Lithuanian-Byelorussian Soviet Socialist Republic], that is, the attempt to unite Lithuania and Byelorussia into a Grand Duchy in the Bolshevik style.... He had a post of some sort in the Lithuanian

branch of the Comintern. They all became victims of Stalin's purges. I am not sorry for them. I am sorry only for Katarzyna, and this is why I will write about her no more. . . .

I had heard before Besedovsky's revelations were published about the significant role which my brother-in-law had apparently played in the abduction of Savinkov.[2] A year after Savinkov was seized, the Bolsheviks managed, by way of the notorious "Trust," to entice and abduct another great enemy, a former agent of the Intelligence Service, Captain Sydney George Reilly. . . . Apparently, Romuś Pilar had a hand in the Reilly abduction scandal, too. . . .

My brother-in law—let me keep this designation to the end—Romuś, that is Baron Roman Pilar von Pilhau, a well-known agent and head of the Minsk GPU, was liquidated during Stalin's purges.

I am not going to wring my hands over Stalin's crimes for this reason, as the contemporary political fashion dictates, nor am I going to demand that yet another Bolshevik be posthumously "rehabilitated." (1964)[3]

1910

Mackiewicz became a pupil at the Winogradow school, which offered a classical education.

These were the times of captivity.

Everyone was enslaved: the children of Mr. and Mrs. X and those of Mr. and Mrs. Y came from Polish homes and this is why Polish speech, Polish laughter, and Polish joy resounded at the ice rink, while janitors in Russian peaked caps addressed them: Master Kazio, Master Józio, Master Henio, or Miss Jadzia. . . .

Kolya, Petya, and, the youngest of them, Masha Morkhov lived not far from the ice rink, but they did not come with skates. Their father was a minor railway clerk, Russian and Orthodox; he did what he could, working in order to educate his children, and the boys were at a school which taught science. So they would only come and look from afar. Once Kolya brought skates and stood, holding them now in one hand in a woolen glove, now in the other; he stood thus for an hour or so, devouring the rink with his eyes, until he became cold and went home. The ice rink was private. Quite understandably, it would not do to admit everyone. The Morkhov children did not belong to polite society, no one invited them, and no one would talk to their parents. These were the times of the bleak Russian captivity, so the Polish children had to enjoy themselves, if only on the ice rink, isolated from the "East." Kolya, Petya, and Masha stood far away, beyond a fence; in fact, no one prevented them from looking on. The children of Mr. and Mrs. X and those of Mr. and Mrs. Y were brought up well enough not to allow themselves any teasing remarks or jokes. . . .

Mrs. Morkhov was in this instance merely a mother. She did not dare to enter the drawing room, when invited nonchalantly by the maid, but remained in the hallway, and this was proper. Mrs. Morkhov could at most have been seen in the study.

She came to ask whether it would not be possible for her children to use the ice rink at least occasionally, at least on Sundays. She apologized that her Polish wasn't good. . . .

The lady of the house, with the genuine kindliness of well-reared people, said, of course. If the children have no other . . . naturally, always . . . She spoke Russian badly, so the conversation could not last long. She proffered a piece of paper and extended her hand.

"Ochen', ochen' blagodarna" [Most grateful indeed]. . . .

We spoke Russian well enough, and there, among the old trees of the park, in the frosty air, the cries of joyful children were heard more often than precise phrases in the languages of two nations, of which one ruled and the other was oppressed; in addition, the Russian language would occasionally be permitted. (1935)[4]

1914

Antoni Mackiewicz died.

In its origins, the First World War had nothing to do with Polish problems. It was born of German rivalry with France, Britain, and Russia and from Austria's troubles with Serbia. But the outbreak of hostilities in August 1914 automatically breathed fresh life into the Polish Question. For the first time since 1762, Berlin was at war with St. Petersburg. The solidarity of the partitioning powers, scarcely ruffled during the nineteenth century, was broken at last. For the first time since the Napoleonic period, the Polish lands were to be turned into an international battleground. In Silesia and Galicia, and later on in Byelorussia and Polesie, the Eastern Front was to bring the Polish people into direct contact with the conflict, and with all the ideas and horrors of the day. For the first time in history, mass conscript armies were to be raised by each of the three Empires. Unprecedented demands were to be made on the civilian population, straining their loyalties to the utmost. The Polish lands were not merely the theatre of operations. They were the area where Russia and the Central Powers were forced to compete for the minds and bodies of their Polish subjects.

As the prospect of an early verdict receded, each of the contestants felt obliged to outdo its rivals in the lavishness of the promises which each hoped would win Polish support. In 1914–16, the Tsar, the Kaiser, and the Emperor-King proposed mounting degrees of autonomy. By 1917, the President of the United States, the Provisional government in Petrograd, and even the leader of the Bolsheviks declared themselves in favour of Polish independence. In 1918, they were copied by France, Italy, Japan, and, last of all, Great Britain. Most of these declarations were pious invocations, with no chance of implementation by the men who made them. The Germans alone were in a position to turn their words into deeds but failed to do so very effectively.

Yet the spectre of independence, once raised, could not be laid. Over the four years of the war, the political atmosphere was transformed. The habitual disillusionment of previous decades was gradually replaced by a vague but fervent expectancy. Among the Poles themselves, optimists felt elation at the tempting prospects which the fickle fortunes of battle presented. Pessimists felt appalled at the certainty that fratricidal slaughter was unavoidable. There were tens of thousands of young Poles in each of the armies.[5]

1915

On 5 September, the Germans took Wilno and occupied it until January 1919. The Winogradow school was evacuated to Moscow. Mackiewicz became a pupil of a Polish school organized by Stanisław Kościałkowski, a renowned historian, who later became a professor at the Stefan Batory University in Wilno.

1918

In October of that year, I was still in Wilno. A febrile atmosphere already prevailed. No one could sit still on a school bench. The colored caps of the Dowbor Army soldiers were seen everywhere, and their spurs resounded. On October 20, some disturbances occurred and ended in bloodshed. German soldiers and policemen smashed standards and banners. A thousand-strong crowd in Cathedral Square was dispersed by mounted police. Naked sabers shimmered in the sun of the fair autumn day. Right before my eyes, next to the Cathedral tower, a Dowbor man, Czyż, fell, ferociously stabbed with a bayonet by a Prussian rough, but he did not let go of the standard. (1925)[6]

The Polish Republic came into being in November 1918 by a process which theologians might call parthenogenesis. It created itself in the void left by the collapse of three partitioning powers. Despite Molotov's assertion, it was not created by the Peace of Versailles, which merely confirmed what already existed and whose territorial provisions were limited to defining the frontier with Germany alone. It was not the client state which the Allied governments had been preparing to construct in 1917–18 in collaboration with Dmowski's National Committee in Paris. It was not the state which the Bolsheviks hoped to construct as their Red Bridge with revolutionary Germany. And it was not the puppet Poland which Russia, Germany, and Austria had variously proposed in the course of the Great War. It owed its procreation to no one, not even to the Poles themselves, who, fighting with distinction in all the combatant armies, had been constrained to neutralize each other as a political force.

The collapse of all established order in Central and Eastern Europe condemned the infant Republic to a series of nursery brawls. In 1918–21, six wars were fought concurrently. The Ukrainian War, which started in Lwów in November 1918 and ended with the collapse of the West Ukrainian Republic in July 1919, established Polish control over East Galicia as far as the River Zbrucz. The Posnanian War with Germany, which erupted on 27 December 1918, was settled by the Treaty of Versailles on 28 June 1919, but the Silesian War, prosecuted intermittently through the three Risings of 16–24 August 1919, 19–25 August 1920, and 2 May–5 July 1921, was not settled until the Silesian Convention, signed in Geneva in 1922. The Lithuanian War, which disputed possession of the city of Wilno (Vilnius), began in July 1919 and continued in practice to the truce of October 1920; in theory, in the absence of a formal peace treaty, it continued throughout the interwar period. The Czechoslovak War, launched on 26 January 1919 by the Czechoslovak invasion of Cieszyn (Těšín) in abrogation of a local agreement, was terminated by Allied arbitration on 28 July 1920. Minor conflicts in Spisz (Spiš) and elsewhere in the Carpathians persisted until 1925. Gravest of all was the Soviet War, which alone threatened the Republic's existence. This was an ordeal by fire, which left an enduring mark.[7]

1919

On 1 January, a schoolboy, not yet seventeen years old, volunteered to take part in the war against the Bolsheviks. He served in the Tenth Cavalry Regiment of the Lithuanian-Byelorussian Division and was subsequently—at his own request—transferred to the Thirteenth Regiment under Major Dąbrowski. In this war, Kuban Cossack and Russian volunteers also fought on the side of Poland. Mackiewicz's association with them had an impact on his later literary work and his political views.

> The Polish-Soviet War had implications far beyond those which most textbooks allow. It was not related to the Russian Civil War, which proceeded concurrently on other fronts; it was not waged by the Poles as part of Allied Intervention in Russia, and cannot be described as "The Third Campaign of the Entente." For the government of Piłsudski, who preferred the Bolsheviks to the Whites in Russia, it was fought to maintain the independence of non-Russian areas of the former Tsarist Empire. For the government of Lenin, it was fought to re-create that Empire in socialist guise and to spread the Revolution to the advanced capitalist countries of Western Europe. It was caused in the first place by the Germans' withdrawal from the intervening zone of occupation, the *Ober-Ost*, in February 1919, and continued without a break until 12 October 1920.
>
> The Soviet War grew out of the first unplanned skirmish, which occurred at Bereza Kartuska in Byelorussia on 14 February 1919. In the first phase, in 1919, the initiative lay with the Poles. Piłsudski's home city, Wilno, was recaptured in April

and Minsk was taken in August. Yet, in the autumn, in spite of urgent pleas from the Entente, Polish support for the advance of Denikin's Whites against Moscow was expressly withheld. Peace talks miscarried owing to mutual suspicions over the future of the Ukraine. In 1920, the action expanded dramatically. Over one million men were deployed on a swiftly moving front stretching from Latvia in the north to Romania in the south. From January onwards, the Red Army was constructing a huge strike force of 700,000 men on the Berezina. On 10 March, the Soviet Command gave orders for a major offensive to the west under the 27-year-old General, Mikhail Tukhachevsky. But Piłsudski nipped these preparations in the bud. A sharp attack at Mozyrz in March, the daring march on Kiev launched on 24 April, and the fiercely contested Battle of the Berezina in May all served to delay the Soviet advance. Then, in the summer, fortunes changed. Budyonny's First Cavalry Army smashed its way through the Polish lines in Galicia in June, and on 4 July Tukhachevsky broke out from the Berezina. "To the West!" ran his order of the day. "Over the corpse of White Poland lies the road to world-wide conflagration." By the beginning of August, five Soviet armies were approaching the suburbs of Warsaw. The situation was critical. Allied diplomatic intervention had failed to produce an armistice. The frontier line proposed by the British government, the so-called Curzon Line, was rejected by Poles and Soviets alike. The British refused to give Poland military assistance despite their clear obligation to do so. The French declined to reinforce their small Military Mission. . . . A vociferous propaganda campaign, under the slogan "Hands off Russia," led world opinion astray at a time when Soviet Russia was laying violent hands on its Polish neighbour. . . . At the very moment when the enemy was pausing to deliver the final blow, the Polish Army re-formed in a manoeuvre of daring complexity. . . . Three Soviet armies were annihilated. The rest struggled eastward in total disarray. This was the "Miracle of the Vistula."[8]

The Germans evacuated Vilna on January 2, 1919, and local Polish authorities, reinforced by aid from Warsaw, took over the city. . . .

Polish control of Vilna was itself short-lived. Polish forces evacuated the city on January 5, and that night the Red Army moved in. Vilna now became the capital of the Lithuanian Soviet Socialist Republic, headed by two former Lithuanian Social Democrats. . . . This, too, however, proved to be only an interlude, and when the Lithuanian state proved not viable, the Communists merged it with the Belorussian Soviet Republic. Vilna then became the capital of the so-called Litbel Republic. In five months, the city had seen five different "sovereigns."

Although a scant hundred kilometers separated Vilna from Kaunas, the city to which the Lithuanian government had retreated, the Bolsheviks were unable to advance further. German aid enabled the Lithuanians to remain in Kaunas, and in February the Bolsheviks were themselves forced to retreat. . . .

On April 19, Polish troops entered Vilna, and, after three days of fighting, the city was under the complete control of Piłsudski's forces.⁹

Eighteen- and nineteen-year-old people were already rendered blasé by an atavistic fear of cavalry charges and bayonet assaults; trenches, lice, physical and moral dirt; in order to lift the spirits, and also because of the patriotic mood of the time, a lot was being said about the ups, but there was silence at the very beginning about the downs. But how unmitigated those downs were before the independent state emerged: one man lost the roof over his head, another got drunk and fell under the inn table; into cocaine, brothels, unemployment. When I recall the generations of outcasts on both sides of the Bolshevik border, all those Remarques who crawled out from under the barbed wire, both their own and that of the enemy and who were not destined to put together a single short story about that life. . . . (1960)¹⁰

1920

On 15 July, the Thirteenth Regiment covered the retreat of the Polish Army from Wilno, which had fallen to Budyonny.

Europe first became acquainted with the Vilna question in the summer of 1920. . . . The question, simply stated, concerned the possession of the city of Vilna and its environs. The Poles asserted that the city was Polish in culture. Lithuanians claimed it as their historic capital. There were also other interested nationalities: the Jews, a self-conscious and aware group who formed a large part of the city's population, and the Belorussians, who could probably claim a majority of the peasants in the surrounding countryside but who had a relatively weak consciousness of their national identity. Nor should one forget the Germans and the Russians. German troops had occupied Vilna from September 1915 until January 1919, and in 1920 Berlin still had a strong interest in supporting the Lithuanians against the Poles. In Moscow, the Bolsheviks were now assuming the role of legal heirs of the Tsars, the rulers of Vilna from 1795 to 1915. . . .

The heart of the matter lay in the confusion as to what, by 20th-century standards, could properly be called "Lithuanian." An ancient and distinctive Lithuanian language existed, studied by philologists for keys to the mysteries of Indo-European linguistics. A modern nationalism had now developed, based on that language, and its exponents claimed to be the heirs of the medieval Grand Duchy of Lithuania.

The boundaries of the Grand Duchy, however, had extended far beyond the territory now encompassed by the Lithuanian language. . . .

In the 1860s, "Lithuanian" was more a territorial designation than an ethnic one. A Pole from Vilna would call himself a Lithuanian in order to distinguish himself from the Poles of *Korona,* i.e., of the Polish Kingdom. . . .

Western observers in 1921 and 1922 noted the absence of any particular national consciousness on the part of the rural population of the Vilna region, but such comments still provide no assurance that the Lithuanians could "reeducate" this population in the spirit of Lithuanian nationalism. Given the mixture of languages in the region, the population could just as easily become ardent Belorussians or Poles. . . . Nevertheless, the Lithuanian nationalists could not conceive of a Lithuania without Vilna as its capital.

The Lithuanian nationalists of the early 1900s were working to reverse a trend of centuries, not only in Vilna but throughout the entire region which they claimed. . . .

Although the Lithuanians at times seemed to be aware that history was working against them, for the most part they insisted that their task was the "reestablishment" of the Lithuanian state. . . .

The Lithuanian nationalists faced formidable hurdles. . . .

Since Lithuanian was generally the language of the peasantry, and since the landed nobility in Lithuania was mainly Polish in culture, national conflicts merged with social and economic conflicts as the Lithuanian nationalists called for land reform. . . .

On the eve of World War I the Lithuanian national movement, while growing, remained relatively unknown even in St. Petersburg. The Lithuanians' claims to Vilna, moreover, were virtually a secret, shared only by the nationalist intellectuals and their Polish opponents. To the casual observer, Vilna appeared to be a Polish city. Its architecture, showing Gothic, Baroque, and classical influences, testified to its historic ties with the West. The city's administration was in the hands of the Poles. Services in the city's many Roman Catholic churches were held in Polish. Lithuanian influences were not to be seen. When German forces first entered Vilna in September 1915, their commander referred to the city as "the jewel of the Polish crown."[11]

1921

The Treaty of Riga between Poland and the Soviet Union, signed 18 March, ended the Polish-Bolshevik War.

Mackiewicz began to read biology at Warsaw University. He maintained that it was precisely this subject which made him understand the absurdity of nationalisms.

> It is true that I suffer from atrophy of the sense of nationalism. For me, anti-Semitism and Philo-Semitism are equally alien, as much as any other phobia or philia with regard to any nation. Not that they are good or evil; they simply do not enter my tissues. My education and my imagination make me a biologist. I am surprised that people may devote so many years in their youth to general studies and to pro-

fessional studies and arrive at the most antiscientific conclusions on their completion. (1974)[12]

1922

His first literary work, "From the Depths of the Białowieża Forest," appeared on 2 September in the 28th issue of the Wilno daily publication the *Słowo* [The Word].

> There are now few places free from the human swarm. There are no woods and virgin steppes in this Europe, which smells of gases and airplane fuel; but there is still one spot—a demesne, at least apparently virgin, because if one looks at it from the top of a 60-meter tower, it appears as a huge billowing ocean of green treetops, it seems to be a country wild and free as the dream of a poacher... this is the Białowieża Forest....
>
> The Forest is vanishing! The Forest is no longer what it was in the past. In the shadows of the thicket a ruthless struggle continues between avaricious people and millions of tranquil trees. (1922)[13]

1922–1939

Mackiewicz worked on the *Słowo*, whose editor-in-chief was his elder brother, Stanisław. His journalistic interests were extremely broad, but he most frequently applied his ever-restless pen to the fight against the Polish authorities, who endeavored to annihilate the multinational and multifaith mosaics of the former Grand Duchy of Lithuania in the name of "Polish national interests."

> The bureaucratic ravenousness of our institutions does not know any limits or bounds. It alters, adapts, and amends everything which catches its eye. Orders, directives, announcements, and decrees shower various ideas from a true horn of plenty onto the heads of the unfortunate citizens. (1923)[14]

1924

Mackiewicz wedded Antonina Kopańska. The marriage broke up after a few years.

1930–1939

Mackiewicz tried to advocate a Polish-Lithuanian accord in order to restore the "Great Lithuania," which would, in an alliance with Poland, become a power capable of withstanding Soviet designs in the east of Europe.

Nowhere in the world are there two so diametrically opposing phenomena as the idea of a great state promulgated by Witold and the current raison d'état of the Republic of Lithuania. We can describe this fundamental difference as follows: Witold sought the support of Poland because his goal was a Great Lithuania, whereas nowadays Kowno [Kaunas] does not want a Great Lithuania because it does not want to be supported by Poland. . . . Indeed, Witold's Lithuania does not in the least resemble the existing Republic of Lithuania. Witold's idea was directed at "de-nationalization," at the destruction of nationalistic separatisms in the name of state interests, while the present Kowno tries to subjugate Lithuania's interests and limit it exclusively to the interests of narrow nationalism of a small part of Witold's state. (1930)[15]

1931

Pan Poseł i Julia [The Deputy and Julia], a comedy in three acts about the gulf between the private lives of politicians and their ideas of "moral improvement," written together with Kazimierz Leczycki, was staged by the Lutnia Theatre in Wilno.

1932

Mackiewicz's mother died.

1933

Mackiewicz met, and on 3 May 1939 married, Barbara Toporska (born in 1913), a journalist who worked on the *Słowo*.

With three colleagues, he co-authored a political novel, *Wileńska powieść kryminalna* [The Wilno Detective Story], satirizing an influential Wilno coterie. It was published by the *Słowo* in installments, then in book form, and published again by Kontra (London) in 1995.

1935

From the estate, from the stables, from the garage, park, the tennis court, or, more precisely, from the very veranda of the manor—800 meters to the border. When in the evening one plays bridge in the drawing room, when one listens to the radio or flirts rocking gently in a deckchair, or, when one is to return a ball in a game of tennis, it seems that one's hand will stop during a smash, that the racket will not hit the ball, because one wonders: how is it possible that 800 meters away lies a land which is the same, yet completely different, different as never before, mysterious, topsy-turvy, usurped, inaccessible, hungry, shackled, hostile? (1935)[16]

1936

A collection of Mackiewicz's short stories, *16-go między trzecią i siódmą* [On the 16th, Between Three and Seven], was published.

> Our paper is fighting Communism and all of the symptoms . . . which lead or may lead to it. I would like this fight to be unrelenting and therefore steadfast. In this fight we should not favor those who hid their heads under the student hats of "bourgeois" universities, nor those who conceal their faces in the red flags of organizations which are supported even by the so-called competent and authoritative circles. On the contrary, we also consider it our duty to reproach those "circles" for their tolerance, for their overt or covert patronage of that movement. Because this movement takes against any spiritual or material ideals, against the tradition of these ideals and against the basis of the outlook which we consider our own, good and purposeful, against the cultural achievements of generations, not only of our own people but of the whole of mankind.
>
> I said that I would like this fight to be unrelenting because I myself think that we wage it in too humane a manner, too leniently. . . .
>
> We should fight Communism to the death. . . . And in a fight to the death no handicaps are given.
>
> In a war against Communism it would be precisely the giving of handicaps on our part if we did not apply this equally dangerous weapon which is used by the belligerent "International": ruthlessness and obstinacy. . . .
>
> No stimuli born out of a non-Communist outlook, which taken together result in various forms of solicitous concern, exist in the mode of combat against us in which Communism is engaged. . . . In the Soviet Union, people are condemned for crimes which in the Christian outlook are good deeds. . . . Humanitarianism is fought against, and religion is persecuted.—The Communists see us as people who have no right to be treated on a par with them or to take part in any discussion. If they call us, as they usually do, "the White bandits," they are not consistent in this instance, because, in contrast to the age-old tradition and practice of the entire civilized world, they place bandits and criminals above political offenders.
>
> This is not a temporary method, nor is it a phenomenon of a period of transition. This is a wrought iron, unremitting system for the destruction of our world, for our eradication the way weeds are eradicated, without mercy or the respect which is due to adversaries in regular combat. . . .
>
> The Third International has not stopped the war, either in theory or in practice. The Communists subvert our life, destroy our industrial plants, stir up our villages, and wreck our state organism. This offensive is met here by a method of action worthy of another adversary but futile against Communism. A method hemmed in by a long line of handicaps, "bourgeois prejudices"—and this is indeed a bad method. . . .

> We should use the same wrought-iron, unremitting system . . . we should put the Communists below criminals, and we must not become soppy over a youth in a student hat or over a prewar Communist activist. We must not show a soft heart, allow any handicap, or make any compromise! . . .
>
> This is not any "eye for eye" teaching. God will forgive us. We are waging a war against Communism, and religions permit us to kill in war. And only such combat against a system of that nature, even if in the end it does not prove to be successful, will in any event be proportionate. (1936)[17]

1938

Bunt rojstów [The Revolt of the Marshes], a selection of reportage-articles written for the *Słowo* and printed there, was published in book form under the paper's own imprint.

> Mackiewicz's book is gloomy, but it contributes to the body politic in a most significant manner, as it fights falsehood, the cutting of corners and inertia. So many books that are meaningless and stupid are being published in Poland at present, but this first-rate analysis has not found a publisher! It will be attacked and greeted with silence, and well-known people will be called up against it. Famous writers will be summoned, along with common hacks, and, should arguments be lacking, derision will do, as never before against any book in the independent Poland. Because no book has been arrogant enough to state so much truth. And we are not in the habit of forgiving such things.[18]

> Blind bureaucracy, personal ambitions, raising the protective shield of state authority, the brain-idleness of officials, and people's obdurateness. The awful specter of a totalitarian system, which permeates, pervades, penetrates the thicket, the woods, the soul, the smallest matters, those most insignificant and least appropriate for a store of state energy to be spent on. (1939)[19]

1939

On 17 September, the Red Army invaded eastern Poland. Mackiewicz fled to Kaunas, the capital of Lithuania.

> The German-Soviet Treaty of Non-Aggression, drafted by the Soviets on August 20, was approved by Hitler on the very same day and signed in Moscow on August 23, 1939. The pact simplified Germany's options by removing haunting thoughts of a revived Entente in response to Hitler's planned military aggression against Poland. The secret protocol attached to the pact set the price the USSR charged for its benign neutrality in the forthcoming war: Bessarabia, Estonia, Latvia, and the better part of

Poland, up to and including half of its capital, Warsaw. . . . The Soviet side, its lesser military contribution notwithstanding, was the main author of all Russo-German documents sealing Poland's fate in the late summer and early autumn of 1939. Indeed, the final frontier between the USSR and Germany, quite different from that originally proposed in the August Pact of Non-Aggression, was drawn in the end according to Stalin's new wishes. Presumably unwilling on second thought to split ethnically Polish territories, and having changed his mind about the desirability of allowing the existence of a rump Polish state between Russia and Germany (because either might lead to undesirable Soviet-German friction), Stalin proposed that the Lublin voivodeship and the rest of the Warsaw voivodeship extending to the Bug River be added to the German share of Poland. In exchange, he wanted Lithuania. . . . The new territorial arrangements were finalized in the German-Soviet Boundary and Friendship Treaty signed by von Ribbentrop in Moscow on September 28.[20]

On October 10 *Pravda* carried a lead article about the conclusion of negotiations with the government of Lithuania that resulted, among other things, in the Soviets returning the city of Wilno and the neighboring area to Lithuanian sovereignty.[21]

On 28 October, the Lithuanian Army entered Wilno.

This, which once was a state, and subsequently a tradition of "The Two Nations," finally collapsed in the years 1920–1921. Afterwards, Polish-Lithuanian relations were unvaryingly stagnant: neither peace, nor war, until a well-known Polish ultimatum, after which a more or less normal neighborly coexistence followed. This was a very short period, interrupted by the outbreak of the Second World War. The Lithuanian Republic never renounced her claims to Wilno, at the same time begrudging Poland the ultimatum, so, when the balance was tipping decidedly in Germany's favor, one could have expected the Lithuanians to enter the Wilno region. Yet, this did not happen. In the Polish-German conflict, Lithuania stood emotionally on the side of Poland, and politically she was neutral. It seems certain, however, that in the event of a German failure, she would have openly sided with Poland and the Allies in order to recover Kłajpeda, which Hitler had seized. . . .

On 17 September 1939, when the Soviet Union treacherously assaulted Poland, Lithuania's stance did not change, but one could say that it assumed instead a form of chivalry rarely encountered in political relations between states. Both Polish Forces and civilians fleeing to Lithuania were received hospitably, despite years of altercations. Of the three Baltic states, Lithuania alone did not expel the Polish envoy and continued to recognize the sovereign Poland.

But events develop at a deadly pace. . . . The Soviets compel Lithuania by force into a "treaty of friendship," at the same time thrusting Wilno upon her, although she does not want it and tries to prevent this at all costs. She does not want it not because she has renounced any claims to it, and she tries to stop this from happening, not because she does not want Wilno but because the form of the treaty which was thrust upon her, along with Wilno, actually deprives her of sovereignty and puts her under the sway of the Soviets.

In Kowno [Kaunas], however, strict press regulations are in force, so nothing gets into the papers about what has been going on behind the scenes, about the dramatic negotiations in Moscow. . . . a small Lithuania, at the mercy of the Soviet colossus, accepts the treaty, puts on a brave face, hides the loss of part of her sovereign rights behind the official demonstration of joy because of the "recovery" of Wilno, and marches into the formerly Polish territory from which today . . . Soviet forces are retreating. (1947)[22]

Mackiewicz returned as soon as the Lithuanians entered Wilno, and, on 25 November, began to publish the *Gazeta Codzienna* [The Daily Newspaper], as both publisher and editor-in-chief. He strove for the character of the realm to be preserved, but, because of Lithuanian nationalism, which proved to be extraordinarily zealous, he had to battle against the draconian censorship and suspicions of Lithuanian officials.

At first it became clear to everybody that in a certain corner in the east of Europe, unless there is an independent Poland, neither an independent Lithuania nor an independent Byelorussia may exist. Well, nor independent Baltic states. This was indeed a case of organic connection. The only recipe for the future seemed, therefore, to be a return to the old idea of mutual support and common interests. I thought, when claiming rights to my legacy from the Grand Duchy of Lithuania (indeed, every man has this right with regard to his country) in its capital, Wilno, that this program would be both the only logical conclusion being drawn from the fatal mistakes made in the years 1918–22 and, first and foremost, the only decent resolution not in the interests of Poland but actually in the interests of Lithuania. To put it more precisely, in the interests of all the lands and all of the people inhabiting the area of the former Grand Duchy. This was to have been the ideological, or the ideal, premise of the *Gazeta Codzienna*. I am saying "was to have been" and not "was," because . . . the authorities of the Republic of Lithuania did not allow these ideals to spread. (1954)[23]

On 30 November, the Soviet Union attacked Finland and the Winter War thus began. Finland's heroic resistance against the Soviet aggression was reported in the *Gazeta Codzienna* under headlines in large print, despite constant clashes with Lithuanian censors who were afraid of annoying the Soviets.

I was at that time the editor-in-chief and publisher of one of two Polish papers in Wilno. Our worst enemy, common enemy, was doubtless the Bolsheviks. We were not behind the iron curtain yet, but already behind iron bars. Lithuanian public opinion held a rather correct view that, at this moment, it was firing not on the Maginot Line but closer, on the Mannerheim Line, which would directly decide the fate of all of us. The Lithuanian press still took the liberty of taking a more or less pro-Finnish stance, but we . . . were not permitted even that much! One day we were barred from placing news about Finland in a prominent place, so I ordered that Soviet news be printed in small type in a prominent place and Finnish news in a secondary position but set in bold. They prohibited the use of bold type for Finnish dispatches. They prohibited the use of the adjective "heroic" in headlines referring to the Finns. They prohibited any political articles on the subject of the Finnish war. If this was the attitude of the Lithuanians toward the cause which was after their own heart, you can easily imagine how restricted we were with regard to subjects which were not to the liking of the press control office! At first I kept petitioning the authorities and fighting against censorship. As a result . . . the Government in Kowno [Kaunas] decided to prevent me from editing any journal anywhere within the borders of the Republic of Lithuania. (1947)[24]

1940

In May, Mackiewicz was prohibited from publishing anything.

15 June—the second Soviet occupation.

Mackiewicz lived in poverty, working as a woodcutter and carter.

> Huge windows of railway stations, for years day and night viewing the city beyond the forecourt, in time becoming opaque with dust. In addition, on the outside a spider had spun its web, so I looked through it, as if through prison bars, on the most vile rally in which a crowd of people can take part: a submissive herd was cheering the loss of freedom and the arrival of a yoke and feigning joy. The justification was that the majority did not even know the reason for this rally. But they knew with all certainty and conviction that they were there and that they would take part in every subsequent rally, that they would not refuse their participation, humbly and submissively, in everything which would be required of the "working masses" in the future. Just to be included in these "masses." Otherwise there would be a threat of losing a job, of persecution, jail, hunger, the gates of the NKVD. The odious fear for a ruble in their pocket, for their own skin, milk for a child, the right to look at one's own yard, fear—the least exalted of human feelings—was a triumphal gate for the delegates returning from Moscow: the gate adorned with red flags. (1947)[25]

On the 14th and 15th of July 1940, Wilno and its vicinity (occupied by the Soviets for the second time since the beginning of the war) elected their respective National Assemblies (together with the rest of Lithuania, Latvia, and Estonia, which the USSR had invaded that summer). On 15 December 1940, local soviets were chosen in the Western Ukraine and Western Belorussia. Finally, on 12 January 1941, together with other Baltic states and Bessarabia, which had been swallowed during the summer of 1940, the Lithuanian electorate sent its representatives to the Soviet of the Union and the Soviet of Nationalities.[26]

I did not take part in the first Bolshevik election, nor in the second; never, never did I fly a red rag outside my house; never did I attend any meeting or rally, never did I march at any demonstration; I was summoned four times to contribute money to a loan [to support the Red Army—*editor*]—I refused. . . . I was on my own then, the only one in the parish . . . [among] people softened into jelly under Soviet rule. This is why I cannot stand it when one of those . . . today proffers political directions or civic admonitions and criticism, when, during the Bolshevik era, he unquestioningly walked in the first row, held a nicely paid post "in order to protect our assets," gave speeches here and there, contributed to this or that paper, and ran around with a star on his forehead or in his lapel. (1941)[27]

Sitting behind the windowpane of a café in this city centre, one was as if in a box in an incomprehensible theater. People on the sidewalk were going to and fro, and in the middle of the road Soviet trucks, flat, painted green, went in this and that direction, carrying other people, that is, those already seized. They went to various addresses indicated by the NKGB, took families marked on the list, or only some members of those families, proceeded to another house, passed each other by, went forth again. In this manner, one could see acquaintances, close and distant, people known by sight only, occasionally relatives. There were lots of people in the streets. As we went to this table in the café, so they went out at dawn, because it was safe in the streets. People were not yet taken from the streets. They were taken from homes at night, before dawn, from work at any time during the day. Everything that was happening was seen by everybody; the peace was kept, and there was a deathly stillness. Some bizarre form of order reigned in the usual Bolshevik chaos, and perhaps this was the least comprehensible thing. (1947)[28]

1941

22 June—the outbreak of the German-Soviet war.

In July, the German occupation authorities proposed that Mackiewicz edit a paper in Polish. He refused categorically.

In the *Goniec Codzienny* [Daily Herald], a paper published by the Germans in Polish, Mackiewicz placed a few texts, including "Moja dyskusja z NKWD" [My Discussion with the NKVD] and "Prorok z Popiszek" [The Prophet From

Popishki], which he later adapted for use in the novel *Droga donikąd* [Road to Nowhere]. These publications constituted the basis for the accusations of collaboration with the Nazis.

> I do not agree that the Germans are the worst enemy. The Bolsheviks are worse, because they are more dangerous to any nation. For the simple reason that no Pole can simultaneously be a German. . . . But every Pole can simultaneously be a Communist. . . . We fabricate reality, on occasion putting an equal sign between the German and Soviet occupations. The German occupation makes heroes of us, while the Soviet one makes filth of us. The Germans shoot at us, and the Soviets take us with their bare hands. We shoot at the Germans and lick the Soviet asses. There is thus no equivalence, but the opposite. I agree, however, that the alternative of seeking a concord with the Germans would be absurd. . . . It is the fact that the Germans fight the Soviets which makes the most effective pro-Soviet propaganda. If we were to seek a concord with them, we would, therefore, engage not in anti-Bolshevik but in pro-Bolshevik activity. (1968)[29]

1941–1942

He wrote a book about the Lithuanian occupation and the Soviet invasion, *Prawda w oczy nie kole* [The Truth Does Not Hurt]. The only extant typewritten copy was found in 2002 and was published by Kontra in the same year.

1943

In May, having been invited by the Germans and having obtained the permission of the Polish underground (the Home Army) authorities, he traveled to Katyń in order to witness the exhumation of the bodies of Polish officers murdered there by the Soviets. On his return, he gave an interview to the *Goniec Codzienny* [Daily Herald], headed "Widziałem na własne oczy" [I Saw This With My Own Eyes].

In the autumn he was a chance witness to a massacre of Jews in Ponary, which he later described in the reportage "Ponary-Baza" and in the novel *Better Not to Talk Aloud*.

1944

In May, he and his wife made their way to Warsaw in order to evade the second Soviet occupation.

> The time in our region when leaves begin to fall from trees is usually associated with the time of winds. When one walks with the wind, the leaves run behind; when one

is departing, quitting the country, they are as faithful doggies, which roll along the ground, accompanying one awhile for the last farewell; or as tamed birds, fledglings—russet, yellow, brown—comically and clumsily bouncing in an elongated flock and clinging to boots or to a trouser leg. The wind will blow, and the autumn leaves, in their childlike fervor, assume a demeanor which suggests that they had no intention of ever abandoning the exile but would indeed roll after him to the end of the earth, and they even daringly overtake him on the path. In particular, the maple leaves spin around on their bent legs and rustle so much that the path seems to be alive. You cannot trust them, however. The entire rabble will stop suddenly and lie flat in the mud. (1948)[30]

In Warsaw, shocked by the extent of the pro-Soviet mood and the optimism of the underground authorities, the Mackiewiczes clandestinely published three issues of *Alarm*, a periodical in which they argued that the defeat of Germany on the Eastern Front, before its surrender in the West, would quench all hope of the independence of any country in the East of Europe, including Poland, because they would all be occupied by the Soviets. This was obviously contrary to the policy of the Polish Government in Exile.

In the autumn, the Mackiewiczes reached Cracow, where he wrote a political tract entitled *Optymizm nie zastąpi nam Polski* [Optimism Won't Be a Substitute for Poland]. The pamphlet was discovered in 2005 and published by Kontra in the same year, along with two other political tracts, written in 1969 and 1976.

> There is no analogy between the German occupation of the years 1939–45 and the 1939–41 Soviet occupation. There is no analogy between the German method and the Soviet.—Against the Germans—there was a war. A terrible war, but a war. In this war, rightly or wrongly, the whole of Poland took part, and she had to draw conclusions from those barbarous conditions which Hitler had imposed upon her, and which he did not conceal but plastered on every corner and every entrance: murder, destruction, prison, camps. . . .
>
> There was a terrible stillness within the boundaries of the Soviet Union. There was no war. There was no blackout in anticipation of foreign bombers. There was no curfew. There was "joy." Placards and photos of smiling faces were displayed in the streets. Banners announced that we constantly thank Stalin for something or other. Processions marched with these banners. Everybody was addressed as "citizen." There was equality, monotony, and boredom. War communiqués were arriving from another world. In the streets there were no armored patrols ready to open fire. There were no announcements about those executed, and if somebody learned by chance

about the fact of an execution, he would keep this information to himself rather than repeat it to another. (1947)[31]

1945

18 January—the Red Army was approaching Cracow. The Mackiewiczes escaped "from liberation" to the West.

> We left Cracow, my wife and I . . . with one small suitcase, on foot, and later by various means, because we promised ourselves: "Never again under the Bolsheviks." After innumerable adventures we reached Vienna. (1974)[32]

> It was 18 January 1945. The only route from Kraków still left free led to Kalwaria [Calvary]. In the city, warehouses were already being broken into, German shops and canteens plundered. From Długa Street the continuous fire of a heavy machine gun was heard.
>
> I would have preferred to walk across this city with my eyes shut in order not to see those cheery faces. We were walking briskly. The snow was crunching, the sky became clear, the sun was shining. Faster, faster! The absurdity of this delight on the occasion of the Bolsheviks entering royal Cracow was breathtaking. The suitcase was not heavy, but it was hard to walk. The sun was warm, even though it was January, and drops of sweat were running down the face, under the collar, like insufferable ants. (1948)[33]

> War is war, and many of us bore it in trenches, in ditches, acquiring hemorrhoids on cavalry saddles, hid the head in a helmet and raised the shoulders when bullets swished, were afraid for themselves, with a subliminal sense of aversion to the necessity of movement, or found oblivion and defense in action and contraction. But the war against women and children, unleashed recently on every front, is terrible! Terrible not for humanitarian and rarefied reasons but because of its unwritten rules, which bind those who take part in it. The rules had previously been clear to the soldier. Let us take as an example something as natural as crawling: one concentrates in a single effort to do it more swiftly and nimbly. If a Bronek crawling on one's right, or a Wacek on one's left, got it in his back, let the stretcher-bearers or sawbones with red crosses worry about it. For me, a crater is what matters, a ditch, a tree, a haystack, and the distance of a hundred meters. But can a father crawl faster if his wife and child behind cannot keep up with him in this crawling? Why did the staff sergeant not lecture us about this in the barracks? Did he forget? Didn't he know? It was not in the rules? Aaaa . . . perhaps. Because at the present moment this is a thing of the foremost tactical importance, inextricably linked to defense, which is not the defense of oneself, nor is it a fear for oneself only. (1948)[34]

They reached Rome, where Mackiewicz, commissioned by the Research Section of the Second Polish Corps under the command of General Władysław Anders, prepared a white book about the Katyń crime, first published in 1948 as *Zbrodnia katyńska w świetle dokumentów* [The Katyń Crime in the Light of Documents].

> At the time of the Fascist republic, every Italian loved the Poles. That is to say, a prevailing majority of the inhabitants loved the Poles as enemies of the Germans, and the Fascist minority loved the Poles as enemies of the Bolsheviks. Unfamiliarity with the language would save from saying the wrong things. . . .
>
> In April 1945, when the great "liberation" occurred, the situation changed as if someone had cut butter with a sharp knife. The Fascists began to hate us as obvious allies of the democracies, and the rest of the Italians soon began to hate us as enemies of Bolshevism. (1948)[35]

An arbitration board of the Association of Polish Journalists cleared Mackiewicz of the collaboration charge.

The *Orzeł Biały* [White Eagle] in Rome published the "Ponary-Baza" reportage.

1946

Mackiewicz began to contribute regularly to émigré publications, including *Lwów i Wilno*, *Wiadomości* [The News] (from 1947), and *Kultura* (from 1951). His output over the forty-year period in exile is enormous.

1947

In April, the Mackiewiczes moved to London.

> The main question, the principal question, which no one wishes to ask in an "awkward" manner is: ought we to fight against the enemy, the invader, or not?
>
> Only the answer to this principal question may lead us to the secondary questions: along with whom? How? And when? . . .
>
> By the fight against the enemy I understand an open fight, and not one of circuitous references as pursued at present. A state of war against the invader does not imply, as some try to ridicule it, "an assault on the atom bomb with a stanchion." But it implies a moral stance which would restrain the present-day downward slide of the whole nation. . . .
>
> I cannot imagine how it is possible, in the long run, to educate the people politi-

cally without indicating an "awkward" border between concepts as rudimentary as "ally" and "enemy," "loyal" and "traitor," "our own man" and "enemy agent." Yet, we know from experience that the boundary between these concepts is becoming blurred. It is becoming more blurred day by day. And the so-called "opposition" in Poland, which calls a Moscow agent, Bierut, "the President of the Polish Republic," the Soviet occupation "the Reborn Poland," and the lands taken by the Bolsheviks for reasons of political strategy "Recovered Territories," is a classic tangent to that blurred boundary. (1947)[36]

1951

The Katyn Wood Murders, the first book on the subject, was published in English and translated into several languages.

1952

The U.S. Congress Select Committee to Conduct an Investigation of the Facts, Evidence, and Circumstances of the Katyń Forest Massacre heard Józef Mackiewicz in his dual capacity of witness and expert.

1955

The Mackiewiczes moved to Munich, where they remained until the end. They lived in poverty, on meager royalties.

He published *Droga donikąd* [Road to Nowhere], "a powerful, traditionally realistic novel on a most untraditional subject: life in Lithuania as it was being converted into a republic of the Soviet Union."[37]

Also that year, *Karierowicz* [The Careerist], a psychological novel, without political references, even though the story begins in the later stages of the Polish-Soviet war, was published.

1957

Kontra [Contra], a novel about the Cossacks, both citizens of the Soviet Union and political émigrés, who fought against the USSR in the Soviet-German War but were subsequently handed over by the Allies in accordance with the Yalta agreement, was published.

1962

Sprawa pułkownika Miasojedowa [The Colonel Myasoedov Affair] chronologically opens a great novel cycle, but it spans the entire period during which the other novels are set. It is the story of the well-known, at one time, case of Sergey Myasoedov, who was hanged in 1915 as a traitor, and the aftermath, until the bombing of Dresden.

> In my view, it was a crime to destroy Hitlerism along with the most beautiful German cities, which were subjected to devastating bombardment. Nazism should have been destroyed but cities left intact. (1955)[38]

At his own expense, Mackiewicz published *Zwycięstwo prowokacji* [The Triumph of Provocation].

> Those people who . . . secretly cherish illusions about the idea of Communism as "poorly accomplished but beautiful in principle" are unlikely to take to this anti-Communist manifesto by Mackiewicz.[39]

> This book destroys many Communist myths which, paradoxically, survived the fall of Communism. This is one of many reasons why it constitutes most instructive reading in the twenty-first century.[40]

1964

Mackiewicz's collection of short stories *Pod każdym niebem* [Under Every Sky] was published. Supplemented by a few short stories from the 1936 volume *16-go między trzecią i siódmą* [On the 16th, Between Three and Seven], it was republished in 1989, with an afterword by Barbara Toporska, under the title *Ściągaczki z szuflady Pana Boga* [Cribbed From God's Drawer].

> Perhaps there is still something for which a man's soul, weary of "mass culture," will unwittingly yearn. This is the longing for a life governed by the law of a one hundred percent "private man." There is no doubt that such a life is closer to paradise than any other. After all, God gave man free will. Therefore, do what you please. There is no question that this law has a reactionary, counterrevolutionary nature, but it provides the possibility of escape—if only in memories—from the collective of today. (1962)[41]

1965

Mackiewicz published *Lewa wolna* [Clear on the Left], a novel about the Polish-Soviet War of 1920.

1969

Mackiewicz published *Nie trzeba głośno mówić* [Better Not to Talk Aloud], an epic sequel to *Droga donikąd* [Road to Nowhere] and a panoramic view of the Nazi occupation and the maze of underground resistance networks that opposed each other as much as they fought the Germans. The largest underground organization, the Home Army, although linked to the Polish Government in Exile, facilitated the "liberation" by the Red Army.

1972

W cieniu Krzyża [In the Shadow of the Cross], a book analyzing the conciliatory policies of John XXIII toward Communism, came out.

> President Roosevelt, through his policies, helped to surrender half of Europe and half of Asia to international Communism. President Kennedy, by his policy of "peace," clearly aimed at the consolidation of the status quo achieved by Communism. Of all the American Presidents, Kennedy followed in Roosevelt's footsteps the most earnestly. Why should this fill us with such joy that after his tragic death we had to be in mourning?
>
> With regard to John XXIII, let us remember: the Communists murdered 55 bishops, imprisoned 109, expelled 90 from their dioceses; murdered 12,800 priests, imprisoned 32,500, forced 15,700 to renounce their ministry; they closed down 31,000 churches, 1,600 monasteries, 3,000 seminaries of all Christian denominations and nationalized 5,000 Roman Catholic schools; it is estimated that of the total number of people sent to camps, 10 million were persecuted for their religious beliefs. Communism has been striving, and is still striving, to destroy any faith in God and says so openly. Pope John XXIII was the first pope who considered it possible to exchange congratulatory telegrams and messages of goodwill with the leader of international Communism and to receive his envoy and his son-in-law. And he raised peaceful coexistence with the Communist system almost to the level of a tenet of Christian duty.
>
> Why should this delight us so much and prompt us to outdo those who have vested interests in this in trying to elevate the late John XXIII almost to sainthood?
>
> Whatever we say about President Kennedy's foreign policy and his real intentions, it will not change the fact that, since Roosevelt, his has been the policy with the most significant compromises with the Soviet bloc. Whatever we say about the real objectives and intentions of John XXIII and about the fraudulent use of those intentions by every Moscow *Pravda,* which bade farewell in a black frame when he was called to heaven by Providence, the fact remains that outwardly this Pope's deeds constituted the gravest compromise since Bolshevism emerged and possibly the weightiest compromise in the history of the Roman Catholic Church. Even if we do not wish to call Kennedy's policy surrender and the stance of John XXIII a moral disarmament, we

have to concede that both the policy and the stance are generally known by the name of "coexistence." This is to say, contrary to the policy of liberation, to the policy of independence, to the policy of restoring freedom to peoples, countries, and states which are at present in Communist captivity. And, in any event, allowing for the possibility of different interpretations, it is a policy which delays this liberation.

For the Western world, which is not captive but free, this is a policy compatible with its profound wishes and hopes. Leaving aside Communists, crypto-Communists, and fellow-travelers of every description, this policy suits the bourgeoisie who want their humdrum peace, the merchants who want to trade with Communists, the industrialists who want to sell their products to Communist states, socialists who have to demonstrate their anticapitalist "progressiveness," democrats who solicit votes, conservatives who in a habitual aversion to any revolution against the strong see this today in . . . the counterrevolution; it particularly suits intellectuals who professionally dabble in pro-Sovietism, and, of course, the so-called youth who have to overtake the older generation in everything, including conformism. Briefly, without providing a complete list, it suits adherents of the so-called real politics, "sensible" politics, "flexible" politics. In the free world, everybody prefers to take a drive to the seaside or to the mountains, with a girlie, in a Mercedes or a Ford, and is terrified by the nightmare of driving a tank in order to liberate anyone. This is clear and quite understandable.

This policy should not, however, suit the peoples who are in the clutches of international Communism. Yet, not just in Polish émigré publications but also in those which represent other captive nations in the fellowship of wretched exiles, we see the same syndrome of joining the "coexistentialists" of all countries in the elevation of those two men to the status of providential human beings.

Considering the causes of this phenomenon, I have reached the conclusion that it is the result of a competition, in a manner of speaking, which emerged after the Second World War. It is a bidding down. The Western world tries to outbid international Communism in slogans, and we are trying to outbid the slogans of the Western world. Whoever shrugs at these tactics is considered devoid of the sense of political "realism." I am concerned that this race of catchwords, which sound increasingly more accommodating, might obscure completely the actual reality and lead us all together along a path not to the liberation of the "East" but to the captivity of the "West." (1964)[42]

1975

Mackiewicz published, as a sequel to the previous book, *Watykan w cieniu czerwonej gwiazdy* [The Vatican in the Shadow of the Red Star], which assesses the pontificate of Paul VI.

1984

Publication of *Droga Pani* . . . [Dear Madam . . .], a selection of articles and essays by Józef Mackiewicz and Barbara Toporska.

A selection of narratives and reportage-articles, *Fakty, przyroda i ludzie* [Facts, Nature and People], with an introduction by Barbara Toporska, was also published.

1985

31 January—Józef Mackiewicz died in Munich.

20 June—Barbara Toporska died. The ashes of both were deposited in London.

Notes

CHAPTER 1. "CENSORED"

1. V. D. Spasovich, "Rech' v zashchitu Alekseya Kuznetsova," *Izbrannye trudy i rechi*, Avtograf, Tula, 2000, 254.
2. Salvatore Quasimodo, "To the New Moon," *Complete Poems,* translated by Jack Bevan, Anvil Press Poetry, London, 1983.
3. *Życie Warszawy* [Life of Warsaw], October 27, 1959.
4. *Tygodnik Powszechny* [Everyone's Weekly], October 1, 1961.
5. Carl J. Burckhardt, *Meine Danziger Mission 1937–1939,* Verlag Georg D. W. Callway, Munich, 1960, 125; 340.
6. *Polityka,* June 17, 1961.
7. *Politicheskii slovar',* Gospolitizdat, Moscow, 1958.
8. *Visti Tsentralnoho Vykonavchoho Komitetu UkSSR* [Information Bulletin of the Central Executive Committee of the Ukrainian SSR], no. 144 (June 25, 1938).
9. Translated by Anthony Bower.

CHAPTER 2. DOES RUSSIA STILL EXIST?

1. I. A. Kurganov, *Natsii SSSR i russkii vopros* [The Nations of the USSR and the Russian Question], Possev, Frankfurt am Main, 1961, 168.
2. *Rabochaya pravda* [Workers' Truth], July 16, 1913.

3. Fedor Stepun, *Byvshee i nesbyvsheesia* [The Fulfilled and Unfulfilled], Chekhov Publishing House, New York, 1956, vol. 1, 276.

CHAPTER 3. BETWEEN BOLSHEVISM AND NATIONALISM

1. *Kratkaya istoriya grazhdanskoi voiny v SSSR* [A Short History of the Civil War in the USSR], Gosudarstvennoe Izdatelstvo Politicheskoi Literatury, Moscow, 1960, 296–97.
2. Josef Mienski, "Die Gründung der Weissruthenischen SSR," *Sowjetstudien,* Munich, 1956, no. 1.
3. A. I. Denikin, *Ocherki russkoi smuty* [Essays on Times of Troubles in Russia], Knigoizdatelstvo "Mednyi vsadnik," Berlin, 1926, vol. 5, 185–86.

CHAPTER 4. MIKASZEWICZE

1. Lenin, *Polnoye sobraniye sochineniy* [Collected Works], fifth ed., Izdatelstvo Politicheskoi Literatury, Moscow, 1967, vol. 50, 329.
2. *Robotnik* [The Worker], 1919: May 29; May 30; May 31; June 3; June 4.
3. Józef Sieradzki: "Po Białowieży i Mikaszewiczach: 3: Lenin chciał pokoju," *Przegląd Kulturalny* [Cultural Review], Warsaw, 1958, no. 4.
4. Bernard Andreus [Jerzy Niezbrzycki], *Polska a "kapitalistyczna interwencja" w stosunku do ZSSR* [Poland and the "Capitalist Intervention" in the USSR], Biblioteka "Orła Białego," Rome, 1945, 16.
5. Lenin, *Pravda,* January 21, 1933.
6. Ibid.
7. Lenin, *Polnoye sobraniye sochineniy,* fifth ed., vol. 39, 207.
8. Cf. Tadeusz Kutrzeba, *Wyprawa Kijowska 1920 roku* [Kiev Expedition], Gebethner i Wolff, Warsaw, 1937, 27.
9. Ibid., 30.
10. Julian Marchlewski, *Rosja proletariacka a Polska burżuazyjna* [Proletarian Russia and Bourgeois Poland], Wydawnictwo Komunistyczne "Trybuna," Moscow, 1921, 18.
11. Viscount D'Abernon, *The Eighteenth Decisive Battle of the World,* Hodder and Stoughton, London, 1931, 10–11.
12. L. Degtiarev, *Politrabota v Krasnoi Armii v voennoe vremia* [Political Work in the Red Army During the War], Moscow, 1930.
13. Julian Marchlewski, *Voina i mir mezhdu burzhuaznoi Polshei i proletarskoi Rossiei* [War and Peace Between Bourgeois Poland and Proletarian Russia], Gosudarstvennoe Izdatelstvo, Moscow, 1921, 21.
14. *Times,* London, February 14, 1920.
15. Pavel Milyukov, *Rossiya na perelome* [Russia at the Turning Point], Paris, 1927, vol. 2, 226.
16. Grigory Rakovsky, *Konets Belykh* [The End of the Whites], Izdatelstvo "Volya Rossii," Prague, 1921; Aleksandr Valentinov, *Krymskaya epopeya* [Crimean Epic], vol. 5 of the *Arkhiv russkoi revolyutsii,* Berlin, 1922.
17. Bernard Andreus, *Polska a "kapitalistyczna interwencja,"* 35.
18. A. I. Denikin, *Ocherki russkoi smuty,* vol. 5, 181.
19. Mieczysław M. Rakowski, *Polityka,* October 21, 1961.

CHAPTER 5. "GOMUŁKAISM" (NATIONAL COMMUNISM) OF THE TWENTIES

1. *Politicheskii slovar',* 388.
2. *Entsyklopediya ukrayinoznavstva* [Encyclopaedia of Knowledge About Ukraine], New York and Munich, 1949.
3. Juliusz Mieroszewski, *Kultura,* Paris, 1961, no. 12, 6.
4. Stepan Vytvytsky and Stepan Baran, "Ukrainski zemli pid Polshcheyu" [Ukrainian Territories Under Polish Rule], *Entsyklopediya ukrayinoznavstva.*
5. *Kultura,* Paris, 1961, no. 12, 12.

CHAPTER 6. THE FIRST GREAT PROVOCATION ABOUT THE ALLEGED "EVOLUTION OF COMMUNISM"

1. Ryszard Wraga, *Wiadomości* [The News], London, 1961, no. 37.
2. Yuri Annenkov, "Vospominaniya o Lenine" [My Memories of Lenin], *Novyi Zhurnal* [New Journal], New York, vol. 5 (1961), 146–47.

CHAPTER 7. THE SECOND PHASE OF NATIONAL COMMUNISM

1. Jan Szembek, *Journal, 1933–1939,* Librairie Plon, Paris, 1952, 404.
2. L. M. Chassin, *L'Ascension de Mao Tse-toung,* Paris, 1953.
3. Burckhardt, *Meine Danziger Mission 1937–1939,* 72.
4. Stanisław Kopański, *Wspomnienia wojenne* [Reminiscences of War], Veritas, London, 1961, 30.

CHAPTER 8. ALLIANCE OR COLLABORATION WITH THE SOVIET INVADER?

1. Tadeusz Katelbach, *Rok złych wróżb (1943)* [The Year of Ill Omens], Instytut Literacki, Paris, 1959, 27, 59.
2. Jan Rzepecki, *Wspomnienia i przyczynki historyczne* [Memoirs and Historical Materials], Czytelnik, Warsaw, 1956, 267–68, 274, 276.
3. *Po prostu,* June 9, 1957.
4. *Ostatnie Wiadomości* [The Latest News], Mannheim, July 9, 1961; *Dziennik Polski* [The Polish Daily], London, September 3, 1949; *Dziennik Polski,* June 1, 1957.
5. Jerzy Putrament, "Pół wieku" [Half-a-Century], *Przegląd Kulturalny,* Warsaw, January 25, 1962.
6. *Jutro Polski* [Poland's Morrow], London, 1947, no. 19.
7. HAK [Henryk Kleinert], "Trzy rodzaje uchodźców" [Three Kinds of Refugee], *Myśl Państwowa* [Thoughts of the State], London, 1954, no. 1.

CHAPTER 9. THE ORIGINS OF "PAX"

1. Wojciech Żukrowski, *Życie Warszawy,* January 22, 1962.
2. *Kuźnica Kapłańska* [The Priests' Forge], 1955, no. 4.
3. *Kuźnica Kapłańska,* 1954, no. 20.

CHAPTER 10. PHARISAISM VERSUS SUBVERSION

1. *Życie Warszawy,* February 3, 1959.
2. *Tygodnik Powszechny,* September 4, 1960; Stomma's Sejm speech, *Życie Warszawy,* October 22, 1960; Stomma, *Tygodnik Powszechny,* February 6, 1961; Rev. Mieczysław Maliński, *Tygodnik Powszechny,* February 5, 1961; *Tygodnik Powszechny,* September 4, 1960.
3. [Stomma, speaking on ZNAK's behalf], *Życie Warszawy,* May 20, 1961.
4. Rev. Mieczysław Maliński, *Tygodnik Powszechny,* May 21, 1961.

CHAPTER 11. THE SECOND GREAT PROVOCATION

1. Lenin, *Polnoye sobraniye sochineniy,* fifth ed., vol. 38, 162.
2. *Głos Ludu* [The People's Voice], May 6, 1945.
3. *Nowe Drogi* [New Paths], 1956, no. 10.
4. *Pravda,* July 23, 1959.
5. *Pravda,* September 5, 1959.

CHAPTER 12. ALONG THE ROAD OF CLASSIC "POPUTNICHESTVO" [FELLOW-TRAVELING]

1. *Dziennik Polski,* October 27, 1961.
2. *Dziennik Polski,* August 30, 1961.
3. *ŻycieWarszawy,* August 11, 1959.
4. *Ostatnie Wiadomości,* November 3, 1957.
5. *Dziennik Polski,* January 25, 1961.

CHAPTER 13. THE GERMAN COMPLEX

1. *Kultura,* 1961, no. 12.
2. *Dziennik Polski,* June 15, 1961.
3. *Dziennik Polski,* April 19, 1962.
4. Quoted here from the London *Dziennik Polski* of August 29, 1961.

CHAPTER 15. THE REAL GERMAN THREAT

1. *hvp,* November 15, 1961; March 14, 1962.
2. *hpv,* December 6, 1961; January 31, 1962; ibid.

CHAPTER 17. PATHOS VERSUS PESTILENCE

1. Winston Churchill, *The Aftermath: The World Crisis After 1918,* Thornton Butterworth, London, 1929, 72–73.

CHRONOLOGY

1. Kyril FitzLyon and Tatiana Browning, *Before the Revolution. A View of Russia Under the Last Tsar,* Allen Lane, London, 1977, 52.
2. Grigori Besedovsky, *Revelations of a Soviet Diplomat,* Williams & Norgate, London, 1931.
3. Józef Mackiewicz, "Mój szwagier—szef G.P.U." [My Brother-in-law—a GPU Chief]," *Wiadomości,* 1964, no. 12.
4. Mackiewicz, "Ślizgawka" [The Ice Rink], *Słowo* [The Word], Wilno, 1935, no. 156.
5. Norman Davies, *God's Playground. A History of Poland,* Clarendon Press, Oxford, 1981, vol. 2, 378–80.
6. Mackiewicz, "Wspomnienie" [A Reminiscence], *Słowo,* 1925, no. 272.
7. Davies, *God's Playground,* 393–94.
8. Ibid., 394–98.
9. Alfred Erich Senn, *The Great Powers, Lithuania and the Vilna Question 1920–1928,* E. J. Brill, Leiden, 1966, 16–18.
10. Mackiewicz, "Casus: Marek Hłasko" [The Case of Marek Hłasko], *Dodatek Tygodniowy Ostatnich Wiadomości* [Weekly Supplement to the Latest News], Mannheim, 1960, no. 5.
11. Senn, *The Great Powers,* 1–6.
12. Mackiewicz, "Michał Chmielowiec jakim Go znałem" [Michał Chmielowiec as I Knew Him], *Wiadomości,* 1974, no. 35.
13. Mackiewicz, "Z ostępów leśnych Białowieży" [From the Depths of the Białowieża Forest], *Słowo,* 1922, no. 28.
14. Mackiewicz, "Zmiana uprzęży dorożkarskiej" [New Harness Requirements for Horse-Drawn Carriages], *Słowo,* 1923, no. 28.
15. Mackiewicz, "Maior Dux Lituaniae," *Słowo,* 1930, no. 30.
16. Mackiewicz, "Słońce świeci nad granicą" [The Sun Is Shining Above the Border], *Słowo,* 1935, no. 194.
17. Mackiewicz, "Bierzmy przykład z *Cichego Donu*" [Let Us Take an Example From *Quiet Flows the Don*], *Słowo,* 1936, no. 124.
18. Ksawery Pruszyński, *Wiadomości Literackie* [Literary News], Warsaw, February 27, 1938.
19. Mackiewicz, "Ponura tajemnica nie stotalizowanego pustelnika" [The Gloomy Mystery of a Nontotalized Hermit], *Słowo,* 1939, no. 216.
20. Jan T. Gross, *Revolution from Abroad: The Soviet Conquest of Poland's Western Ukraine and Western Belorussia,* Princeton University Press, Princeton, 1988, 8–13.
21. Ibid., 72.
22. Mackiewicz, "Jak to było z Litwinami" [How It Was Under the Lithuanians], *Wiadomości,* 1947, no. 33.
23. Mackiewicz, "O pewnej, ostatniej próbie i o zastrzelonym Bujnickim" [About a Certain Last Attempt, and About the Assassinated Bujnicki], *Kultura,* 1954, no. 11.
24. Mackiewicz, "Jak to było z Litwinami."
25. Mackiewicz, "Zaczynamy gnić" [The Rot Is Setting In], *Wiadomości,* 1947, no. 24.
26. Gross, *Revolution from Abroad,* 109.
27. Mackiewicz, "Moja dyskusja z NKWD" [My Discussion with the NKVD], *Goniec Codzienny* [Daily Herald], Wilno, 1941, no. 6.

28. Mackiewicz, "Łapani jak psy" [Being Caught Like Dogs], *Lwów i Wilno,* London, 1947, no. 30.
29. Mackiewicz, *Nie trzeba głośno mówić* [Better Not to Talk Aloud], Instytut Literacki, Paris, 1968.
30. Mackiewicz, "Na drogę do Kalwarii" [Leaving for Calvary], *Lwów i Wilno,* 1948, no. 57.
31. Mackiewicz, "Łapani jak psy."
32. Mackiewicz, "Z teczki: niefortunne losy" [From the 'Inauspicious Lot' File], *Wiadomości,* 1974, no. 44.
33. Mackiewicz, "Na drogę do Kalwarii."
34. Mackiewicz, "Masakra" [The Massacre], *Lwów i Wilno,* 1948, no. 60.
35. Mackiewicz, "W Mediolanie" [In Milan], *Lwów i Wilno,* 1948, no. 61.
36. Mackiewicz, "Dlaczego nie mogę wziąć udziału w ankiecie" [Why I Cannot Take Part in the Survey], *Lwów i Wilno,* 1947, no. 43.
37. Czesław Miłosz, *The History of Polish Literature,* Macmillan, New York & London, 1969, 525.
38. Mackiewicz, "List do Szołochowa" [A Letter to Sholokhov], *Wiadomości,* 1955, no. 1.
39. P. Szathamáry István, "Adventures of Deaf and Dumb Blind Men Vis-à-vis the Evolution of Communism," *Kommentár,* Budapest, 2007.
40. Pálfalvi Lajos, "Contra. Only the Truth Is Interesting," *Magyar Nemzet Magazin,* Budapest, September 1, 2007.
41. Mackiewicz, "O książce Michała K. Pawlikowskiego" [About a Book by M. K. Pawlikowski], *Wiadomości,* 1962, no. 23.
42. Mackiewicz, "Kennedy i Jan XXIII" [Kennedy and John XXIII], *Wiadomości,* 1964, no. 7.